Italian Politics and Nineteenth-Century British Literature and Culture

Italian Politics and Nineteenth-Century British Literature and Culture

Patricia Cove

EDINBURGH
University Press

Edinburgh University Press is one of the leading university presses in the UK. We publish academic books and journals in our selected subject areas across the humanities and social sciences, combining cutting-edge scholarship with high editorial and production values to produce academic works of lasting importance. For more information visit our website: edinburghuniversitypress.com

© Patricia Cove, 2019

Edinburgh University Press Ltd
The Tun – Holyrood Road, 12(2f) Jackson's Entry, Edinburgh EH8 8PJ

Typeset in 11/13 Adobe Sabon by
IDSUK (DataConnection) Ltd, and
printed and bound in Great Britain.

A CIP record for this book is available from the British Library

ISBN 978 1 4744 4724 9 (hardback)
ISBN 978 1 4744 4726 3 (webready PDF)
ISBN 978 1 4744 4727 0 (epub)

The right of Patricia Cove to be identified as the author of this work has been asserted in accordance with the Copyright, Designs and Patents Act 1988, and the Copyright and Related Rights Regulations 2003 (SI No. 2498).

Contents

List of Illustrations

Series Editor's Preface

'Victorian' is a term, at once indicative of a strongly determined concept and an often notoriously vague notion, emptied of all meaningful content by the many journalistic misconceptions that persist about the inhabitants and cultures of the British Isles and Victoria's Empire in the nineteenth century. As such, it has become a by-word for the assumption of various, often contradictory habits of thought, belief, behaviour and perceptions. Victorian studies and studies in nineteenth-century literature and culture have, from their institutional inception, questioned narrowness of presumption, pushed at the limits of the nominal definition, and have sought to question the very grounds on which the unreflective perception of the so-called Victorian has been built; and so they continue to do. Victorian and nineteenth-century studies of literature and culture maintain a breadth and diversity of interest, of focus and inquiry, in an interrogative and intellectually open-minded and challenging manner, which are equal to the exploration and inquisitiveness of its subjects. Many of the questions asked by scholars and researchers of the innumerable productions of nineteenth-century society actively put into suspension the clichés and stereotypes of 'Victorianism', whether the approach has been sustained by historical, scientific, philosophical, empirical, ideological or theoretical concerns; indeed, it would be incorrect to assume that each of these approaches to the idea of the Victorian has been, or has remained, in the main exclusive, sealed off from the interests and engagements of other approaches. A vital interdisciplinarity has been pursued and embraced, for the most part, even as there has been contest and debate amongst Victorianists, pursued with as much fervour as the affirmative exploration between different disciplines and differing epistemologies put to work in the service of reading the nineteenth century.

Edinburgh Critical Studies in Victorian Culture aims to take up both the debates and the inventive approaches and departures from convention that studies in the nineteenth century have witnessed for the last half century at least. Aiming to maintain a 'Victorian' (in the most positive sense of that motif) spirit of inquiry, the series' purpose is to continue and augment the cross-fertilisation of interdisciplinary approaches, and to offer, in addition, a number of timely and untimely revisions of Victorian literature, culture, history and identity. At the same time, the series will ask questions concerning what has been missed or improperly received, misread, or not read at all, in order to present a multi-faceted and heterogeneous kaleidoscope of representations. Drawing on the most provocative, thoughtful and original research, the series will seek to prod at the notion of the 'Victorian', and in so doing, principally through theoretically and epistemologically sophisticated close readings of the historicity of literature and culture in the nineteenth century, to offer the reader provocative insights into a world that is at once overly familiar, and irreducibly different, other and strange. Working from original sources, primary documents and recent interdisciplinary theoretical models, Edinburgh Critical Studies in Victorian Culture seeks not simply to push at the boundaries of research in the nineteenth century, but also to inaugurate the persistent erasure and provisional, strategic redrawing of those borders.

Julian Wolfreys

Acknowledgements

My deepest gratitude belongs to Alison Chapman, whose thoughtful guidance made this research possible. Thank you! I owe the inspiration for this project to Marjorie Stone: thank you for pointing me toward Post Office spying. Many thanks to Rohan Maitzen, Judith Thompson, Lisa Surridge and Deborah Stiles for encouragement along the way. To the graduate students at the University of Victoria, Aaron Bartlett, Eric Henwood-Greer, Janice Niemann, Heidi Rennert, Emily Scott and Peter Wilson: thank you for travelling with me for part of this journey. To the participants at the North American Victorian Studies Association 2015, 2016 and Florence 2017 conferences and the Association of Canadian College and University Teachers of English 2016 and 2018 conferences, thank you for listening and questioning. My thanks to the blind reviewers who responded helpfully to these chapters and to the many at Edinburgh University Press from whose hard work this book benefited, especially Julian Wolfreys, Michelle Houston, Ersev Ersoy and James Dale. I appreciate the research assistance provided by the University of Victoria Libraries and Dalhousie University Libraries and by librarians Elaine MacInnis, Jennifer MacIsaac, Shirley Vail, Lara Wilson and Trish LeBlanc. I am grateful for the friendship of my generation of early career researchers; thank you for being kind. Finally, to my family and friends and to those I've lost, *grazie mille*.

This research was supported by the Social Sciences and Humanities Research Council of Canada. Without the generous support of a SSHRC postdoctoral fellowship, which I held at the University of Victoria, I could not have embarked on this project. A version of Chapter 3 appeared previously as 'Spying in the British Post Office, Victorian Politics and Wilkie Collins's *The Woman in White*', by Patricia Cove, *Journal of Victorian Culture*, copyright © Leeds

Trinity and All Saints College, reprinted by permission of Taylor & Francis Ltd, <http://www.tandfonline.com> on behalf of Leeds Trinity and All Saints College. Digital reproduction for Figure 1.1 is from the W. K. Morrison Special Collection of the J. B. Hall Library at the NSCC Centre of Geographic Sciences.

Introduction: Italian Unity and International Alliances

In summer 1860, Italian patriot and Garibaldian fighter Alberto Mario looked across time and geographical distance from newly liberated Sicily to imagine the volunteer force's future success in pushing the repressive Bourbon monarchy out of mainland Neapolitan territory. However, the retrospective account of his 1860 optimism, published in his English-language memoir, *The Red Shirt* (1865), develops a tension between the hope that preceded Giuseppe Garibaldi's conquest of mainland southern Italy and the disillusionment borne out by the subsequent losses sustained by democrats like Mario, who saw their territorial and political gains absorbed into the moderate, state-driven movement directed by the northern Italian Kingdom of Piedmont-Sardinia, which annexed southern Italy within months. For Mario,

> Throughout the months of June and July the smile of victory, the miraculous stories of the recent battles fought and won, the unrivalled beauty of the scene, the intoxicating perfumes wafted from the surrounding gardens, the radiant countenance of the victor, enthralled us. Garibaldi . . . was a magician. Faith in the future was boundless; the passage to Naples, the entry into Rome, the storming of Verona, were spoken of as certainties ere the winter should set in. The place, the time, the events, produced a sort of delicious ecstasy which annihilated distances and transformed facts . . . And even now, when four disenchanting years have swept away belief and hope, there are times when I seem to stand upon that terrace, spell-bound still, believing in the reality of the future which thence arose to view.[1]

Mario's personal, English-language intervention in the public representation of the Italian political and cultural movement known as the Risorgimento, or resurgence, and the new Kingdom of Italy to which the movement gave birth reveals three points crucial to this study. First, Mario's decision to publish his memoir in English establishes an international, English-speaking audience for Risorgimento writing, a market upon which his British wife, Jessie White Mario, built a decades-long career.[2] Second, Mario's account navigates an emotional blend of romantic investment in the Risorgimento and 'disenchant[ment]' with the process and outcome of Italian unification.[3] Much of the British and English-language writing in this study negotiates a similar mixture of commitment and disaffection, with varying degrees of optimism, complacency and cynicism about the Risorgimento's intertwined independence, democratic and nationalist movements. Finally, Mario's participation in a print effort to shape international understandings of what occurred during and after Garibaldi's campaign demonstrates his continued involvement in a political contest to control the Risorgimento's public image and promote his own political agenda even after the culmination of Risorgimento conflict in 1859–60 and Italy's official unification in 1861. The political clashes within and beyond the Italian peninsula that led to the 1859–60 wars and accompanying revolutions persisted in the new, ostensibly unified Italy.

The Risorgimento revolutionised the map of Europe to create a new nation-state; yet, the political tensions inherent in the movement and its cultural representations reveal that forging a new state demands both making and unmaking, knitting together new bonds, while wrenching others apart. *Italian Politics and Nineteenth-Century British Literature and Culture* combines a broad, transnational approach to Risorgimento history with attention to specific points of impact between Italian politics and British print culture, to argue that the Risorgimento also reshaped nineteenth-century British political, literary and cultural landscapes. Crossing borders, political divides and genres, this study examines the sites at which a cross-section of British literature, including works by Elizabeth Barrett Browning, Mary Shelley and Wilkie Collins, intersects with journalism, travelogues, parliamentary records and pamphlets, to establish Britain's imaginative investment in this seismic geopolitical realignment. As the Risorgimento reshaped Europe's geopolitical reality, it also reframed how the British saw themselves, their politics and their place within Europe.

Examining four political focal points of British engagement with the Risorgimento in its four chapters, this study excavates the unsettling and pervasive fusion of political optimism and disaffection produced in nineteenth-century British literature and print culture through the collision of British and Italian politics. The shockwaves of the Italian independence movement forced the British to rethink conventional attitudes towards political revolution, Britain's responsibilities towards its neighbours and myths of British freedom and stability: even as the Risorgimento became the 'foundation story' that 'ma[de] nation-state creation seem the inevitable, and morally correct, outcome of what was, in reality, a political struggle for power' within Italy,[4] British sympathy with Italian reform and revolutionary efforts facilitated criticism of perceived abuses of power within Britain and encouraged the development of a cosmopolitan political identity, which together challenged insular notions of Britain's leadership in European democracy. However, as unification failed to live up to the ideals it was inspired by and as its human cost became increasingly evident, British and Anglo-Italian writers also exhibited disillusionment with the Italian cause and disenchantment with romantic notions of Italy across the century.

Making Italians? The Historiography of Unification

Risorgimento historiography is fraught with the paradoxical vision that sees nineteenth-century Italy as, on the one hand, a colonised nation that pre-dated the state that gave it political volition, and, on the other, a culturally and politically divided post-unification territory lacking national cohesion, or an 'imagined political community',[5] to legitimise its geopolitical existence. Scholars view the Italian peninsula both as a 'geopolitical situation of cohesion in diversity and fragmentation, and a cultural dimension unrelated to a unitary state'[6] throughout the nineteenth century and as 'a state in search of a nation' after unification.[7] Thus, the Risorgimento's nation-making process continued after unification, with various setbacks and failings. One crucial impediment to Italian unity was the absence of a shared language, literate population and reading public. Historian Lucy Riall summarises the dilemma Italian nationalists faced when circulating their messages:

> most people spoke a series of regional dialects which could . . . be very different from literary Italian. French or the local dialect were more widely spoken than Italian in Piedmont (both Cavour and the Piedmontese king[8] spoke much better French than Italian). According to one estimate, there were around 600,000 Italian speakers at the time of unification, that is, about 2.5 per cent of the total population. Nevertheless, . . . [d]ialects spoken in central Italy . . . were very similar

to literary Italian, so that the actual figure for 'Italian' speakers may be closer to three million people, or between 10 and 12 per cent of the population. In much of Italy, moreover, Italian was the official administrative language.[9]

Furthermore, as Riall outlines, trade barriers, resistance to mass production, the slow development of modern transportation systems and an inflexible rural–urban divide prevented the growth of a pan-Italian reading public, all of which 'had a clear impact on the spread of a sense of imagined community within the peninsula'.[10] Low rates of literacy and Italian fluency persisted after unification. Suzanne Stewart-Steinberg identifies 75 per cent of the population as illiterate and estimates that only 0.8 per cent of Italians could speak the language,[11] while Adrian Lyttelton argues that after unification literate, native Italian speakers comprised less than 2.5 per cent of the population.[12] Regardless of the variations in these estimates, historians agree that the conditions for creating a shared political culture and an engaged, modern reading public did not exist at unification.

Many historical narratives of the Risorgimento and the early Italian constitutional monarchy, then, present Italy as a failure, a nation-state unable to consolidate itself against political division and regional diversity. Stewart-Steinberg prefaces her study of post-unification *italianità*, *The Pinocchio Effect: On Making Italians*, with the claim that Italian history after 1861 'is the history of a fragile political structure in search of a national culture that would authenticate and legitimate it'.[13] Lyttelton, similarly, traces the effects of post-unification regional discontent on the Italian nation-state,[14] concluding that Italy exhibited a 'persistent unease about the incompleteness of the transformation accomplished, and about the failure to bring about the "nationalization of the masses", or to create a strong national identity'.[15] While the Risorgimento's imagined pan-Italian community appeared strong enough to motivate the independence movement, geopolitical unification could not complete the nation-making process.

For some scholars, however, Italy's diversity was the source of its historical strength and Italian political culture's cultivation of a sense of internal fragmentation and powerlessness at least partly constituted the Risorgimento's ideological content and Italy's national identity. Roberto Esposito's history of Italian philosophy, *Living Thought*, celebrates the fact that '[n]othing deep and intrinsic binds Italian philosophy to the Italian nation';[16] even Italian political thought can be 'prestatal' or 'framed in terms of resistance to the state'.[17] Early modern Italy's political and cultural diversity, he argues, allowed Italian philosophy to project a universality that extended its relevance beyond the peninsula: 'Without political boundaries and without a center, Italy remained a formidable land of development, dissemination, and cross-pollination of the great, single European culture whose scope and importance was not national, because it went beyond the nation'.[18] In political terms, the Risorgimento was, in Riall's words, 'a movement of political opposition',[19] a form of resistance to the existing Italian states. The *italianità* that emerged at unification, furthermore, was constituted by the new nation-state's very lacks, according to Stewart-Steinberg, who argues that 'the formulation of an Italian national self was predicated on a language that posited marginalization and powerlessness as fundamental aspects of what it meant to be modern Italians'.[20] The political discourse of division and oppositionalism noted by historians is, then, central to Italian nationalism.

Distinguishing between history-from-above – the history of the international diplomacy and conflict that resulted in the Kingdom of Italy's creation – and the historiographical re-evaluations offered by Risorgimento cultural historians such as Alberto Banti allows us to confront the apparent paradox that Italy before unification might have been a nation without a state, while Italy after unification was a state struggling to become a nation. Historians recognise that, as Derek Beales notes, 'unification was an affair of war and diplomacy rather than of peaceful development towards national consciousness';[21] in Riall's words, 'united Italy was the creation of kings not of the people'.[22] Yet, the Risorgimento prepared the ground for unification in international political culture by putting pressure on diplomats and politicians and presenting unification as a political inevitability; for Beales, the Risorgimento was most important as 'part of a European movement of reformists, liberals and nationalists'.[23] Furthermore, the language of failure that infiltrated post-unification Italy originated in the component of decline that is fundamental to the concept of *risorgimento*:[24] in Risorgimento culture, 'the nation is . . . under threat, and Italy's more recent past must be written as a story of decadence, foreign domination and internal divisions'.[25] Imagery of decay and rebirth, like *The Red Shirt*'s fusion of optimism and betrayal, lingers in the post-unification political consciousness that emphasises Italian uneasiness and fragmentation.

Risorgimento discourse, then, is a politically contested field. For Riall, the existence of a post-unification language of division and disappointment speaks to the extent of the Risorgimento's success in penetrating national consciousness, as well as a continued fight for a political voice on the part of those, like Mario, who might benefit from the Risorgimento discourse's blend of hope and victimisation:

> the 'failure' of Italy reflected the significant economic, social and political challenge of national unification but it was also the result of a polemic, in which the political loser(s) sought to denigrate and diminish the achievements of the victorious side. The effect of this polemic on the national discourse was to maintain at its very centre the persuasive contrast between a poetic vision of national belonging and the prosaic disenchantment of Italy's governments; . . . the contrast which had been such a powerful weapon in the hands of the political opposition during the Risorgimento was to remain in place after the unification of Italy . . .
>
> The crucial point to recognise, however, is not so much that Italy was an unsuccessful nation as that it was a politically divided one. In many ways, the emphasis on a failed Italy in this political conflict, the strong focus on national heroes and national martyrs, on national 'resurgence' and national betrayal, points us to the overwhelming victory of the Italian nationalist discourse.[26]

It is not my intention to simplify the difficulties of making Italians by reconciling the tensions within the Risorgimento and the nineteenth-century Italian nation-state, but, rather, to open up a space for contradiction within the discussion that follows, with the goal of recognising the diversity and contested nature of Risorgimento thought and cultural production. Though democrats such as Giuseppe Mazzini and Giuseppe Garibaldi dominated the Risorgimento propaganda of the 1830s, 1840s and, to a lesser degree, 1850s,[27] the constitutionalist Piedmontese Prime Minister, Camillo Benso di Cavour, finally harnessed the movement for Piedmont's territorial gain. Yet, Cavour's success in doing so did not erase the more radical, dissenting voices that continued to fight for a more democratic vision of Italy after unification.

Furthermore, the act of interpreting the Risorgimento is itself political. As Riall's study of the Garibaldi myth that developed in Risorgimento propaganda and popular culture indicates, the Risorgimento's major figures and events were immediately and subsequently interpreted to suit various political purposes. Riall explains that different versions of Garibaldi's conquest of southern Italy and Piedmont's annexation of the territory corresponded to the views of different stakeholders, such as the democrats who lost the ideological fight at unification, the liberals whose version became official history and mid-twentieth-century historians, respectively:

> There are different memories of the Thousand and its aftermath. The first is a Risorgimento tale of triumph and tragedy: a small group of heroic men overthrow oppression and liberate their enslaved 'brothers', only to be betrayed and defeated by a number on their own side. The second sees the events of 1859–60 as a single, happy continuum: the story of Garibaldi being 'the right man in the right place at the right time', and of opposing political views compromising and coalescing at the right point and with the right objective – Italian unification. Finally, there is the more recent interpretation of the events of 1860 by historians. For them, 1860 was a form of civil war, a moment of intense political conflict and social instability, the results of which were actually damaging to national unity.[28]

Consciousness of this historiographical debate allows us to trace the contrasting interpretations of the Risorgimento while acknowledging their biases and insights.

The same diversity and dissention appears in nineteenth-century British responses to the Italian question. The Risorgimento, with its compelling martyrs, campaigns and propagandists, captured international attention across the nineteenth century, as well as official and unofficial participation by governments and citizens across Europe and around the world. As Lauren M. E. Goodlad's *The Victorian Geopolitical Aesthetic* explores, 'multiple modes of "worlding" . . . informed nineteenth-century experience'.[29] Though Goodlad focuses on the intersections between realist representation and global capital, cosmopolitanism and empire, the Italian cause took a prominent place in an international web of nineteenth-century sites of civic engagement. Maurizio Isabella's work on early Risorgimento exiles demonstrates that '[t]he networks of liberals and revolutionaries to which the Italian diaspora belonged testify to the development of a Europe-wide and also transatlantic civil society, whose objectives and political beliefs transcended national boundaries'.[30] Inspired by revolutions and wars of independence in Spain, Greece and Latin America,[31] Italian patriots and refugees in turn made their cause a flashpoint within a cluster of democratic, independence movements, capitalising on the liberal international's 'belief in international solidarity and in the interconnectedness of all movements for emancipation worldwide'.[32] Moreover, sympathy with the Risorgimento was cultivated in transatlantic liberal, republican and antislavery discourse.[33]

The British public was a crucial ally for Risorgimento activists, though British opinion was also contested. British writers and public figures who explored support for the Risorgimento in print include voices as varied as Elizabeth Barrett Browning, William Gladstone, Benjamin Disraeli, Thomas Carlyle and W. J. Linton. The extent of British engagement with Italy may be traced to the perceived 'special relationship' between England and Italy[34] that has been discussed in depth in Anglo-Italian studies. For Manfred Pfister, British and Italian identities are mutually constitutive: '"Englishness" or "Britishness" and *Italianità* . . . are staged both within each culture and, more importantly, in joint performances of difference across cultural borders'.[35] As Maura O'Connor amply shows in *The Romance of Italy and the English Political Imagination*, the British were vital participants in the process of imagining an Italian nation:

> The inspiring beauty of the Italian peninsula, with its rich historical associations and sublime landscapes, lent itself to this English enterprise of romantically recasting Italy as a nation. The idea of a unified Italian nation loomed so large in the English imagination that it took on different, and sometimes competing, political forms and representations.[36]

Yet, this process was as much about projecting British political ideology, and particularly liberalism, onto the Italian peninsula in an imaginative act of self-definition, as it was about Italian geopolitical realities. In O'Connor's words, 'English men and women laid claim to the historical greatness that was once Rome's while simultaneously infusing their various (and sometimes competing) narratives of an Italian nation with English liberal ideals'.[37] In the Victorian liberal age, Annemarie McAllister notes, the British press developed a self-endorsing 'narrative of English aid to Italy', while the public revelled in the 'vicarious excitement of a liberation, at a safe remove'.[38] Italy's geographical distance from Britain and the Risorgimento's potential to develop along moderate, constitutionalist lines allowed British observers to frame the Italian movement as an emulation of Britain's liberal, constitutional monarchy and to invest the Risorgimento with political meaning for the British ideal of progress and mid-century context of debate over reform. Though many Italians, especially the liberal exiles whom Isabella tracks in *Risorgimento in Exile*, considered British constitutionalism a viable political model for Italy,[39] Riall cautions readers that 'sympathy for Italy in Britain, as well as in France and the USA, masked a distinct sense of cultural and political condescension'.[40] Meridianist and self-interested constructions of Italy within the mutually constitutive Anglo-Italian relationship are as much a recurring feature of the works discussed in this study as is the liberal international's discourse of cross-border solidarity.

British interest in the Risorgimento, then, reflects a number of positions and priorities within British political culture. Considering Alfred Tennyson's seemingly inconsistent enthusiasm for both the Risorgimento and the British Empire, Matthew Reynolds notes that

> the Risorgimento was so compelling to English imaginations that it was harnessed by many mutually contradictory causes: extension of the franchise (Garibaldi was honorary president of the National Reform League); the coming Republic (Swinburne); monarchical constitutionalism (the *Quarterly Review*); even apocalyptic prophecy.[41]

Most groups in British society, historians argue, could find some component of the Risorgimento to support, ranging from opposition to Austrian, Papal and Neapolitan government among the upper ranks to working-class sympathy with republicanism.[42] For Riall, the example of Gladstone's transition from Tory to Liberal politics through his interest in the conditions in Neapolitan prisons illustrates how Italy 'was essentially a "safe" and workable way for middle- and working-class liberals to assert their own identities and beliefs'.[43] The 800-member Society of the Friends of Italy, established in 1851 and consisting of 'Middle-class liberals, free traders, parliamentary reformers, radicals, intellectuals, Chartists, Dissenters, and secularists',[44] reflected the cross-class progressive coalition characteristic of the mid-Victorian liberal age. The British, furthermore, participated extensively in fundraising, and, to a lesser extent, in volunteering, for Garibaldi's 1860 southern campaign.[45] Yet, Italy was more than a blank canvas on which the British envisaged their political projects; Risorgimento leaders also influenced and provided support to more radical members of British society. After the failure of the Chartist movement in the late 1840s, Isabella notes, 'Mazzini provided disillusioned or demoralised Chartists, especially those of the younger generation, with a new and appealing programme of moral regeneration'.[46] Public support for the Risorgimento in Britain, then, could include an inconsistent concoction of liberal complacency, radical internationalism, meridianist self-satisfaction and celebrity worship.

Furthermore, opposition to the Italian cause was high within important segments of British society, especially among conservatives, who feared that an Austrian defeat would unsettle the balance of power, help Napoleon III's Second French Empire and promote revolution, and among Catholics, whose allegiance remained with the Pope.[47] In the colonised British territory of Ireland, donations and volunteers to support the Papal States in 1860 surpassed British material support for Garibaldi[48] and riots occurred corresponding to crises in the Italian movement.[49] Nonetheless, some sympathy for Italian independence existed among Irish nationalists such as Sydney Morgan, the Anglo-Irish writer featured in Chapter 1, and members of the Mazzinian Irish movement, Young Ireland.[50] This illustrates that the Risorgimento remained 'deeply divisive', rather than garnering unanimous support.[51]

In addition, the Risorgimento's outcome sowed new seeds of discontent among radical supporters in Britain, just as it alienated Italian democrats like Mario. Though the constitutionalist victory in Italy might seem to confirm the success of the British model of government, for some Piedmont's expansion and Cavour's political triumph over republicans and federalists in Italy indicated a lack of solidarity within the Italian independence movement and liberal international and the perceived betrayal of the radical cause by the moderates with whom democrats like Garibaldi had temporarily aligned themselves. Marcella Pellegrino Sutcliffe's *Victorian Radicals and Italian Democrats* argues that

> [t]he connection between the victory of the Italian moderates and reaffirming the British monarchical constitution as a model for all nations is a constant which weaves its way through decades of historiographical interpretations, leaving little opportunity to test whether some British observers were in fact disappointed with the turn that events took in 1860.[52]

Pellegrino Sutcliffe, in turn, examines the disaffection of radical British Risorgimento supporters in depth. This range of British responses to the Risorgimento's process and outcome – including optimism, self-congratulation and discontent – appears in the varied, multifaceted familial and romantic metaphors of alliance and solidarity developed in British literary and print culture, to which I now turn.

Metaphors of Union, Allegories of Alliance

As the above discussion illustrates, Risorgimento myths and figures contained a flexibility that allowed British and Anglo-Italian observers to identify the Italian cause with their own political values. Unlike the immediate, radical threat associated with revolution in France, the Italian peninsula was at a safe distance from Britain and was often perceived as a lesser sibling emulating liberal British constitutionalism. Imagining Italy in terms of corporeal and familial metaphors for the state allowed British observers to almost immeasurably shape, revise and manipulate their representations of unification and international solidarity to accommodate any political position. One of the fullest non-fiction visions of a Risorgimento family romance is Theodosia Garrow Trollope's *Social Aspects of the Italian Revolution* (1861), collecting her eyewitness Florence correspondence for the *Athenaeum* during and after the 1859 Second War of Independence and simultaneous Tuscan revolution. Several others also contributed to the contested domain of the Italian family romance in novels, short stories and poetry, establishing literary writing as another field for debate about the Italian independence movement and its relationship to British politics and culture.

Garrow Trollope's *Athenaeum* correspondence, the work of a self-proclaimed 'eye-and-ear-witness of the circumstances',[53] emphasises optimism in the opening declaration, 'We have made at Florence a revolution with rose-water' (1). Her 'rose-water' contrasts particularly with the French Revolution's 'blood-tinted hues',[54] from which British liberals like Garrow Trollope wished to distance themselves and the Italian cause. The short-lived *Tuscan Athenaeum* (1847–8), edited by then Theodosia Garrow's future husband Thomas Trollope in the months leading up to their marriage,[55] cultivated such distance. The 'fiercely pro-Risorgimento' publication targeted a British audience and regularly published Garrow's patriotic poetry.[56] An early *Tuscan Athenaeum* article titled 'A word to those elderly Ladies of both sexes who are afraid of coming into Tuscany, because it is in a state of revolution' stakes its support for the Risorgimento on its difference from French radicalism:

> Tuscany is in a state of revolution, it is true. And it is devoutly to be hoped by every friend of humanity that she may continue to be so . . . But revolutions are dangerous things – it is said – and involve anarchy, massacre and social dissolution . . . The fearful explosion that occurred in France at the end of the last century has coloured the ideas we attach to the meaning of the word *revolution* with its own blood-tinted hues.[57]

A decade later, Garrow Trollope's confidence in her 'rose-water' revolution (1) and Tuscany's incorporation into Piedmont permeates her volume, covering 27 April 1859 to 6 November 1860, even as the bloody battles of the Second War of Independence in Lombardy, rebellions and reprisals in the Papal States and the conquest of southern Italy illustrated the costs of modern warfare.[58] Throughout her correspondence, Garrow Trollope uses customary figures for the modern state – the family and the body politic – to negotiate her partisan Risorgimento support against the movement's real political complications and in particular her suspicion of intervening diplomats and international power players. Her November 1860 Preface argues that 'revolutionary times in Florence [are] so essentially different from any record of similar events in the cities of Northern Europe' (vi). Yet, the correspondence nonetheless draws on the representational legacies of British Romanticism, inheriting the finely strung, bodily sensibility of her precursors and revising the revolutionary family romance's allegories for the new circumstances of Italian unification, to recast revolutionary history for a new generation.

In celebrating cross-class solidarity and bodily investment in shared patriotic feeling, Garrow Trollope revives the cult of sensibility, a 1790s 'site of contention between radical and conservative discourses'.[59] In her essay on Garrow Trollope's Florence correspondence, Esther Schor marks how Garrow Trollope 'delights in showing the hearts of the people pulsing in unison as they gather for a variety of lavish nationalist spectacles';[60] Garrow Trollope celebrates mass volunteering for the war effort and displays of patriotism as cross-class 'spontaneous offering[s] of every heart' (26). She recalls radical sensibility's early enthusiasm for the French Revolution, for example, in describing a crowd gathered to see a Piedmontese official at Livorno ahead of the Tuscan election:

> [A] voice from the throng, nearly under the balcony, cried aloud, 'Viva Vittorio Emmanuele!' and the mass of humanity hurrahed in reply with hearty goodwill and prolonged hand-clapping, which echoed strangely from the buildings around. Then the same voice again took up the strain with 'Viva la Indipendenza d'Italia!' and then indeed the popular heart was touched to the quick, and sent forth the mighty shout which can come only from the 'great deeps' of a people's strong desire. Many – for I saw them – uttered that cry with clasped hands raised above their heads; many with outspread palms as in an act of supplication. (78)[61]

For Garrow Trollope, the body that participates in Risorgimento politics is an emotional body and the body politic a sensitive body pulsing with shared sentiment, projecting a unity that is also a drive to unify.

Garrow Trollope inherits Romantic sensibility via the Corinne fig-ure, a model for female poetic expression she cultivated across her poetic career. Her self-fashioning as 'a new Corinne'[62] allows her to present herself as a knowing expatriate writer with Italian and British allegiances who can speak for the Risorgimento to British audiences.[63] Germaine de Staël's well-known *Corinne* (1807), plot-ting a 1790s romance between individuals representing Italian and British cultures, acts as a textual bridge between 1790s revolutionary discourse and Garrow Trollope's self-image as a nineteenth-century poetess. Using her Corinne-like sensibility as the basis for her author-ity, Garrow Trollope invests the Risorgimento with emotional reso-nance through her revival of the political family romance Lynn Hunt identifies in French revolutionary culture for the mid-Victorian Italian context. Garrow Trollope's account of 1859–60 investigates a range of radical configurations of the family. For Hunt, one of the French Revolution's central questions was, 'what kind of family romance would replace the one dominated by the patriarchal father?'[64] This question is also crucial to Garrow Trollope's refashioning of Tuscany as it moved from Austrian to Piedmontese control. Justifying what could be construed as a Piedmontese takeover through family meta-phor, Garrow Trollope presents political revolution as generational change and unification as companionate union and assertion of sis-terhood across the Italian peninsula and beyond.

Garrow Trollope presents Tuscany's rejection of her paternal *Babbo*, or Daddy, the Grand Duke, as empowered, female self-deter-mination, most obviously in her narrative of Tuscany's companionate marriage with Piedmont's martial Victor Emmanuel II. However, she also explores concepts of female kinship that transcend national bor-ders, presenting Piedmont as Tuscany's 'elder sister' (36) and rejoicing in Italy's induction into 'sisterhood with the nations' (24), including England, leader of this 'crowned sisterhood' (301). She revises the band of revolutionary brothers associated with French radicalism into a feminised model of political solidarity that takes constitutional Britain as its ideal. However, as Schor indicates, the allegory that envisions 'the new Kingdom of Italy as a marriage between *la bella Italia* and the King of Savoy'[65] dominates the text's family romance, transforming into a fairy tale by the conclusion.[66] Garrow Trollope replaces the French family romance's beheaded patriarchal king, Louis XVI, and the narrowly defined radical fraternity that temporar-ily succeeded him[67] with a more tempered rejection of the patriarch: Tuscany's move from the authority of her paternal Grand Duke into a contractual, voluntary union with a constitutional monarch.

Contained within this marriage metaphor are complexities surrounding political agency, female choice and resistance to interference that show Tuscany's commitment to self-determination in the unification process. After all, feminine Tuscany proposes marriage to masculine Piedmont: 'Yesterday afternoon Tuscany laid her hand trustfully in the manly palm of Victor Emmanuel, and bade him take her for better for worse' (106). This does not mean, however, that a state modelled on heterosexual marriage is universally desirable; Garrow Trollope stresses Tuscany's choice of Victor Emmanuel and warns away others who might force her into an unwanted union. To Austrians and international statesmen, Garrow Trollope writes,

> If you will but suffer sunny little Tuscany to give herself away, as her heart desires, to the gallant Zouave corporal, well and good . . . ; if not, beware how you force her old sovereigns back upon her by bayonet law, for though single-handed she needs must yield to an overwhelming force, she stands now linked in a common bond of danger and of faith with Modena, Parma, and the Legations . . . ; and though she have peaceful olives on her uplands, and bounteous corn and vines garlanding her valleys, she has store of iron in her mountains yet, and . . . Garibaldi, to teach her how to use it! (104–5)

The risks Schor identifies with the analogy between the marriage's 'orgasmic' public consummation when Victor Emmanuel enters Florence[68] and Garibaldi's less welcome entry into Naples[69] are thus perhaps intentional: just as Tuscany chooses 'to give herself away, as her heart desires', she can choose to transform herself – with the help of Garibaldi and her Italian sister states – into a figure of strength to counter the myth of debased, feminised Italy fetishised in the Romantic literature that obsessively paraphrased and translated early modern Italian poet Vincenzo da Filicaja's famous sonnet, 'Italia, Italia! O tu cui diè la sorte', best known in English through Lord Byron's translation as

> Italia! oh Italia! thou who hast
> The fatal gift of beauty.[70]

In Garrow Trollope's metaphor, power shifts from the patriarchal Grand Duke to the mature, strengthened daughter figure, Tuscany, not to the bridegroom, Victor Emmanuel, whose presence in Florence depends upon her invitation.

However, Garrow Trollope draws on Filicaja's familiarity to further her optimistic picture of the 'rose-water' revolution (1). Unlike Elizabeth Barrett Browning, who argues in *Casa Guidi Windows* (1851) that conventional descriptions of physically mutilated, dying Italy are

> all images
> Men set between themselves and actual wrong,[71]

Garrow Trollope revives and revises the scarred Italian body politic in a concrete, wartime context. Recognising the costs of occupation and unjust government, she contrasts Naples and Venice with powerful Tuscany. Naples 'yet groans, throbs, and trembles, convulsively inarticulate, under the pressures of the red right hand of tyranny' (98); Austrian-ruled Venice is similarly 'scourged, mangled, and bleeding from every vein' (132). However, Garrow Trollope pairs with suffering Naples and Venice an Italian body politic building physical strength and acquiring resistance to disease in the war's aftermath. The war and subsequent unification efforts illustrate a conflict between political renewal and the deadening status quo. After the disappointing 'paralytic peace' (79) Napoleon III reached with Austria at Villafranca, Garrow Trollope maintains that

> the living principle will never cease to work till it have driven out the remnants of the old tyranny, as surely as the healthy, living flesh drives out the splinters of the unskilfully removed arrow-head which has pierced and angered it. (60)

Political health depends on detecting and removing the internal damage that could lead to infection and spread throughout the living body from within.

Images of new birth underlie this presentation of the healthy body politic. Unification is Italy's 'birthright' (74) and the infant state of Tuscany must undergo physical trials that help develop its constitutional strength:

> Baby states, like baby mortals, have to run through a perilous round of maladies before arriving at the condition of compact and vigorous health, which enables them to stand alone among their fellows, and thrive and hold their own, even to the exchanging of many a sound buffet with any interloper who dares encroach on their nursery privileges. We – I speak for collective Tuscany – are, in truth, a promising infant,

and require but little physic. We have passed in a short time through many threatenings of infantile disorder, and are all the better for stoutly rejecting the sleepy syrups, weakening diet, persuasive lozenges, and infinitesimal poisons prescribed by our high and mighty M.D.s, in solemn consultation assembled, who shake their learned heads, and foredoom us to all the horrors of rickets, atrophy, and convulsions, because we will obstinately overturn their carefully-concocted messes, and shout lustily for plenty of fresh air and wholesome mother's milk to plant us firmly on our baby legs. (157–8)

Just as the marriage contract underlies the shift from *Babbo*'s authority to voluntary alliance with Victor Emmanuel, the image of the baby state empowers the feminine by stressing the maternal role in guiding the family romance's generational change and creating healthy renewal in the body politic.

Garrow Trollope, then, unites her female-centred family romance to existing Risorgimento discourse, which emphasises family. Italian cultural historian Alberto Banti shows, for example, that in Mazzinian thought,

> The lexicon of family and kinship is of paramount importance ... in moulding what is taken to be the essence of the community; and the bond is ... both 'biopolitical', in the sense that it is structured around the nation's capacity to reproduce itself down the ages, and 'affective', in the sense that it is structured around the deepest emotional ties that reinforce relations in a community (of mothers and fathers with their children, of brothers with brothers, and of wives or fiancées with their men).[72]

Garrow Trollope's emphasis on sorority, maternity, healthy birth and the celebratory ritual of national marriage presents a uniquely female-centred Risorgimento to her British audience. At least one reader accepts and builds on this model of feminine contribution to national health, investing Garrow Trollope's eyewitness work with a similar gendered discourse of political care. According to Thomas Trollope, *The Examiner* claimed that:

> Better political information than this book gives may be had in plenty; but it has a special value which we might almost represent by comparing it to the report of a very watchful nurse, who, without the scientific knowledge, uses her own womanly instinct in observing every change of countenance and every movement indicating the return of health and strength to the patient ... She has written a very vivid and truthful account.[73]

Garrow Trollope's vision of a revitalised Italy, it seems, successfully counters the conventional imagery of gendered Italian debasement familiar to her audience.

Six months after Victor Emmanuel's metaphorical marriage with Tuscany, a new feminine figure, Italy the female champion, emerges from her struggle as a heroic revision of Filicaja's trope to close the volume:

> New-wakened Italy, like some fated champion of heroic days in his solemn vigil of arms, has had to wrestle for the life with many a weird shape of enchantment; and to stagger under many a fierce buffet dealt in the dark by hands unseen, while she bided her time and fought her way step by step towards light and deliverance. Now, at last, standing on high ground and looking trustfully forward, with the glory of the new morning on her face, the path of that six months' pilgrimage lies dimly behind her, a maze of crag, ravine, quagmire, and tangled wood, in comparison with which, the way yet to be passed seems smooth and pleasant. (271)

The trials of infant Tuscany, now the married and matured heroine Italy, prepare her for the future, in Garrow Trollope's final paragraph: 'So, with steadfast heart, amid many perils, fixing her eyes upon the ever nearer goal, and helped onwards by the efforts of friends and foes, goes Italy bravely to the accomplishment of her Olympic race!' (309). Garrow Trollope empowers female Tuscany with self-determination; in her further transformation into the courageous new Italy, Garrow Trollope also allows her to absorb, through her union with martial Victor Emmanuel, under Garibaldi's tutelage and alongside her sororal allies, the characteristics of a masculine heroism that prepare her to embark on her adventures as a new nation-state.

However, metaphors of union and new national birth are flexible. Alternative readings of unification, the Wars of Independence and other moments in Risorgimento history propose more sceptical family metaphors and visions of the new body politic. In D. G. Rossetti's 'After the French Liberation of Italy' (1859?),[74] a monstrous Italian body politic is born from a major power's political ambition and self-interest. Through the sonnet's 'elaborate sexual conceit',[75] Rossetti, son of Italian exile Gabriele Rossetti, presents the Italian nation brought into being through war between France and Austria as a 'birth'[76] engendered through the sinful coupling of a 'lust[ful]', masculine France and a promiscuous, 'submissive' (11) Europe. In this variation of 'the old topos of rape as a vehicle for conquest'[77] familiar from Filicaja, the temporary 'throes of longing' that motivate the pair (6) result in the birth of Italy, 'An harlot's child, to scourge her [Europe] for her sin' (14). Rossetti's cynical reaction to Italian state formation reflects the major players' political opportunism in the Second War of Independence: Napoleon III's peace at Villafranca, which failed to include Piedmont; the exclusion of Venice and the Papal States from united Italy; and France's annexation of Nice and Savoy. The sonnet's prostituted Europe, like a 'bought body' (13), invites France to physically reshape it according to French desires and the incomplete Italy that results is Europe's punishment for its surrender to French territorial ambition. Unlike in Garrow Trollope's family romance, Italy does not participate in this version of events: her martial Victor Emmanuel II, empowered female Tuscany and robust infant state are replaced by a predatory Napoleon III, a submissive Europe and a new-born Italy that is a geopolitical 'scourge' (14). Rossetti's discomfort with this venal coupling absorbs an established trope of Italian Risorgimento writing, which 'typically condemned any contact between the heroine, representing the *patria*, with the foreigner, who was generally seen as a threat to the purity and honour of the community'.[78] France was one major outside player in nineteenth-century Italy, occupying the peninsula under the first Napoleon, laying siege to the short-lived Roman Republic in 1849, allying with Piedmont against Austria in 1859 and garrisoning Papal Rome against Italian invasion until Napoleon III's fall in 1870. Yet, Austria was an even more direct interloper in Italy; Austrian rule in Lombardy and Venetia lasted from the 1815 restoration until the 1859 and 1866 wars, respectively.

Unsurprisingly, British writers also tested out the possibility of rapprochement between Italy and Austria using similar familial metaphors. In George Meredith's *Vittoria* (1866), depicting the 1848 Milanese revolution and 1848–9 First War of Independence, the Milanese repudiate any suggestion of unity between Austrians and Italians. The idea that an Italian woman could love an Austrian soldier is 'monstrous' to the heroine Vittoria,[79] and when the conspirator Barto Rizzo recruits his wife to seduce an Austrian soldier to gather intelligence, the republican Carlo Ammiani recoils from the 'incestuous horror' of an embrace he witnesses.[80] Though Carlo's disgust originates with the two figures' representative and irreconcilable national and political dissimilarity, the description of their coupling as 'incestuous' points to the embeddedness of the taboo against Italian–Austrian alliance and the intimacy between occupier and occupied under imperial rule. Anthony Trollope's topical short story, 'The Last Austrian Who Left Venice' (1867), sets a courtship plot during the 1866 Third War of Independence, part of the broader Austro-Prussian War, which precipitated Venice's incorporation into Italy after over half a century of Austrian rule. Carlo Pepé, a secret Garibaldian volunteer, and his friend, Austrian Captain Hubert von Vincke, disagree amicably about politics; yet, as the 1866 struggle approaches their friendship becomes strained, particularly when von Vincke proposes to Carlo's sister, Nina. Despite von Vincke's intimacy with the family, this marriage is 'madness' to Carlo,[81] who argues that von Vincke is 'unfit', 'Not personally, but politically and nationally. You are not one of us; and now, at this moment, any attempt at close union between an Austrian and a Venetian must be ruinous'.[82] The couple eventually marries after the Austrian forces withdraw from Venice. However, the von Vinckes remove to Trieste, demonstrating that although Trollope can imagine cultural reconcili-ation in personal terms, this is only possible when military occupa-tion ends and must occur away from the historic site of hostility.

Though Britain did not directly intervene in Italy, British observers also explored the possibility of Anglo-Italian alliance. Well-known Anglo-Italian courtship plots occur in de Staël's French-language, Romantic-era blockbuster *Corinne* and its Victorian re-visioning, Barrett Browning's *Aurora Leigh*.[83] Meredith tests out versions of Anglo-Italian alliance in his first novel featuring Vittoria, then known as Emilia Alessandra Belloni, in *Sandra Belloni* (1864). Emilia sees her lover Wilfrid as a representative of English intervention against Austrian rule in Lombardy, signified by her music master: she sighs, 'My English lover! I am like Italy, in chains to that German'.[84] Simi-larly, for Emilia's admirer, British Risorgimento supporter Merthyr Powys, Emilia is 'Italy in the flesh'.[85] Wilfrid's decision to join the Austrian army and betray Emilia with another woman represents a failed Anglo-Italian alliance. British writers also used marriage meta-phors to explore the possibility of international disengagement, mir-roring their government's official neutrality. The eponymous hero of Benjamin Disraeli's *Lothair* (1870), set during the 1867 Mentana episode, when Garibaldi's democratic volunteers attempted to take Rome,[86] is torn between his Roman Catholic guardian, Cardinal Grandison, and the compelling Italian revolutionary, Theodora. Though Lothair fights on the democratic side, Theodora dies and Lothair finally marries the neutral English aristocrat Lady Corisande, indicating his withdrawal from the theatre of European revolution. Lill Tufton, the fickle heroine of Henrietta Jenkin's '*Who Breaks – Pays*' (1861), similarly retreats from her engagement with the Italian exile Giuliani to marry the conservative English baronet, Sir Frederick Ponsonby. Lill's entanglement with the Risorgimento does not end with this marriage, however; separating from Sir Frederick in jealousy of his former lover, Lill finds herself in Genoa under siege in the aftermath of the 1849 Battle of Novara,[87] where she is killed by a stray bullet only hours before her planned reunion with her husband. For Lill, withdrawal from Italian affairs does not mean an escape from their consequences. Through Lill's courtship plot, Jenkin tells her readers that hesitation and vacillation carry their own penalties in love and politics.

Arthur Hugh Clough's epistolary verse novel *Amours de Voyage* (1858) more fully explores the consequences of neutrality through the tourist Claude, who witnesses the 1849 siege of the Roman Republic by French forces. Hesitating in his romance with fellow tourist Mary Trevellyn and his political stance towards the siege, Claude, an observer, is placed at the centre of a debate surrounding Britain's international responsibility towards its neighbours that crystallised around Risorgimento conflict. Citing Mazzini's well-known arguments against British neutrality,[88] Renzo D'Agnillo suggests that 'both Clough and Claude, as representatives of England, become the antagonistic protagonists of a silent ideological confrontation, played out on a subconscious level'.[89] As Christopher M. Keirstead argues, 'Like the British Foreign Office, Claude reveals that as an English citizen he just watches';[90] in fact, by blaming France for intervention and Britain for non-intervention, Claude fails even to commit to doing nothing.[91] Claude's studied neutrality reveals competing urges within the liberal self, as the cross-border solidarity imagined by the liberal international conflicts with individual self-interest. He excuses his own inaction by pointing out a tension between patriotic sacrifice and personal security, arguing that

> Sweet it may be and decorous perhaps for the country to die, but
> On the whole we conclude the Romans won't do it, and I shan't.
>   (II, 46–7)

Yet, he also identifies with Rome's collective action, writing, for example, 'we are fighting at last' (II, 95), despite his nonparticipation.

Thus, Claude vicariously assumes privileged access as a witness to the Roman revolution, although his passivity becomes increasingly crippling. He retreats from Rome and his affair with Mary, but continues to identify with Rome's fate, imagining his personal, romantic defeat as a parallel to the public fall of the Roman Republic:

Rome is fallen; and fallen, or falling, heroical Venice.
I, meanwhile, for the loss of a single small chit of a girl, sit
Moping and mourning here, – for her, and myself much smaller.
    (V, 115–17)

Giving up on his love with the statement, 'I will go where I am led, and will not dictate to the chances' (V, 179), Claude also accepts Papal Rome as a political inevitability:

Politics farewell, however! For what could I do? with inquiring,
Talking, collating the journals, go fever my brain about things o'er
Which I can have no control. No, happen whatever may happen,
Time, I suppose, will subsist; the earth will revolve on its axis;
People will travel; the stranger will wander as now in the city;
Rome will be here, and the Pope the *custode* of Vatican marbles.
    (V, 188–93)

This abdication rings false, given Claude's early claim that he 'nor meddle[s] nor make[s] in politics' (II, 16); Claude's fate is not a defeat, but a confirmation of his status quo, his refusal to engage. The malaise Clough identifies at the heart of modern life in *Amours de Voyage* also lies at the centre of the liberal British citizen Risorgimento propagandists worked so hard to engage.

As these chapters illustrate, the British did engage, and on an immense scale. British and Anglo-Italian responses to the Risorgimento reveal a complicated print contest that played out over decades, across high literary modes, pamphlets and propaganda, memoirs and travel writing, parliamentary debates and reports, journalism and emerging genres. The breadth of texts that addressed the Risorgimento establishes the movement's significance for the evolution of forms and genres such as sensation fiction, the historical novel and the lyric against the contemporary polemical and journalistic non-fiction writing in pamphlets and the periodical press. As the Risorgimento geopolitically re-mapped Europe, its reverberations in British print helped to reshape Britain's literary and political cultures; the wide-ranging and diverse British responses to Italian democratic and independence efforts show the centrality of Italian politics within the nineteenth-century British imagination.

The discussion that follows excavates some of the major collision points between Italian politics and nineteenth-century British literature. The four chapters examine four concrete, political focal points of British engagement with the Risorgimento, moving between two crucial turning points that reshaped Europe's geopolitical map, the

1815 Congress of Vienna and the 1861 creation of the Kingdom of Italy. Chapter 1 analyses Romantic-era responses to the Congress of Vienna in the period leading up to and following the 1820–1 uprisings in the Two Sicilies and Piedmont, with attention to Lady Morgan's travelogue *Italy* (1821) and Mary Shelley's historical novel *Valperga* (1823). Morgan and Shelley place Italy, a cluster of minor European states, within a broad, European context of cultural appropriation, imperialist territorial expansion and failed diplomacy to interrogate the discourse of Italian decay against the concrete realities of the peninsula's fragmented history and post-Napoleonic present. Chapter 2 explores the re-imagining of the Italian refugee during the early Risorgimento, between the emergence of Giuseppe Mazzini's Young Italy movement and the waning of the democratic wing's influence after 1848. This Chapter focuses on two English-language novels by Italian refugee Giovanni Ruffini, a former Young Italy member who fictionalises his own involvement in the movement in 1830s Piedmont and flight into exile in *Lorenzo Benoni* (1853) and depicts a returned Sicilian exile's participation in the 1848 revolutions in *Doctor Antonio* (1855), to argue that Ruffini makes exile a constitutive feature of Italian political identity and re-writes the Italian landscape by mapping out the tracks of the dispossessed patriots who were expelled from their homes and communities during this period.

The final two chapters concentrate on works produced during and after the climax of the Risorgimento in 1859–60. Chapter 3 discusses Wilkie Collins's sensation novel, *The Woman in White* (1859–60), focusing on representations of spying as they relate to the development of the Gothic and to the 1844 Post Office Espionage Scandal, during which the British public learned that its government was opening Mazzini's private letters and passing their contents to continental authorities. The crisis in mid-Victorian liberalism that occurred as a result of the scandal, evident in the ensuing parliamentary and print debates, is transposed into the emerging literary genre of sensation fiction with the publication of *The Woman in White*. Chapter 4 traces the traumatic impact of the 1859 Second War of Independence and its aftermath in Elizabeth Barrett Browning's *Poems Before Congress* (1860) and *Last Poems* (1862). Despite voicing enthusiastic support for unification efforts led by Napoleon III and Cavour, Barrett Browning's poems also recognise the Risorgimento's failures and costs. 'Napoleon III. in Italy', 'Mother and Poet', 'Died . . . ', 'The Forced Recruit' and 'A Tale of Villafranca Told in Tuscany' explore the uses and limits of lyric utterance in EBB's political project of representing the Risorgimento, using familial and intergenerational motifs to demonstrate how a performative poetic voice that ushers Italy into being comes into conflict with the historical trauma that often precludes speech and severs the correspondence between words and deeds.

These case studies of British engagement with Italian politics highlight the diverse and contradictory responses to Italian nationalism through the interventions and mediations of the outside voices of those who often could not claim citizenship or membership in the incipient nation that emerged as a result of the movement. In constructing a British Risorgimento imaginary, these writers participate in politics and nation-making obliquely. Morgan, Shelley, Garrow Trollope and Barrett Browning are women writers without any rights of citizenship; Shelley, Garrow Trollope and Barrett Browning also wrote as Anglo-Italians, expatriates who were neither fully British nor precisely Italian. Morgan was an Anglo-Irish writer whose interest in Italy highlights her position as a colonial subject, while Barrett Browning first published many of her Italian poems in the United States, demonstrating both her international readership and her fraught relationship with British audiences. Finally, Ruffini was an Italian refugee based in Paris who published in Britain and wrote in English for a British public. The voices of outsiders and figures of cultural hybridity – women, expatriates, exiles, Anglo-Italians and Anglo-Irish – shape this nineteenth-century print debate about self-determination, citizenship and political rights.

Furthermore, Risorgimento cultural production features a tension between a discourse of rooted nationalism and an internationalist emphasis on mobilities and cross-border cooperation. Even Mazzini, who transformed romantic nationalism into a republican political brand, cultivated international revolutionary networks and cross-border collaboration. Banti describes Mazzinian thought in essentially romantic nationalist terms, arguing that 'in Mazzinian rhetoric we find an appeal to history, genealogy, blood, land, and the nation's honour'.[92] Yet, tension between a romantic nationalist concept of the nation as a rooted community grounded in culture and biological relationship and an internationalist, republican political discourse that informed the Italian question exists within Mazzini's own writings. Mazzini, after all, saw 'the *nation*' as 'an intermediary between humanity and the *individual*'[93] and envisioned 'the formation of a *United States* of Europe'[94] as the next stage of his republican political project following national independence. From a critical perspective, viewing a nationalist movement in internationalist terms allows for the recognition of dialogue, dissent and opposition within the political discourse that envisioned an Italian nation-state. As Good-lad and Julia M. Wright describe it, 'an internationalist standpoint evokes contingent spaces of social, politico-economic, and cultural interaction – including the importance of non-state actors'.[95] This study explores how international exchange, empathy and interventions existed alongside and within the Italian nationalist movement. Throughout the British and English-language writing discussed here, forms of mobility and circulation take a central place. These comprise the exchange of political ideas; the movement of people, including refugees, tourists, soldiers and spies; the circulation, and non-circulation, of texts, including letters and books like Morgan's banned travelogue; and the flow of information, troops and arms through communications and travel networks, such as the telegraph and railroad systems that determined the speed with which the 1859 war was conducted and with which international audiences gained access to its latest news. As these chapters demonstrate, the nation-building enterprise of Risorgimento culture was a participatory, international field crossing borders, cultural and print forms, political parties and literary genres, which radically reshaped British culture as it re-drew Europe's borders.

Notes

1. Alberto Mario, *The Red Shirt. Episodes*, p. 9.
2. Jessie White was a Mazzinian propagandist, lecturer, nurse during Garibaldi's campaigns, Italian correspondent for the American periodical *The Nation*, biographer and collector of Risorgimento papers. The couple spent their engagement in Sant'Andrea prison in Genoa for participating in Giuseppe Mazzini's plot to stage uprisings across Piedmont corresponding to Carlo Pisacane's unsuccessful 1857 expedition to southern Italy. For more, see Elizabeth Adams Daniels, *Jessie White Mario: Risorgimento Revolutionary* and Maura O'Connor, *The Romance of Italy and the English Political Imagination*, pp. 93–115.
3. Mario, a republican federalist, opposed the new nation-state's centralisation and its constitutional monarchy.
4. Lucy Riall, *Risorgimento: The History of Italy from Napoleon to Nation State*, pp. 39, 40.
5. Benedict Anderson, *Imagined Communities: Reflections on the Origin and Spread of Nationalism*, p. 6.
6. Diego Saglia, 'Hemans's Record of Dante: "The Maremma" and the Intertextual Poetics of Plenitude', p. 129.
7. Suzanne Stewart-Steinberg, *The Pinocchio Effect: On Making Italians (1860–1920)*, p. 1.

8. Camillo Benso di Cavour, Prime Minister of Piedmont-Sardinia and first Prime Minister of Italy, and Victor Emmanuel II, first King of Italy.
9. Lucy Riall, *Garibaldi: Invention of a Hero*, p. 136.
10. Ibid.
11. Stewart-Steinberg, *The Pinocchio Effect*, p. 2.
12. Adrian Lyttelton, 'The National Question in Italy', p. 99.
13. Stewart-Steinberg, *The Pinocchio Effect*, p. 1.
14. Lyttelton, 'The National Question', pp. 99–100.
15. Ibid. p. 100.
16. Roberto Esposito, *Living Thought: The Origins and Actuality of Italian Philosophy*, p. 19.
17. Ibid. p. 21.
18. Ibid. p. 20.
19. Riall, *Risorgimento*, p. 38.
20. Stewart-Steinberg, *The Pinocchio Effect*, p. 2.
21. Derek Beales, *The Risorgimento and the Unification of Italy*, p. 84.
22. Riall, *Risorgimento*, p. 146.
23. Beales, *The Risorgimento and the Unification of Italy*, p. 92.
24. Riall, *Risorgimento*, p. 40.
25. Ibid. p. 124.
26. Riall, *Garibaldi*, pp. 386–7.
27. By the 1850s, Mazzini's continual involvement in plots against the Italian regimes, including Piedmont, compromised him in much public opinion. Garibaldi, by contrast, worked with Cavour and Victor Emmanuel to achieve unification at the expense of his more radical, republican political goals. Cavour's untimely death in 1861 contributed to Piedmont's inability to consolidate its territorial victory politically. The term Risorgimento was popularised by the title of Cavour's newspaper, *Il Risorgimento*, founded in 1847 under King Charles Albert's liberalisation of press freedoms. Alison Chapman, 'On *Il Risorgimento*', p. 3.
28. Riall, *Garibaldi*, p. 268. For more on southern Italy's annexation, see Riall, *Garibaldi*, pp. 223–4. Cavour annexed Naples and Sicily despite his disinclination towards pan-Italian unification because Garibaldi's conquest of the south forced his hand: 'In order to control the apparent inevitability of national unification, Cavour was forced to become its main architect'. Riall, *Garibaldi*, p. 269. Cavour's 1859–60 territorial ambitions were focused on Austrian-held Lombardy-Venetia.
29. Lauren M. E. Goodlad, *The Victorian Geopolitical Aesthetic: Realism, Sovereignty and Transnational Experience*, p. 34.
30. Maurizio Isabella, *Risorgimento in Exile: Italian Émigrés and the Liberal International in the Post-Napoleonic Era*, p. 23.
31. Ibid. p. 31. Garibaldi first came to public prominence as a guerrilla fighter in 1840s Uruguay. For more on his South American career, see Riall, *Garibaldi*, pp. 37–46.
32. Isabella, *Risorgimento in Exile*, p. 92.

33. Several of Elizabeth Barrett Browning's Risorgimento poems were initially published in the American periodical *The Independent*, for example. Garibaldi lived briefly in exile in New York, alongside other Italian activists, and White Mario toured America in the 1850s, lecturing to primarily abolitionist audiences, before becoming the Italian correspondent for *The Nation*. For more on transatlantic, expatriate networks of Risorgimento support, see Alison Chapman, *Networking the Nation: British and American Women's Poetry and Italy, 1840–1870*.

34. Annemarie McAllister, *John Bull's Italian Snakes and Ladders: English Attitudes to Italy in the Mid-Nineteenth Century*, p. 199.

35. Manfred Pfister, 'Performing National Identity', p. 9.

36. Maura O'Connor, *The Romance of Italy*, p. 1.

37. Ibid. p. 3.

38. McAllister, *John Bull's Italian Snakes and Ladders*, pp. 196, 6.

39. Isabella, *Risorgimento in Exile*, pp. 111–50.

40. Riall, *Garibaldi*, p. 143.

41. Matthew Reynolds, *The Realms of Verse 1830–1870: English Poetry in a Time of Nation-Building*, p. 203.

42. Maurizio Isabella, 'Italian Exiles and British Politics Before and After 1848', p. 78.

43. Riall, *Garibaldi*, p. 144.

44. Isabella, *Risorgimento in Exile*, p. 211.

45. Riall, *Garibaldi*, pp. 294–5, 297.

46. Isabella, 'Italian Exiles', p. 72.

47. Nick Carter, 'Introduction: Britain, Ireland and the Italian Risorgimento', pp. 15–19.

48. Ibid. p. 8.

49. Anne O'Connor identifies the March 1859 Galway riot with the tension leading up to Italy's Second War of Independence and the September 1862 Tralee riot with the Battle of Aspromonte. Anne O'Connor, 'An Italian Inferno in Ireland: Alessandro Gavazzi and Religious Debate in the Nineteenth Century', p. 139. 'Garibaldi riots' also occurred in 1862 London between Garibaldi supporters and Irish Catholics and the 1866 Newcastle riot corresponded to the Third War of Independence. Carter, 'Introduction', pp. 17–18.

50. See Michael Huggins, 'A Cosmopolitan Nationalism: Young Ireland and the Risorgimento'.

51. Carter, 'Introduction', p. 15.

52. Marcella Pellegrino Sutcliffe, *Victorian Radicals and Italian Democrats*, p. 3.

53. Theodosia Garrow Trollope, *Social Aspects of the Italian Revolution, in a Series of Letters from Florence, Reprinted from the* Athenaeum; *with a Sketch of Subsequent Events up to the Present Time*, p. 6. Subsequent citations will appear parenthetically in the text.

54. Quoted in Giuliana Artom Treves, *The Golden Ring: The Anglo-Florentines 1847–1862*, p. 30.

55. October 1847–January 1848.

56. Chapman, *Networking the Nation*, p. 55.

57. Quoted in Treves, *The Golden Ring*, p. 30.

58. Garrow Trollope primarily covers Tuscany, but her first letter is dated 'April 27, 1859' (1), the day after war was declared and the date on which Tuscany's Leopold II was overthrown.

59. Chris Jones, *Radical Sensibility: Literature and Ideas in the 1790s*, p. 6.

60. Esther Schor, 'Acts of Union: Theodosia Garrow Trollope and Frances Power Cobbe on the Kingdom of Italy', p. 97.

61. Compare, for example, Helen Maria Williams's triumphant description of the French Revolution's first anniversary celebrations. Helen Maria Williams, *Letters Written in France* [1790], pp. 64–5.

62. Thomas Adolphus Trollope, *What I Remember*, p. 168.

63. See Chapman, *Networking the Nation*, pp. 123–32.

64. Lynn Hunt, *The Family Romance of the French Revolution*, p. 5.

65. Schor, 'Acts of Union', p. 91.

66. Ibid. p. 100.

67. For a discussion of French revolutionary fraternity, see Hunt, *The Family Romance*, p. 13.

68. Victor Emmanuel 'entered Florence' on 'A memorable day, and a memorable night, to all who witnessed his reception and saw our beautiful Florence in her bridal attire' (257). See also Elizabeth Barrett Browning, 'King Victor Emanuel Entering Florence, April, 1860' [1860/1862], in *Last Poems*, pp. 65–9.

69. Schor, 'Acts of Union', pp. 98–100.

70. Lord Byron, *Childe Harold's Pilgrimage* [1818], IV, 370–1. Felicia Hemans also translated the sonnet as 'Italia! thou, by lavish Nature graced' (1818). Felicia Hemans, *Felicia Hemans: Selected Poems, Prose, and Letters*, p. 143.

71. Elizabeth Barrett Browning, *Casa Guidi Windows*, I, 43–4.

72. Alberto Mario Banti, 'Sacrality and the Aesthetics of Politics: Mazzini's Concept of the Nation', pp. 61–2.

73. Quoted in Trollope, *What I Remember*, p. 256.

74. According to the *Rossetti Archive*, the first manuscript copy, housed in the British Library, may have been written in 1859. The first publication date is 1911.

75. Tobias Döring, 'Imaginary Homelands? D. G. Rossetti and his Father between Italy and England', p. 271.

76. D. G. Rossetti, 'After the French Liberation of Italy', l. 13. Subsequent citations will appear parenthetically in the text by line number.

77. Döring, 'Imaginary Homelands?', p. 272.

78. Isabella, *Risorgimento in Exile*, p. 90. Isabella cites Banti; see Banti's description of Francesco Hayez's paintings for an example. Banti, 'Sacrality and the Aesthetics of Politics', pp. 68–73.

79. George Meredith, *Vittoria*, p. 353.

80. Ibid. p. 139.

81. Anthony Trollope, 'The Last Austrian Who Left Venice', p. 61.
82. Ibid. p. 62.
83. Other re-workings include Felicia Hemans's 'Corinne at the Capitol' (1827) and 'Woman and Fame' (1829). Felicia Hemans, *Felicia Hemans*, pp. 351–2, 355–7. For relevant readings of *Aurora Leigh*, see Sandra M. Gilbert, 'From *Patria* to *Matria*: Elizabeth Barrett Browning's Risorgimento' and Alison Chapman, 'Poetry, Network, Nation: Elizabeth Barrett Browning and Expatriate Women's Poetry'.
84. George Meredith, *Sandra Belloni; Originally Emilia in England*, p. 149.
85. Ibid. p. 300.
86. See Riall, *Garibaldi*, pp. 349–52.
87. The final battle of the First War of Independence between Piedmont and Austria, after which Charles Albert abdicated.
88. See, for example, Giuseppe Mazzini, 'The European Question: Foreign Intervention and National Self-Determination (1847)', in *A Cosmopolitanism of Nations: Giuseppe Mazzini's Writings on Democracy, Nation Building, and International Relations*, pp. 193–8; 'Concerning the Fall of the Roman Republic (1849)', in *A Cosmopolitanism of Nations*, pp. 208–12; and 'Europe: Its Condition and Prospects' (1852).
89. Renzo D'Agnillo, '"Now in Happier Air": Arthur Hugh Clough's "Amours de Voyage" and Italian Republicanism', p. 108.
90. Christopher M. Keirstead, *Victorian Poetry, Europe, and the Challenge of Cosmopolitanism*, p. 50.
91. Arthur Hugh Clough, *Amours de Voyage*, II, 23–5. Subsequent citations will appear parenthetically in the text by canto and line numbers.
92. Banti, 'Sacrality and the Aesthetics of Politics', p. 68.
93. Giuseppe Mazzini, 'Toward a Holy Alliance of the Peoples (1849)', in *A Cosmopolitanism of Nations*, p. 125.
94. Giuseppe Mazzini, 'Against the Foreign Imposition of Domestic Institutions (1851)', in *A Cosmopolitanism of Nations*, p. 136.
95. Lauren M. E. Goodlad and Julia M. Wright, 'Introduction and Keywords', in *Victorian Internationalisms*, n. pag.

Chapter 1

Romantic Italy and Restoration Politics: Romantic Poetry, Lady Morgan's *Italy* and Mary Shelley's *Valperga*

In 1820, Lord Byron wrote to Italian insurgents in Naples to volunteer his services in their fight for political rights 'without any other motive than that of sharing the destiny of a brave nation'.[1] This imagining of Italy as a 'brave nation' with an unfolding 'destiny' marks a significant shift from Byron's hopeless 'lament'[2] for a fallen state in 'Venice. An Ode' (1818) or the 'grie[f]' William Wordsworth expresses in considering that

> even the Shade
> Of that which once was great, is passed away

in 'On the Extinction of the Venetian Republic' (1807).[3] The motif of political resurrection after a period of death or decay is encoded in the emerging discourse of Italian national rebirth and in British imaginative responses to Italy's awakening revolutionary consciousness. Yet, the tropes of decay and rebirth that occur across British Romantic poetry about Italy tend to elide contemporary history in favour of a distant, idealised past and an imminent but imagined future. By contrast, prose works by Mary Shelley and Lady Morgan, well known as Sydney Owenson before her marriage, historicise Italy, to acknowledge how outside influence and occupation shaped the peninsula and how Italy mediated the major European powers' views of themselves and each other. Morgan and Shelley thus present an alternative to the abstract, ideological projections onto the Italian peninsula offered in much of the British poetry of the Napoleonic period and restoration. For Morgan and Shelley, Italy is contingent on complex existing outside and internal power structures and hosts a range of competing political ambitions and agendas. Although after 1815 British Romantic writers appear to turn

away from France and look to Italy's past and future for inspiration
for their political hopes, Italy, in fact, comes to mediate British attitudes towards the legacies of the French Revolution and Napoleon's
Empire. Likewise, British encounters with Italy are framed by an
intricate network of pan-European alliances, power structures and
struggles. Positioning Morgan's *Italy* (1821) and Shelley's *Valperga*
(1823) against symbolic poetic representations of fallen and reborn
Italy reveals a heightened awareness of political complexity and
international context in Romantic-era responses to the Italian peninsula's revolutionary potential and place within the post-Waterloo
balance of power.

Within the Romantic political discourse of resurgent Italy, then,
Morgan and Shelley carve out a representational space that respects
Italy's diversity and acknowledges its contingency on international
geopolitics. Though Morgan and Shelley support pan-Italian unity
and Italy's elevation to the status of nationhood, they also explore
the results of Italy's fragmentation within their political projects
of crafting a revolutionary anti-imperialism that promotes minor
powers against restoration Europe's dominant centralised nation-
states and Empires. Offering alternatives to a newly masculinised
Romantic literary culture and 'hegemonic' concept of the nation-
state founded on romantic nationalism's 'emphasis on the organic
relationship between nation and state, allied to a localist attention
to the folkloric connection between people and place',[4] Morgan and
Shelley negotiate the continuities and conflicts among cross-border
unity, local sovereignty and anti-imperialist resistance in their literary interventions in Italian politics. Italian unity provides a start-
ing point for reclaiming autonomy against imperialist, territorial
expansionism; yet, for Shelley in particular, internal Italian forces of
expansion also threaten local sovereignty. Taken together, Morgan
and Shelley clarify some of the contradictions that emerge in Risorgimento politics in the subsequent decades: though the concept of an
Italian nation-state is a potential weapon against outside imperialist
incursions into Italy, it could also subordinate Italy's rich and diverse
local and regional cultures to strategic projects of territorial acquisi-
tion and ideological assimilation. In placing the minor Italian states
against imperialist powers like Austria, France and Britain, Morgan
and Shelley recognise how Romantic Italy's access to 'the dignity of
a nation'[5] was contingent upon the European balance of power that
took shape after 1815.

'Land of Departed Fame!': British Poetry and
Romantic Italy

What became the Risorgimento myth of national and political
regeneration following a period of decay maps onto the brand of
revolutionary Romantic thought that emerged after Waterloo, most
famously in P. B. Shelley's 'Ode to the West Wind' (1820), which
suggests that the path to rebirth lies only through the kind of political death Wordsworth identified in Venice. Shelley's speaker begs
the autumn wind to 'Scatter' and plant his revolutionary thought
throughout the earth, 'Like withered leaves to quicken a new birth'.[6]
Political decay thus inevitably and naturally leads to regeneration
through the destruction of the old, dead dispensation. Shelley's
imagery of apocalyptic natural forces and the building momentum
created by the interlocking rhyme of his Italian *terza rima* form com-
bine to usher in a revolutionary world. For radical second-generation
Romantics, the betrayal of republican hopes in France meant finding
a new hope for the republican legacy of the 1790s after 1815: Italy,
oppressed, occupied and divided by neighbouring powers before,
during and after the Napoleonic period, offered fertile territory for
planting the seeds of insurrection.

'Italy' as a unified state or distinct geopolitical entity did not
exist in 1815; with the Congress of Vienna, the peninsula was
divided among reactionary monarchies (the Kingdom of the Two
Sicilies and the Kingdom of Piedmont-Sardinia); the Papal States;
direct Austrian possessions (Lombardy-Venetia); and Habsburg-
ruled Austrian client states (the Grand Duchy of Tuscany and the
Duchies of Parma, Lucca and Modena). The formerly independent Republics of Venice and Genoa were incorporated into the
Austrian Empire and Piedmont, respectively (Figure 1.1).[7] Yet, the
concept of 'Italy' did have meaning to the peninsula's inhabitants
and the Romantic writers travelling in Italy or looking on from a
distance. As Diego Saglia notes, '"Italy" stood for a geopolitical
situation of cohesion in diversity and fragmentation, and a cultural dimension unrelated to a unitary state'.[8] Just exactly what
composed that 'cohesion' and defined that 'cultural dimension',
however, remained in constant negotiation, with Romantic writers
from across Europe participating in constructing the nineteenth-
century idea of Italy.

Figure 1.1 *Italy*. (Source: *New Universal Atlas of the World*, J. Morse and S. Morse [New Haven, 1822]. Digital reproduction from the W. K. Morrison Special Collection of the J. B. Hall Library at the NSCC Centre of Geographic Sciences, <https://nscc.cairnrepo.org/islandora/object/nscc:506>.)

Italy was also an experimental space for Romantic writers defining their own national and cosmopolitan identities. After 1815, the territory of the traditional, aristocratic Grand Tour was also a place of radical exile from conservative Britain and an opportunity for the extension of liberal and revolutionary political thought beyond the Napoleonic period. Though Jeffrey N. Cox notes that '[t]he turn to Italy is a defining characteristic of what we know as second-generation romanticism',[9] Romantics did not abandon the concerns of 1790s radicalism: revolution, republicanism and the example – and warning – of France. For second-generation Romantic writers, consideration of Italy was part of the cultural and political struggle that defined the post-Napoleonic period; for expatriates in particular, representations of Italy and Italianness were responses to what Maria Schoina describes as 'a crisis in politics and culture' that corresponded to 'an age of failed revolutions, imperial reaction and struggling nations'.[10] Italy in the early restoration period provided a new field for grappling with the pan-European legacies of revolution and reaction of the previous twenty-five years.

The decayed Venice trope of Wordsworth's 'On the Extinction of the Venetian Republic' features the contrast between historical Italian greatness – Venice's absolute sovereignty and position as both ancestor and heir to republican ideals as 'the eldest Child of Liberty' – and its supposed current degradation, as an occupied city ceded by one Emperor to another, a worthless pawn in European-wide war.[11] As Riall explains, the term *risorgimento* 'ironically . . . reflects, and bestows on Italy, a sense of national decline which is largely missing in other western European nationalist movements'.[12] Though the fallen Italy literary trope is not unique to the Romantic period, the extent to which former Italian republics lay prostrate before the warring imperial powers of France and Austria gave new political emphasis to Italy's classical and medieval ruins in the early nineteenth century. Italy's fall, to Romantic writers, was primarily political. Invaded by republican France, incorporated into Napoleon's domains and carved up by the victorious allies after Napoleon's defeat, Italy lost what liberty and independence had remained to its states after 1815. Byron describes Italy as 'the throne and grave of empires'[13] and P. B. Shelley calls the peninsula 'the corpse of greatness'.[14] For Felicia Hemans, Italy was a 'Land of departed fame!', a

> Proud wreck of vanish'd power, of splendour fled,
> Majestic temple of the mighty dead!
> Whose grandeur, yet contending with decay,
> Gleams thro' the twilight of thy glorious day.[15]

The revolutionary period, then, consolidated Italy's political death for Romantic writers. As Joseph Luzzi argues, the period saw 'Italy's transition from Europe's "museum" to its "mausoleum"'.[16] Romantic-era interest in Italy could be understood as a mournful appropriation of its cultural and political heritage that fails to endow full political consciousness to real, nineteenth-century Italians:

> Many foreign writers believed . . . that Italy's monumental past . . . represented the privileged historical source of their own individual nations and cultures. In linking themselves to this storied Italian past, authors tended either to ignore or to dramatize the shortcomings of contemporary Italy, which emerged paradoxically in the Romantic age as the culturally impoverished antithesis of its own illustrious heritage.[17]

Luzzi's comments point out the ways in which Italian history became a European-wide inheritance for Romantic writers, shifting its legacies away from modern Italy. According to Schoina, furthermore, expatriate identity construction pre-empted Italian states and people in British imaginings:

> Italianness was decontextualized from its geographical-cultural reality and was intimately infiltrated into British narratives and keyed to various British concerns, such as the forging of British identity, the rise of the English middle-class, and the envisioning, by a group of Romantic liberal intellectuals, of a European/universal cultural, political and social reform.[18]

For Schoina, the 'Anglo-Italian' comprises 'a cartography of intersecting and interacting identity positioning, which conditions, to a large extent, the map of post-Waterloo British Romantic Italy'.[19] The Italian peninsula, these critics suggest, is taken up by Romantic writers as a testing-ground for their own claims for cultural ascendancy, national and cosmopolitan identity and political relevance, including the relevance of self-imposed exile.

British writers in particular often viewed contemporary Italy through the lens of their cultural and political appropriations of its history. Some considered themselves the heirs to Italy's glorious past, a view that contributed to British support of the Risorgimento across the century. During the war years, Erik Simpson writes, 'British national propaganda . . . presented the Britain fighting Napoleon as analogous to ancient Rome but not to modern Italy'.[20] Many considered Britain to be Italy's ally and protector in the Napoleonic

Wars. In *The Restoration of the Works of Art to Italy* (1816), for example, Hemans calls upon the Italian Muse to 'Awake', but not to re-claim past Italian greatness; instead, Italy must praise and thank Britain for restoring the artworks stolen during the war and protecting Italy's glorious history.[21] Hemans's poem becomes an occasion for praising contemporary British heroism at Waterloo, where, she argues,

> th'avenging sword,
> Won the bright treasures to thy fanes restored.[22]

This discourse erases modern Italians from their own civilisation, appropriating historical Italian liberties and transforming them into British constitutional freedoms, then projecting British institutions back onto Italy as models. Mary Shelley's fantastical short story, 'Valerius: The Reanimated Roman' (1819), in which a resurrected ancient Roman disdains modern Italians as the fallen usurpers of Roman glory and turns for friendship to a young British woman, illustrates the ease with which the British assume the Roman mantle.[23] Though Britain did not intervene territorially on the Italian peninsula like France or Austria,[24] then, its ideological intervention – subscribed to by liberal and republican writers in varying degrees – attempted to shape Italian political discourse, often directing it away from revolutionary republicanism and towards liberal constitutionalism.

As a model for constitutional liberty, however, Britain also betrayed both the Italian population it purported to support and its own political values. While commanding Britain's occupation forces in Sicily during the Napoleonic Wars, British Lord William Bentinck advocated Italian independence under the post-war settlement; however, at the Congress of Vienna, Foreign Secretary Lord Castlereagh subordinated British constitutionalism to the nation's continental interests.[25] For anti-Castlereagh Romantic writers, Britain's guilt had to be expunged. Byron contrasts Britain's post-war celebration with Rome's 'lament', describing the restoration settlement as 'the betrayal of Genoa, of Italy, of France, and of the world'.[26] Italy's betrayal, Byron continues, is analogous to post-war repression within Britain, as part of an attempt by the established powers to enforce a pan-European reactionary status quo:

> What Italy has gained by the late transfer of nations, it were useless for Englishmen to enquire, till it becomes ascertained that England has acquired something more than a permanent army and a suspended

Habeas Corpus: it is enough for them to look at home. For what they have done abroad, and especially in the South, 'Verily they *will have* their reward', and at no very distant period.[27]

Byron's warning against relinquishing principles in support of the balance of power and public safety is heightened by his subscription to the concept of a special relationship between Britain and the Italian states; Venice, the victim of French and Austrian imperial policy, is also injured by Britain's failure to intervene in support of a sister state. In Canto IV of *Childe Harold's Pilgrimage* (1818), Byron exclaims,

> [Venice's] lot
> Is shameful to the nations, – most of all,
> Albion! to thee: the Ocean queen should not
> Abandon Ocean's children; in the fall
> Of Venice think of thine, despite thy watery wall.[28]

Non-intervention on behalf of a friend, Byron indicates, equals complicity in a policy that could lead to further political decay across Europe, rather than to rebirth. For the cosmopolitan Byron, who defined himself through his exile, criticism of British policy was a key piece in the puzzle of Anglo-Italian identity formation.

Despite the fallen Italy trope, Romantic writers also invested the Italian cause with complex sympathies and hopes, and Italy's political subjection to foreign rule was also the source behind British poets' expectations for its regeneration. Death and resurrection are, after all, mutually reinforcing, not contradictory, states and Romantic-era writers who were disillusioned by the failures of French republicanism and British constitutionalism found opportunity in Italy for a new revolutionary trajectory. Byron, for example, maintains faith in the kind of 'unity of "thought and action"' that later structured Mazzinian Risorgimento propaganda;[29] he writes in *Childe Harold,*

> I do believe,
> Though I have found them not, that there may be
> Words which are things, – hopes which will not deceive.[30]

Byron continually affirms this belief in the power of utterance, including in two 1821 works, *The Prophecy of Dante* and *Marino Faliero*, both encompassing historical Italian subjects. In *The Prophecy of Dante*, Dante describes a past time 'When words were things that came to pass';[31] defending himself against a treason charge, the Venetian Doge Marino Faliero claims,

> true *words* are *things*,
> And dying men's are things which long outlive,
> And oftentimes avenge them.[32]

The resonance of Byron's belief in performative language with his interest in revolutionary political action is heightened in these revisions of *Childe Harold*'s diction; he envisions a world in which human action is driven by and does not belie speech. What Byron describes as Italians' 'still unquenched "longing after immortality", – the immortality of independence',[33] might feed this belief in a revolution that would not betray itself, as the French Revolution had.

Despite such hopefulness, Romantic poets often dehistoricise or elide contemporary Italy by transforming Italy's history into a timeless human inheritance, at once introspectively personal and universalised. For Byron, the abstract natural forces of decay and regeneration serve to fertilise hope for the future:

> Thou [Italy] art the garden of the world, the home
> Of all Art yields, and Nature can decree;
> Even in thy desart, what is like to thee?
> Thy very weeds are beautiful, thy waste
> More rich than other climes' fertility;
> Thy wreck a glory, and thy ruin graced
> With an immaculate charm which can not be defaced.[34]

Such appeals to an abstract Italy, a symbol of past greatness and future fertility, illustrate the tension between Italian historical reality and the supposedly universal and eternal political potential Italy represented. The idealist P. B. Shelley pushes this further, representing an Italy insulated from the post-Napoleonic historical moment. 'Lines Written Among the Euganean Hills' (1819) reveals a conflict between Italian reality and Shelley's political ideals. As Schoina argues, the poem 'revels in abstractions', presenting Italian nature as 'a basis for allegory' and Venice and Padua 'as ideas, rather than as time-bound realities'.[35] In Schoina's reading, despite Shelley's efforts to confront Italy's 'contemporary condition', 'the possible agents of Italy's regeneration are "Freedom", "Liberty", "learning", "reason" and "love", rather than its present inhabitants'.[36] Such poetic responses to Italy as a post-Waterloo home for revolutionary thought suggest that British

Romantic poets like Byron and P. B. Shelley tended to project their ideological concerns onto the Italian peninsula, rather than permitting Italian conditions to shape their political thought.[37]

Indeed, Shelley explains his imaginative, idealistic poetics in the Preface to *Prometheus Unbound*, alongside which 'Ode to the West Wind' originally appeared:

> it is a mistake to suppose that I dedicate my poetical compositions solely to the direct enforcement of reform ... Didactic poetry is my abhorrence; nothing can be equally well expressed in prose that is not tedious and supererogatory in verse. My purpose has hitherto been simply to familiarize the highly refined imagination of the more select classes of poetical readers with beautiful idealisms of moral excellence, aware that until the mind can love, and admire, and trust, and hope, and endure, reasoned principles of moral conduct are seeds cast upon the highway of life which the unconscious passenger tramples into dust, although they would bear the harvest of his happiness.[38]

Using the same universalising 'seeds' and 'harvest' imagery that appears in 'West Wind' and 'Euganean Hills', Shelley privileges imaginative engagement over a concrete political agenda that responds to historical reality.

Although poets like Shelley, Byron and Hemans are drawn to Italy's history and politics after the restoration, then, their work is ultimately about crafting an idea of Italy: Italy as ancestor, sister or heir to Britain; Italy as dying, dead or reborn; Italy as political allegory. This idea neglects the realities of a peninsula fragmented and enriched by the numerous states, cultures, languages and political systems that coexisted within its borders in the early nineteenth century. Privileging abstract ideals and the construction of new national and radical cosmopolitan identities in a geopolitical context shattered by decades of war and testing out an unknown international order, second-generation British Romantics often addressed Italy as a means to an end: that of confronting their own places as thinkers, artists or celebrities in this new world.

'Living, Moving, Breathing, Italy': Contemporary Italian Life in Lady Morgan's *Italy*

Though the decay–death–rebirth trope of Romantic poetry and Risorgimento propaganda is fundamental to the concept of Italian cultural and national resurgence, for Lady Morgan and Mary Shelley Italian liberty encompasses a complex web of political goals, territorial struggles and material realities often absent from British Romantic poetry. My readings of Shelley and Morgan excavate an Anglo-Italian alternative to the self-interested Italian 'cartography' Schoina reveals among Romantic expatriates.[39] For these two, the imaginative map of post-Waterloo Italy is not a product of Anglocentric identity politics: instead, Italian geopolitics structure these writers' responses to the peninsula. For Morgan, contemporary Italy is a unique site of resistance to the major European imperialist powers after 1815. Exploring the uncomfortable space between radical solidarity and centralisation, Morgan examines the concrete and particular cases of the minor Italian states as they adjusted to and chafed against the consolidation of imperial power in restoration Europe.

Morgan and Shelley both propose a view of Romantic Italy that challenges the idealisations found in contemporary poetry via their presentations of the fragmented peninsula's concrete realities. Tilottama Rajan's analysis of *Valperga* alongside the work of historian Jacob Burckhardt illuminates how Shelley uses the cluster of minor powers that was Romantic Italy as 'the scene for her reinvention of the historical novel',[40] offering a reading of the political advantages of approaching revolutionary thought through Italy's fragmented states that equally pertains to Morgan's travelogue. Writing against the nation-building grain of the Scott-style historical novel[41] – and, indeed, her time – Shelley promotes a historiographical 'method' which, 'rather than being organized by a master-narrative, was anti-foundationalist'.[42] For Rajan, Shelley's fictionalisation of 'minor history' in *Valperga* 'deterritorializes what was a reality by Shelley's time: the discourse of the emergent nation-state'.[43] Nineteenth-century Italy was the geopolitical equivalent of the minor history Rajan explores in Shelley's text. A cluster of diverse minor states involved in struggles against the major powers, Italy was occupied by Napoleonic France, divided up by the victorious allies, delivered as a territorial gift to Austria and the pawn of British diplomatic interest in maintaining the balance of power. Italy, then, provided writers engaged with its rich complexity, like Morgan and Shelley, with an opportunity to write against imperialism. According to Roberto Esposito, this history of fragmentation enriches the cultures of the Italian peninsula and beyond, shaping Italy into 'a formidable land of development, dissemination, and cross-pollination'.[44] The very factors that contributed to the Italian peninsula's minor status and vulnerability to cultural appropriation – division, the lack of a power centre, the proliferation of political units and the perceived universality of its culture – also enabled an enriching political experimentation and energising circulation of ideas.

Morgan was an important Romantic precursor to Shelley in this project of exploring Italian complexity, both as a writer whose early career helped to shape the Scott-style historical novel that emphasises the modern British nation-state and as a voice of revolutionary, anti-imperialist resistance to the dominant discourse of romantic nationalism, all the more so since her radical travelogue *Italy* appeared as Shelley wrote her historical novel. The Shelleys loaned Byron their copy of Morgan's controversial earlier travel narrative, *France*,[45] and Mary Shelley read Morgan's *Florence Macarthy* (1818) in 1822, before *Valperga* appeared.[46] She had previously read Morgan's *France* (1817), *The Wild Irish Girl* (1806), *The Missionary* (1811) and *O'Donnel* (1814) in 1816–17.[47] Byron certainly read *Italy*, which he first mentions in a letter to his publisher, John Murray, in 1821.[48] Morgan and Shelley met in person in 1835 and remained 'lifelong' friends;[49] in fact, Shelley gave Morgan a lock of Byron's hair at her request.[50] Shelley, furthermore, cites *Italy* in the Preface to her 1844 travel narrative, *Rambles in Germany and Italy*,[51] and arranged for Morgan to receive a copy, relying on her friend's literary contacts to 'secure a notice in the "Athenaeum"'.[52]

Moreover, as Romantic women writers and successors to the legacies of 1790s radicalism, Morgan and Shelley operate under the same pressures exerted by what Angela Keane terms 'the masculinist myth of the Romantic nation-state'.[53] Linked to a masculinised national literary culture, evident in William Wordsworth's 'organic-pastoral vision of nationality'[54] or Walter Scott's historical fiction,[55] romantic nationalism created 'exclusionary effects' for those, like women, who were not deemed full participants in national culture.[56] For 1790s women writers, Keane argues,

> it is the discourse of the public sphere, not of the nation, which allows them to imagine themselves as participating citizens. It is the discourse of nationality not rationality that turns them into exiles, by naturalising a patriarchal social contract and putting it beyond rational enquiry.[57]

Morgan and Shelley temper the romantic nationalist potential of a united Italy with a civic discourse that emphasises the rights of citizenship, democratic participation and local distinctiveness.

Morgan's engagement with nationalist discourse and travel plots spans her literary career. Like the Italians she depicts within the Austrian Empire, the Irish Morgan was the 'colonized subject' of a neighbouring European power. Yet, with an Irish Catholic father and English Protestant mother, she originated from 'a bilingual, binational, and bireligious household'.[58] As a writer, Morgan exploited the tension between a romantic nationalism she harnessed in support of minor nations like Ireland and Italy and a radical, rational commitment to discourses of citizenship and political representation. As one of the inventors of the national tale genre, Morgan was a literary bridge between 1790s political fiction and the Regency-era historical novel.[59] Featuring plots of border-crossing and contact among representatives of different cultural groups, the national tale on which Morgan built her reputation 'is at once traveler's tale and anticolonial tract',[60] a clear generic relative to the political travelogues of her later career, *France* and *Italy*. Morgan's brand of 'Jacobin-feminist' national tale[61] maps further onto the politics of the later works. Morgan describes her evolution from a writer of 'national novels' to a political travel writer in terms of an expansion of her initial affective nationalism to include a more concrete, internationalist political awareness: 'as an Irish novelist, all my politics lay in my heart: but my subsequent visits to the Continent, by extending the sphere of observation, induced the necessity for research. I saw much, read much, heard much'.[62] The Ireland of the national tale, moreover, is clearly analogous to post-Napoleonic Italy; for Ina Ferris, the national tale is 'a genre of "minor" nations, that is, of small European nations that stand in a certain relation of hostility to a larger and oppressive nation with whose fortunes their own are intertwined'.[63] Though the *Waverley*-style historical novel emerges generically from the national tale, later national tales by Morgan and others resist the centralising, closure-enacting practices of the historical novel, as *Valperga* does. As Katie Trumpener argues convincingly of national tales, 'Problematizing schematic or totalizing explanations of historical causation, they approach history instead as a network of synchronous and nonsynchronous causes, effects, and processes'.[64] Thus, the fact that Shelley read Morgan extensively suggestively highlights the shared political approaches of these two women writers who took up the cause of fragmented Italy in the aftermath of the historical closures imposed by the Congress of Vienna.

The restoration of Europe's so-called legitimate powers after Waterloo seemed to confirm Italian geopolitical degradation for republican writers like Morgan, whose *Italy* follows her travels there in 1819–20, just ahead of the failed 1820–1 insurrections in Piedmont and the Two Sicilies, the precursors to the Risorgimento's mid-century revolutions. Morgan arrived on the Italian scene as a liberal 'celebrity' and *Italy* became an 'international bestseller', running for seven editions and competing in popularity 'with the nine editions of Eustace's *Classical Tour*'.[65] In his work on Italian refugees and the liberal international, *Risorgimento in Exile*, Maurizio Isabella traces a dialogue among Morgan and Italy's 'Romantic intelligentsia', whose thought influenced her travelogue[66] and whose 'mixed' response to *Italy*[67] 'shows the sheer complexity of the intellectual exchanges taking place between traveller and travelled, which challenge mono-directional explanations of the dynamics of the encounters taking place during the Grand Tour'.[68] While Morgan participates in the meridianist discourse that presents Italy as a decayed culture, then, she also recasts the Italian travelogue as a narrative informed by a productive, cross-border circulation of thought that builds upon international political networks and intercultural exchange.

Italy opens with a double-visioned, panoramic perspective on the Italian plains, past and present, that contrasts Italy's origins with its current fallen state:

> The fables of antiquity have assigned to the Peninsula of Italy a golden age; and history, sufficiently vague, but better accredited, has peopled its Eden plains with confederated tribes; and has covered regions with numerous flocks and plenteous harvests, where desolation now reigns over pestilential marshes. (I, 1)

This cliché of ruined Italy lacks the fertility of P. B. Shelley's revolutionary vision; however, Morgan is already poking holes in the fallen Italy thesis by pointing out the 'vague[ness]' of historical accounts and fictive 'fables of antiquity' that shape nineteenth-century judgements against contemporary Italy. Nonetheless, Morgan proceeds to construct a nascent Italian nation across her book that identifies Italian political debasement in its lack of independence and its loss of the republican legacies of its past. She proclaims, for example, that 'Italy fell with Florence' (I, 25) and that with the rise of absolutism 'Tuscany and Lombardy lay benumbed in lifeless torpidity under the house of Austria' (I, 28).

However, the continental powers that invaded, divided and mastered Italy for centuries also have a vested interest in representing the Italian states and people as fallen, as Morgan highlights. Discussing Rome, Morgan writes, 'That it has fallen, is the work of despotism and corruption; and that, like the rest of Italy, it may never rise again from its fearful debasement, is the hope and effort of Allied Sovereigns, their Cabinets, and their dependants' (III, 58). Maintaining the post-Napoleonic balance of power, Morgan suggests, depends upon the established states carving out their spheres of influence on the Italian peninsula: fallen Italy is political propaganda, designed by imperial powers like Austria to keep the Italian states weak. On unfavourable Neapolitan national stereotypes, for example, Morgan argues, 'Conquered nations are always subjects of slander to their foreign masters, who seek to sanction their own injustice by assuming the worthlessness of their victims' (III, 240). Naples under the Bourbons, like her homeland Ireland, was mismanaged through '*the delegated power of foreign despotism*' (III, 199; italic in original). Though Morgan plays with the trope of Italian decay, then, she also exposes its propagandistic value to occupying and despotic powers in Italy.

Internal divisions imposed under the restoration, guaranteed by Austrian administrative rule and influence on the peninsula, are the greatest obstacles to Italian independence according to Morgan, for whom sovereignty and liberty can only be achieved through unison among Italy's states. Morgan describes Austria as Italy's 'grand carver' (I, 452) and argues that administrative divisions on the peninsula and even within Austrian territory are designed by authorities, 'well aware that the unity of the Italian cities would be the grave of German despotism in Italy' (I, 376), to keep Italians at odds with each other. The internal division that enables outside occupation also affects how travellers experience the Italian states. Morgan writes, 'it is wearisome and disgusting to follow these choppings and changings of nations – to behold human society, like the live stock of a farm, set up to auction' (I, 458). Morgan felt the disruptions of internal division first-hand in the check-points set up between and within Piedmont and Lombardy, which

> forcibly illustrate the efficacy of a policy, that insulates the inhabitants of each petty state, and impedes that communication of thought and concentration of interests, which, by effecting the liberation of Italy, would raise it to the dignity of a nation. (I, 115)

Internal division is not simply a symbol of Italian weakness against major European powers, but a strategic policy with real, concrete effects on the lived experience of the peninsula in the early nineteenth century. Furthermore, when coupled with occupation and political repression, fragmentation inhibits rather than allowing for the cross-pollination that Esposito associates with Italian history. For Morgan, the type of nationhood Italians aspire to is a form of political 'dignity' associated with freedom of movement and communication and the unimpeded circulation of ideas, which have been stripped away under the existing regimes. The resonance of her phrase 'the dignity of a nation' (I, 115) with Shelley's exploration of 'the dignity of a human being' in *Frankenstein* further invests Morgan's polemic with the Jacobin language of political rights.[69]

Morgan also grapples directly with Italian culture's propagandistic entanglement with outside European powers beyond Austria. The republican and Napoleonic French occupations and Britain's role in the restoration created more complicated political legacies for Italians and for writers like Morgan who supported Italian independence. While Italy's cultural and political inheritance was central to Romantic writers' interests in a potential republican future, its place within a post-war Europe shattered by conflict among revolutionaries, upstart imperialists and established monarchs also mattered. The Risorgimento, after all, was bookended by two Napoleons and Italy's various nineteenth-century borders and regimes were determined by the outcomes of European-wide military conflicts, at times negotiated without Italian participation, as in the examples of the treaties of Vienna and Villafranca. Just as eventually 'united Italy was the creation of kings not of the people',[70] so too were the early movements for political liberty and independence created through French intervention on the peninsula before 1815. The French Revolution and republican occupation of Italy beginning in 1796 spread revolutionary organisations and republican political discourse throughout the peninsula,[71] as well as an ideology of nation-building based upon shared political principles and civic institutions, rather than shared history or language, which did not exist in Italy.[72] The 'paradoxical situation' created by tension between 'French propaganda' – republican principles and example – and 'French policy' – French interests on the peninsula – made long-term allegiance between supporters of Italian independence and French revolutionaries untenable,[73] and Napoleon's imperialist occupation extended this paradox further. Napoleon united Italy for the first time in modern history as the Kingdom of Italy, creating a discrete national unit for Italians who had traditionally been divided among city states and petty principalities; yet, this Kingdom was simply a colony of his French Empire.[74] Furthermore, French republicanism appropriated and betrayed, but also extended into the present, Italy's historical republican legacies, posing problems to Italian revolutionaries who wished to claim those legacies for themselves. Napoleon's identification with ancient Rome meant that Italians, according to historian Adrian Lyttelton, 'could only express their opposition by repudiating the Roman heritage' and identifying with other Italian civilisations such as the Etruscan and early modern Florentine.[75] Outside European appropriations of Italy's past erased contemporary Italy from its own historical trajectory and made Italian history politically unavailable to Italians in the aftermath of the Napoleonic period.

Morgan's depiction of contemporary Italy illustrates the tension between her admiration for French innovation and the republican legacy and her repudiation of French imperialism. Morgan, whose *France* earned her a pro-revolutionary, pro-Napoleonic reputation, respects the modernisation and cross-border circulation of thought that came with Napoleonic occupation. In fact, she argues that Italy owes its political awakening in part to the vitality injected into the peninsula by Napoleonic rule; at least, Morgan writes, Napoleon's occupation was a 'stirring, bustling tyranny', unlike the post-1815 'lethargic, benumbing despotism' of Austrian and Papal regimes (II, 49). Morgan praises Napoleon for respecting republican values and distinct statehood in some instances, such as that of San Marino, which retained its independence as 'a Republic within a Republic!' (III, 330) under French occupation and, indeed, the restoration (III, 330–8).

Despite her established admiration for the French Revolution and Napoleon, however, Morgan also offers a critique of antiquity focused on the decline from republicanism to imperialism that recurred with Napoleonic rule. According to Morgan, ancient republics were already inclined towards imperialism before Caesar: 'The inherent principle of the Roman government . . . was power, privilege, and knowledge for the few – slavery the most abject for the many' (II, 333). However, the problem lies with the structure of ancient republics and their early modern successors, not, as in the post-Enlightenment French case, with a betrayal of principle:

> Compared to the government by a free, equal, and pure representation, the boasted republics of Greece and Rome were but factious democracies, or tyrannical aristocracies; and the republics of Italy, but tumultuous impulsions towards liberty, overruled by priestcraft, and counteracted by superstition. (I, 428)

For Morgan, classical and early modern republican attempts were failures and could not be taken as models for a nineteenth-century republican movement. Instead, the Etruscan federations are the benchmark of Italian independence and unity. Morgan argues,

> The cause of this [Etruscan] precocity of civilization was a tendency to independence; but its basis was laid in the unity of the people: and when at length the petty principalities loosened the bonds of their federative alliance, and provincial rivalry separated their interests, they fell, and were enslaved. (II, 290)

'Their example, and their fate', she continues, 'should in all ages be the word of the people of Italy' (II, 290). Post-1815 divided Italy, Morgan suggests, cannot achieve independence without a return to the solidarity of the aligned Etruscan states.

Despite her admiration for Napoleon, Morgan firmly establishes her anti-imperialist position in the survey of Italian history with which *Italy* opens. She declares 'that there are no legitimate beginnings of empires; and that all monarchical governments, owing their origin to the wants or the crimes of man, are founded in conquest, or are consolidated by usurpation' (I, 4). Such principles, equally applicable to Napoleon and the so-called Holy Alliance that is Morgan's more immediate political opponent, run through her narrative. Against Austrian rule and the restored regimes, Morgan occasionally frames Napoleon as Italy's 'benefactor' (I, 251); yet she tempers her generally positive portrayal of the former French Emperor with recognition of the revolutionary period's complicated legacies for the Italian states. Italy's imperial colonisation thus contrasts with its perceived earlier liberation by French republican forces; of Lombardy Morgan writes, for example, 'the gorgeous appellation of KINGDOM OF ITALY did not compensate for the loss of that liberty which was not the less cherished because it was new' (I, 120). For Morgan, Napoleon's damage to republican history must be taken into account in any evaluation of Italian politics. For example, she views the 'cruel and contemptuous' (III, 405–6) transfer of Venetia to Austria with the Treaty of Campo Formio as the nadir of Napoleonic treachery towards the Italian people. Thus, for Morgan, the Italian peninsula is not a timeless ideological space onto which a republican future might be projected after 1815; its recent fate, 'to partake in the triumphs and the disasters, the benefits and the evils, of the French revolution' (I, 51), makes it analogous, not an alternative, to revolutionary and imperial France.

Morgan, like Byron, also critiques British policy on the Italian peninsula, focusing on Genoa, a previously independent republic that was ceded to Piedmont under the oppressive House of Savoy with British complicity in 1814 (I, 432–6) and the Two Sicilies, where Britain was most directly involved during the war. After 1815, Morgan emphatically claims, a 'league of invading dictators' infested Naples (III, 285) and Britain's promises of constitutional liberty in Sicily were violated in favour of the imported, absolutist Bourbon monarchy (III, 231–2):

> those unfortunate Sicilians, who, confiding in the promises of Ministers, and the honour of nations, had lent themselves to English politics, were abandoned to sink or swim . . . Every where alike, the same short-sighted and *journalier* policy of the British Cabinet, bungling on from expedient to expedient, has necessitated similar breaches of faith, and violations of solemn engagements; till it has become impossible for an Englishman to leave home, without encountering the execrations of deluded and enslaved nations, and finding the rites of hospitality withheld, wherever strong personal ties do not overcome the gloomy indulgence of national antipathies. (III, 232)

According to Morgan, Sicily's delivery to the Bourbons contributes to the diminishment of British influence across Europe and damage to Britain's brand as a voice of political liberty in international affairs. Accepting imperialism in Italy is akin to practising imperialism elsewhere. Thus, Morgan recognises Britain's failure to project itself back onto Italy as a constitutional model under the restoration and also challenges Britain's mythologised status as the keeper of Italy's ancient and early modern political heritage.[76]

Morgan contrasts her vision for Italian unity, which privileges political solidarity and federalism over centralised power and authoritarianism, with the interference of these imperialist powers. This vision draws on the richness of Italy's diverse regions, cities and populations. The form of *Italy* is episodic, divided by chapter names according to the different cities that Morgan visited during her travels. This form, of course, mirrors Morgan's progress on what is in some ways a traditional Grand Tour. However, in the context of her political commentary about repressive, administrative divisions it also participates in recording the kind of cross-fertilisation Morgan advocates and facilitates in her travels and writings, while also granting each city and region its own, individual place in the overall map of Italy the narrative draws. Morgan, moreover, explicitly applauds movements of loose alliance, like that of the 'confederated tribes' of her opening paragraph (I, 1), over ostensible republics that centralise power among oligarchs and potential tyrants. Each individual city, culture and region in Morgan's Italy enriches the peninsula as a whole. The ban imposed upon Morgan and her book by various authoritarian Italian governments[77] brings her advocacy for the unimpeded, cross-border circulation of individuals and thought into even greater relief. So too does the language of the review of *Italy* in the *Quarterly*, with which Morgan had an oppositional relationship across her career: the *Quarterly* represents itself as a state-aligned corrective authority, developing an extended prison metaphor[78] that sinisterly imagines literary criticism as a form of 'punishment' against political offenders, like the radical Morgan.[79]

For Morgan, then, Italy's concrete diversity generates its revolutionary potential. Although conventional Romantic visions of Venice like P. B. Shelley's 'Euganean Hills' present a city slowly sinking into irrelevance,[80] for Morgan Venice is rising from its recent oblivion: 'The impression is', she writes, 'as of the apparition of a city that had survived the universal deluge! – its inhabitants all gone, and their dwellings but slowly emerging from the "deep of waters"' (III, 363). Morgan leads the shift in political discourse about Italy that permeates Romantic writing beginning in the 1820s, as decayed Italy becomes Italy reborn. Morgan, however, complicates this basic decay–death–resurrection trope. Unlike Byron and P. B. Shelley, Morgan looks for political purpose in ordinary Italian people, not abstract historical cycles. As Stuart Curran argues,

> *Italy* stands alone in its time in English as a record of a bowed but living people, profoundly altered by what was on the whole the liberating experience of French occupation and now thrust back under the combined forces of Papal reaction and foreign despotism.[81]

Morgan suggests that the future of European progress lies with an Italian vitality that is ingrained in its contemporary population: 'living, moving, breathing, Italy, offers the richest harvest to the morality and the politician, that Europe can afford' (I, 214). While she identifies Italy's rejuvenation with this Shelleyan harvest image, Morgan locates the source of Italy's regenerative force in actual Italian life rather than a revitalised ancient or Renaissance legacy or an abstract political principle. Thus, the forces of Italian renewal do not simply play out an inevitable historical cycle, but actively push back against the trends of Morgan's time, determined by the triple alliance's conservatism: 'To retrograde, not to advance', Morgan writes, 'is the order of the times' (I, 297). Morgan insists that she is neither a classicist nor a historian, and that her interest remains with 'living Italy' (II, 292) throughout her book.

In particular, Morgan emphasises living Italians in order to represent regeneration as resistance, growing out of specific contexts of political oppression. Of the Venetians, ruled by Austria from 1797, Morgan writes, 'such is their hatred of the Austrian Government, that it may yet serve as a source of regeneration – a starting-point of resistance' (III, 412). This differs from P. B. Shelley's presentation of Padua as a city inevitably spurred by tyranny to resistance in that for Shelley such resistance is the reaction of natural law,[82] rather than that of a politically engaged population, or the concrete 'hatred' Morgan observes in her travels (III, 412): he writes,

> Men must reap the things they sow,
> Force from force must ever flow,
> Or worse.[83]

Italy, by contrast, remains committed to a concrete political agenda: Morgan's conclusion expands her discussion outwards to evoke a European-wide struggle for constitutional liberty against the 'lawless despotisms' of the established powers (III, 414). In addition to grounding Italian insurrectionary potential in specific historical conditions, then, Morgan presents Italy as a source of political regeneration at the forefront of European anti-imperialist resistance.

For Morgan, in the aftermath of 1815 each Italian region and population has its own grievances with the major European powers and those who govern on the peninsula. Yet, the concrete struggles against oppression and imperialism that she sees emerging in Italy are themselves sources of regeneration as resistance. The peninsula's diversity, according to Morgan, enriches the emerging movement for unity and independence. In Morgan's view, Italians do not await an abstract and idealised awakening, but actively resist the imperialist and nationalist trends of the time, rendering Italy a testing-ground modelling the way forwards for revolutionary republicans across Europe.

'Earth Felt No Change': Mary Shelley's *Valperga* and the Restoration Status Quo

For Morgan, focused on the invigorating present, early modern Italy proved the fatal consequences of the internal contention that continued into her own time (II, 190–1) and the historical successes of tyranny and oligarchy even in supposed republics (III, 365). However, early modern Italy also provided a further complicated template for contemporary Italy as the experimental early modern states presented alternatives to the nineteenth century's centralised, imperialist options.[84] Mary Shelley's *Valperga*, which plots the death of Florentine liberty against the expansionism of petty tyrant Castruccio of Lucca, explores the ways in which medieval republican legacies fail to provide an alternative hope to the French Revolution, itself a failure by the early nineteenth century. At issue for Shelley is what Rajan describes as 'the recoverability of a lost republican moment'.[85] In *Valperga*, the republican principles of medieval Florence are embodied by the aptly named heroine Euthanasia, whose marriage engagement to the Napoleonic tyrant Castruccio ends when the prince threatens her beloved Florence. The solidarity among states that Morgan presents as indispensable to Italian sovereignty could be achieved through such a marriage, should Castruccio give up his imperialistic ambitions. However, Castruccio, tellingly aligned to the Holy Roman Emperor as a Ghibelline, chooses instead to conquer independent Florence, illustrating the threat of internal Italian expansionism.

As *Valperga*'s plot of struggle between republicanism and imperialism suggests, long-term historical movement could be both a liability and a precedent for post-1815 Italy. For Shelley, examining historical Italian successes and failures in *Valperga* was a means of considering republicanism, tyranny and empire in concrete ways. As Betty T. Bennett notes, the first Risorgimento revolutions in Naples and Piedmont occurred while Shelley was writing in 1820–1; both Shelley and her husband 'saw in the concept of renewal the possibility of another wave of political reform that could establish governments dedicated to freedom and republicanism'.[86] Shelley's turn to medieval Italian history in *Valperga* thus explores both the decline from republicanism to imperialism in revolutionary France and the aspirations and difficulties of Italian insurgency in her present. For Shelley, the Italian Renaissance is not just evidence of past greatness, but a potential historical precedent for a new awakening in the present. Her novel opens,

> The other nations of Europe were yet immersed in barbarism, when Italy, where the light of civilization had never been wholly eclipsed, began to emerge from the darkness of the ruin of the Western Empire, and to catch from the East the returning rays of literature and science.[87]

Italy, here, is already an incipient nation and a force of resistance to 'Empire'. Furthermore, the past shows that Italy was resurrected once before from an apparent death-like state that was, in reality, only temporary: 'The spirit of learning, after a long sleep, that seemed to be annihilation, awoke, and shook her wings over her favoured Italy' (16). As resurrection is preceded by death, so is enlightenment preceded by darkness and awakening by slumber.

Yet, instead of confirming the conventional decay–death–rebirth trope characteristic of Romantic writing on Italy, Shelley reverses the direction of this cyclical movement as her novel progresses: the imagery of hopeful resurgence with which *Valperga* opens is replaced with premonitions of death. When Castruccio fights her Florentine allies, Euthanasia can no longer commit to uniting with him, lamenting, 'in that moment I must die, or live a death in life' (113). Later, she despairs to herself on the loss of her youthful love: 'Pulse, and breath, and thought, and all is changed; I must no longer love, – so let me suffer the living death of forgetfulness' (208). Beatrice, a second fictional woman destroyed through loving Castruccio, becomes the novel's voice of hopelessness after suffering violent sexual enslavement in a medieval house of torture as well as imprisonment by the Inquisition. Beatrice's embodiment of decay and her obsession with death reverse the inspired, revolutionary discourse of P. B. Shelley's 'Ode to the West Wind'. She complains, 'I am so unlike what I was when he [Castruccio] saw me, as is the yellow, fallen leaf to the bright-green foliage of May' (272). Rather than imagining time as progressing from autumn to spring, as 'West Wind' does, Beatrice sees herself as inevitably and bitterly declining from her initial spring-like freshness and innocence. Furthermore, Beatrice presents this personal experience as an articulation of natural law, thus extending it outwards beyond herself: 'I see the blight of autumn in the green leaves of spring . . .; all beauty wraps deformity, as the fruit the kernel; Time opens the shell, the seed is poison' (283). Through Beatrice, Shelley challenges her husband's belief in the 'new birth' contained within the seeds of revolutionary thought;[88] 'poison', in *Valperga*, is the more likely yield of a political harvest.

What grows in diseased medieval Italian politics for Shelley is conspiracy and revenge. The awakening to a proto-Enlightenment learning of *Valperga*'s opening transforms into awakenings of vengeful impulses that feed plots for power. The Guelph Bondelmonti, for example, urges Euthanasia to join a conspiracy against Castruccio in order to protect him from himself by arguing Euthanasia 'had forgotten herself awhile, only to awake again with new vigour' (345).

The conspiracy, however, only awakens further rage and retribution, as Castruccio's response shows; he threatens the conspirators, 'They shall feel in every nerve what it is to have awakened me' (364). These cycles of awakenings to hatred end with Euthanasia's death, when the ship carrying her to exile sinks:

> She was never heard of more; even her name perished. She slept in the oozy cavern of the ocean; the sea-weed was tangled with her shining hair; and the spirits of the deep wondered that the earth had trusted so lovely a creature to the barren bosom of the sea, which, as an evil step-mother, deceives and betrays all committed to her care.
>
> Earth felt no change when she died; and men forgot her. Yet a lovelier spirit never ceased to breathe, nor was a lovelier form ever destroyed amidst the many it brings forth. Endless tears might well have been shed at her loss; yet for her none wept, save the piteous skies, which deplored the mischief they had themselves committed; – none moaned except the sea-birds that flapped their heavy wings above the ocean-cave wherein she lay; – and the muttering thunder alone tolled her passing bell, as she quitted a life, which for her had been replete with change and sorrow. (376–7)

A novel that opens with the image of the sun rising to offer Enlightenment to Italy (5), *Valperga* reverses the role of natural forces in Euthanasia's fate and endows nature with the human qualities that produced the political failings of the medieval moment Shelley's novel represents: nature is 'evil', deceptive, a 'betray[er]', a 'destroy[er]' and 'mischie[vous]'. Nature's 'change[s]', far from 'quicken[ing] a new birth',[89] produce only death and 'sorrow' in life (377). For Shelley, the appearance of renaissance with which the novel opens belies the historical reality of political death.

In *Valperga*, as in *Italy*, the struggle for sovereignty and political liberty against repressive, centralised authority extends beyond the Italian peninsula to point to broad political legacies of repression that cross Europe's borders and historical periods and demonstrates the Italian states' contingency on European-wide power struggles and territorial interests. Shelley targets Austrian and French imperialism through Castruccio, tracing nineteenth-century Empires to the late Middle Ages. Shelley is more critical of French occupation in Italy than Morgan:[90] Castruccio's career maps easily onto Napoleon's, as P. B. Shelley noted in a letter to his publisher: 'He was a little Napoleon, and, with a dukedom instead of an empire for his theatre, brought upon the same all the passions and the errors of his antitype'.[91] Castruccio's trajectory does echo Napoleon's move from military leader, to consul, to Emperor; his ally Galeazzo, advising his friend to conquer Florence, urges him to 'give up this old-fashioned name of consul; it is tainted by the idea of that which I abhor – a commonwealth: make yourself a prince' (140). More generally, however, Castruccio's allegiance to the Ghibelline party aligns him to Emperors beyond Napoleon, including Austrian Emperor Francis I, for, as Curran notes, 'the Ghibellines represented an oppressive centralized authority exerted all over Europe and embodied in a single man';[92] more specifically, the Ghibellines are allied to Holy Roman Emperors Henry VII and Louis IV, whose Austrian imperial successors remained in Italy centuries later, when Shelley wrote her novel. Shelley conflates the Austrian and French imperialist legacies on the Italian peninsula and, furthermore, traces imperialist conflict and occupation back to the warring factions, outside aggressors and internal divisions of its destructive past. For both Shelley and Morgan, then, the legacy of the major European powers' intervention in Italy is Italy's true political inheritance. Medieval warring between Italian states allied to outside interests subordinates them to larger political powers, undermines their territorial sovereignty and clears the way for the rise of tyrants like Castruccio, whose presence as an internal expansionist force further destabilises the region.

Like Morgan and Byron, Shelley also challenges constitutionalist Britain's complacency with respect to claims of political guidance provided for nineteenth-century Italy. At times across her career, Shelley highlights the special Anglo-Italian relationship, subordinating the French revolutionary example to a safer and more palatable British constitutional model for Italian political liberty or presenting Britain as historical Italy's heir, as in 'Valerius'. In her 1844 *Rambles in Germany and Italy*, Shelley carefully moderates her Italian sympathies with a dose of British meliorism, as Jeanne Moskal notes: 'the Risorgimento is derived from "the French" . . . only secondarily; its ultimate source is Britain . . . She [Shelley] thus rewrites the historical plot in a way acceptable to her audience'.[93] However, in *Valperga* Shelley problematises the British constitutionalist myth by recognising the political violence that historically inflected the emergence of the multiple stakeholders of British constitutional practice and allowing that violence to impact the Italy of her novel. While *Valperga* cannot confront Britain's influence in nineteenth-century Italy directly, Castruccio's career reflects negatively on English politics. Before he leaves Italy for England as a youth, Castruccio is educated in enlightened thought by Euthanasia's family at Valperga, and then by the wise and peaceful peasant Francis Guinigi. The chapter 'Castruccio in England' (34–42), however, marks a turning point in the future tyrant's education. In England, Castruccio becomes entangled in political infighting among King Edward II, his friend Piers Gavaston and the barons who oppose the King, 'delighted' to have 'found a fitting stage on which he might commence his active career' (36). Castruccio becomes Edward's favourite and, siding with absolute monarchy over stakeholder consensus, agrees to secretly retrieve Gavaston from his exile in Dublin (38–40). Castruccio's first political intrigue at the English court leads to an argument with an English nobleman, against whom Castruccio commits his first murder to avenge an insult (41–2). Far from inheriting Renaissance glory from Italy, England in *Valperga* poisons Italian politics from afar. Though Shelley at times perpetuates the myth of Britain's leadership in European political liberty, then, she does not do so wholeheartedly or uncritically.

Although *Valperga* is set in the distant past, Shelley's novel, like Morgan's travel book, also 'recognise[s] that Italy is peopled by Italians who have an agenda for their own future';[94] placing seemingly anachronistic post-Enlightenment characters, like Euthanasia, in the medieval context is a means of reflecting contemporary political thought in the historical setting. Shelley includes 'covert references' to the 1820–1 uprisings in the novel, mentioning, for example, Alessandria, the location of the March 1821 Piedmontese insurrection that resulted in Victor Emmanuel I's abdication.[95] Such layering of the 1820s on top of the medieval setting recognises the intricacy of Italian politics in Shelley's historical moment. Shelley's choice of the name Euthanasia for her heroine, furthermore, engages with and challenges the rationalist optimism of 1790s Enlightenment political theory from her position in the 1820s. Her father, William Godwin, used the term 'euthanasia' to illustrate what he viewed as inevitable progress towards a perfectible, consensus-based political system. In his 1793 *Enquiry Concerning Political Justice* Godwin argues,

> government cannot proceed but upon confidence, as confidence on the other hand cannot exist without ignorance. The true supporters of government are the weak and uninformed, and not the wise. In proportion as weakness and ignorance shall diminish, the basis of government will also decay. This however is an event which ought not to be contemplated with alarm. A catastrophe of this description would be the true euthanasia of government.[96]

After the failure of rational government in the revolutionary period, however, Shelley re-imagines Godwin's 'euthanasia of government' as the death of republican hopes through the fictional Euthanasia, whose optimism is thwarted by the rise of tyranny and whose voice of reform is stifled when power defeats reason. Thus, *Valperga* challenges the Enlightenment confidence of first-generation Romantics as well as the historical abstractions of the dominant poetic voices of Shelley's own generation, presenting a contemporary political awareness that reflects the complexity of the post-1815 reality within its medieval setting.

For Shelley, then, the political fertility of past, nascent republican moments, including those of medieval Florence and 1790s France, may be an illusion. Several literary critics recognise the 'profoundly pessimistic'[97] outcome of Shelley's novel, often focusing on the feminist failure that Euthanasia represents.[98] However, *Valperga* does not simply project the nineteenth century back into the Italian Middle Ages, but explores different historical manifestations of the struggle between republicanism and imperialism on their own terms; Shelley appeals to a history of republican potential thrown away, a history that exists just as clearly in the Middle Ages as it does in the Napoleonic period and its aftermath. Although some literary critics find in *Valperga* a past in which 'a plurality of future worlds was possible'[99] or, more cautiously, 'a pretext for the hope of recovery that remains just that, a construct, a notion, an idea',[100] Euthanasia's death kills those hopes and forecloses upon alternative futures. However, if 1820s Italy is analogous to medieval Florence, Shelley's contemporaries had a new opportunity to contest the historical closures imposed in 1815: the medieval moment's 'cultural promise'[101] is renewable in the 1820s. Through her choice of historical material for *Valperga*, Shelley resists the centralising and imperialist tendencies of her time; yet she recognises that failure is part of republican history, past and present. Opening up a space for considering Italy's minor states in relation to anti-imperialist resistance is the best that Shelley can offer for the republicanism of the future.

Italy and *Valperga*, written and published in the lead up to and direct aftermath of the 1820–1 uprisings, appeared at a historical hot spot for Italian revolutionary potential. However, little changed in Italy over the next two decades. Shelley's *Rambles* demonstrates a political consistency with Morgan's travel book of over twenty years earlier that suggests the Italian cause remained urgent, but static. Shelley hoped *Rambles* would raise the Italian cause's profile among her British readers:

> I shall be repaid for the labour and anxiety of putting them [her writings] together, if they induce some among my countrymen to regard with greater attention, and to sympathise in the struggles of a country, the most illustrious and the most unfortunate in the world.[102]

The conclusion to *Rambles*, however, apologises on behalf of Italians, who have failed to achieve regeneration and independence by the 1840s, indicating that while the prophetic hope of Italian rebirth that permeates Romanticism remained, so did the fallen Italy motif of the Napoleonic period:

> We must not forget that the people are demoralised and degenerate. The present affords no glimmering light by which we may perceive how the regeneration of Italy will be effected. It is one of the secrets of futurity at which it is vain to guess. Yet the hour must and will come. For there are noble spirits who live only in this hope; and every man of courage and genius throughout the country – and several such exist – consecrates his moral and intellectual faculties to this end only.[103]

The Italian revolution that would produce national sovereignty and unity thus remains as imminent as it appeared in the years immediately following Waterloo.

The political and cultural discourse of Italian rebirth maps consistently onto the trope of a fallen Italy, creating a cyclical pattern of decay, death and resurrection useful for Romantic writers like P. B. Shelley interested in imagining an abstract revolutionary future. However, in *Valperga* and *Italy*, Shelley and Morgan demonstrate that modern Italy exists within a complex network of European-wide political failures, territorial interventions and cultural appropriations that confine the Italian peninsula within an untenable holding pattern after the Congress of Vienna. Thus, for these two writers, nineteenth-century Italy is neither abstractly fallen nor reborn, but context-driven and negotiating its place as a cluster of minor powers within a continent structured by imperial influence and expansionist nation-building. Italy offered a potential site of resistance to the European status quo after the restoration; yet, the peninsula's political stasis from 1815 to the 1840s also intensified the frustration that prepared the ground for the explosion into revolution and war that occurred in the mid-nineteenth century.

Notes

1. Lord Byron, *Byron's Letters and Journals*, vol. 7, p. 188.
2. Lord Byron, 'Venice. An Ode', in *Lord Byron: The Complete Poetical Works*, l. 4.
3. William Wordsworth, 'On the Extinction of the Venetian Republic', ll. 13–14.

4. Angela Keane, *Women Writers and the English Nation in the 1790s: Romantic Belongings*, p. 9.
5. Sydney Morgan [Sydney Owenson], *Italy*, vol. 1, p. 115. Subsequent citations will appear parenthetically in the text by volume and page numbers.
6. P. B. Shelley, 'Ode to the West Wind', in *Poems of Shelley*, vol. 3, ll. 66, 64.
7. See Lucy Riall, *Risorgimento: The History of Italy from Napoleon to Nation State*, pp. 10–11.
8. Diego Saglia, 'Hemans's Record of Dante: "The Maremma" and the Intertextual Poetics of Plenitude', p. 129.
9. Jeffrey N. Cox, 'Re-Visioning Rimini: Dante in the Cockney School', p. 187.
10. Maria Schoina, *Romantic 'Anglo-Italians': Configurations of Identity in Byron, the Shelleys, and the Pisan Circle*, p. 163.
11. Wordsworth, 'Venetian Republic', l. 4. After conquering Venice, Napoleon traded it to Austria in the 1797 Treaty of Campo Formio.
12. Riall, *Risorgimento*, p. 40.
13. Lord Byron, *Childe Harold's Pilgrimage*, III, 1027.
14. P. B. Shelley, 'Lines Written Among the Euganean Hills, October, 1818', in *Poems of Shelley*, vol. 2, l. 148.
15. Felicia Hemans, 'From *The Restoration of the Works of Art to Italy: A Poem*', in *Felicia Hemans: Selected Poems, Prose, and Letters*, ll. 1, 7–10. Subsequent references to Hemans are from the collection, unless stated otherwise.
16. Joseph Luzzi, 'Italy without Italians: Literary Origins of a Romantic Myth', p. 50.
17. Ibid.
18. Schoina, *Romantic 'Anglo-Italians'*, p. 4.
19. Ibid. p. 163.
20. Erik Simpson, *Literary Minstrelsy, 1770–1830: Minstrels and Improvisers in British, Irish, and American Literature*, p. 348.
21. Hemans, *Restoration*, ll. 15, 85–92.
22. Ibid. ll. 87–8.
23. Mary Shelley, 'Valerius: The Reanimated Roman', in *Mary Shelley: Collected Tales and Stories*, pp. 332–44.
24. Britain did, however, station military forces in Sicily during the war.
25. Adrian Lyttelton, 'The National Question in Italy', p. 76.
26. Byron, *Childe Harold's Pilgrimage*, p. 148.
27. Ibid.
28. Byron, *Childe Harold's Pilgrimage*, IV, 149–53.
29. Lucy Riall, *Garibaldi: Invention of a Hero*, p. 29.
30. Byron, *Childe Harold's Pilgrimage*, III, 1059–61.
31. Lord Byron, *The Prophecy of Dante*, in *Lord Byron: The Complete Poetical Works*, II, 2.

32. Lord Byron, *Marino Faliero, Doge of Venice. An Historical Tragedy, in Five Acts*, in *Lord Byron: The Complete Poetical Works*, V, i, 288–90.
33. Byron, *Childe Harold's Pilgrimage*, p. 148.
34. Ibid. IV, 228–34.
35. Schoina, *Romantic 'Anglo-Italians'*, p. 133.
36. Ibid.
37. Schoina argues that 'Shelley's circle sensed the cultural crisis of the post-Napoleonic era and thought it proper to adopt timeless, enduring ideals, myths and classical tales in order to convey truths that would have an impact on the present time'. Maria Schoina, 'The "Poetry of Politics" in Shelley's and Byron's Italian Works', n. pag.
38. P. B. Shelley, *Shelley's* Prometheus Unbound: *The Text and the Drafts*, p. 43.
39. Schoina, *Romantic 'Anglo-Italians'*, p. 163.
40. Tilottama Rajan, 'The Poetry of Philology: Burckhardt's *Civilization of the Renaissance in Italy* and Mary Shelley's *Valperga*', p. 107.
41. Ibid.
42. Ibid. p. 106.
43. Ibid. p. 115.
44. Roberto Esposito, *Living Thought: The Origins and Actuality of Italian Philosophy*, p. 20.
45. 'Lady Morgan's France' appears on a list under the heading 'L. B.' in the endpaper in Mary Shelley's Journal Book II, dated 1816–19. Mary Shelley, *The Journals of Mary Shelley*, vol. 1, p. 285.
46. Ibid. vol. 2, p. 664.
47. Ibid.
48. Byron describes *Italy* as 'a really *excellent* book'. Byron, *Letters*, vol. 8, p. 186. Byron also asks Thomas Moore,

> when you write to Lady Morgan, will you thank her for her handsome speeches in her book about *my* books? . . . Her work is fearless and excellent on the subject of Italy – pray tell her so – and I know the country. I wish she had fallen in with *me*, I could have told her a thing or two that would have confirmed her positions. (Byron, *Letters*, vol. 8, p. 189)

49. The quotation comes from Betty T. Bennett's footnote to a letter Shelley wrote to Morgan in March 1835. Betty T. Bennett (ed.), *The Letters of Mary Wollstonecraft Shelley*, vol. 2, p. 242.
50. Shelley writes to Morgan,

> I send you the *relic* & you may say that I have never parted with *one* hair to any one else. You will prize it – Poor dear fellow – he was very nice the evening I cut it off – which was in August 1822. (Mary Shelley, *The Letters of Mary Wollstonecraft Shelley*, vol. 2, p. 294)

51. Mary Shelley, *Rambles in Germany and Italy, in 1840, 1842, and 1843*, vol. 1, p. x.
52. Shelley, *Letters*, vol. 3, p. 145. For more on Morgan's influence on second-generation Romantic writers, see Julia M. Wright, Introduction, in *The Missionary: An Indian Tale*, pp. 42–3. Morgan's public battles with reviewers are credited with motivating her publisher Henry Colburn's decision to found the *Athenaeum*. See Ina Ferris, *The Romantic National Tale and the Question of Ireland*, pp. 67–8.
53. Keane, *Women Writers and the English Nation*, p. 16. For more detail about the 'array of nationalisms' present within Romantic culture, see Julia M. Wright, 'Nationalist Discourses in the British Isles, 1780–1850', p. 172.
54. Marlon B. Ross, 'Romancing the Nation-State: The Poetics of Romantic Nationalism', p. 59.
55. Rajan argues that 'Shelley was interested in the fragmented political geography of Italy at a time when Walter Scott was using the historical novel in the service of total history to canonize the British nation-state'. Rajan, 'The Poetry of Philology', p. 107. Elsewhere, Rajan contrasts Shelley's emphasis on the lives of fictional women with Scott's 'masculinized historical novels' (Tilottama Rajan, Introduction, in *Valperga*, p. 33). Stuart Curran also briefly argues for Morgan's affinity to Shelley in 'offer[ing] a female-oriented, liberal alternative to Scott's conservative model of the historical novel' (Stuart Curran, '*Valperga*', p. 109).
56. Keane, *Women Writers and the English Nation*, p. 2.
57. Ibid. pp. 6–7.
58. Wright, Introduction, pp. 36, 17.
59. See Katie Trumpener, *Bardic Nationalism: The Romantic Novel and the British Empire*, p. 131.
60. Ibid. p. 142.
61. Ibid. p. 138.
62. Sydney Morgan, *Letter to the Reviewers of Italy*, p. 5.
63. Ferris, *The Romantic National Tale*, p. 49.
64. Trumpener, *Bardic Nationalism*, p. 151. By contrast, the Scott-style historical novel concludes with 'a particular present subsum[ing] the past, with all its historiographical and narrative possibilities' (Trumpener, *Bardic Nationalism*, p. 151).
65. Maurizio Isabella, *Risorgimento in Exile: Italian Émigrés and the Liberal International in the Post-Napoleonic Era*, p. 194.
66. Ibid.
67. Ibid. p. 196.
68. Ibid. pp. 209–10; see also pp. 196–200.
69. Mary Shelley, *Frankenstein or the Modern Prometheus*, p. 46.
70. Riall, *Risorgimento*, p. 146.
71. Ibid. p. 6.
72. See Lyttelton, 'The National Question', p. 63.

73. Ibid. p. 66.
74. Napoleon's Kingdom of Italy excluded the southern peninsula, which became the separate Kingdom of Naples. See Riall, *Risorgimento*, pp. 4–5.
75. 'The later revival of the "idea of Rome" obscures the fact that in its origins the Risorgimento was predominantly anti-Roman' (Lyttelton, 'The National Question', p. 74).
76. Critics such as Donatella Abbate Badin have examined Morgan's critique of British policy in Ireland as analogous to Italian governance. Donatella Abbate Badin, *Lady Morgan's Italy: Anglo-Irish Sensibilities and Italian Realities*.
77. *Italy* was banned in the Papal States, Sardinia and areas of Austrian influence; copies were burned in Turin and Morgan was forbidden entry to the Austrian Empire in 1824. For details on *Italy*'s reception, see Badin, pp. 233–40.
78. Review of *Italy*, pp. 529–30.
79. Ibid. p. 529.
80. P. B. Shelley, 'Euganean Hills', in *Poems of Shelley*, vol. 2, ll. 115–41.
81. Stuart Curran, 'Reproductions of Italy in Post-Waterloo Britain', p. 140.
82. See P. B. Shelley, 'Euganean Hills', ll. 256–84.
83. Ibid. ll. 231–3.
84. Curran argues for Shelley's tendency 'to see in those local medieval city-states such as Florence the beginnings of an essentially republican vision of civic polity that pointed the way for a new political order in post-Napoleonic Europe'. Curran, '*Valperga*', p. 109.
85. Tilottama Rajan, 'Between Romance and History: Possibility and Contingency in Godwin, Leibniz, and Mary Shelley's *Valperga*', p. 99.
86. Betty T. Bennett, 'Machiavelli's and Mary Shelley's Castruccio: Biography as Metaphor', p. 145.
87. Mary Shelley, *Valperga: or, the Life and Adventures of Castruccio, Prince of Lucca*, p. 5. Subsequent citations will appear parenthetically in the text.
88. P. B. Shelley, 'Ode to the West Wind', in *Poems of Shelley*, vol. 3, l. 64.
89. Ibid.
90. See 'The Sisters of Albano' (1828), set in the French-occupied Kingdom of Naples, in *Mary Shelley: Collected Tales and Stories*, pp. 51–64.
91. Quoted in Michael Rossington, Introduction, in *Valperga*, p. ix.
92. Curran, '*Valperga*', p. 108.
93. Jeanne Moskal, 'Gender and Italian Nationalism in Mary Shelley's *Rambles in Germany and Italy*', p. 194. Despite her radicalism, Morgan also notes 'the analogy of the freedom of political institutions [in Italian history] to our own', though her suggestion that the English know little of Italian history indicates that she views modern Britain as a less deserving heir to Italy's past glory than does Shelley in her later career (I, 31).

94. Roderick Cavaliero, *Italia Romantica: English Romantics and Italian Freedom*, p. 64.

95. Nora Crook, '"Meek and Bold": Mary Shelley's Support for the Risorgimento', p. 76. Crook reads Benedetto Pepi as 'a prefiguration of the 1820s Italian ultra-reactionary' and discusses 1831 revisions to *Frankenstein* that transform Elizabeth's father into an Italian patriot imprisoned in Austria just after Silvio Pellico, writer and editor for the liberal newspaper *Il Conciliatore*, was released following ten years in the Austrian prison Spielberg (Crook, pp. 76–8).

96. William Godwin, *Enquiry Concerning Political Justice and its Influence on Modern Morals and Happiness*, pp. 247–8.

97. Jane Blumberg, *Mary Shelley's Early Novels: 'This Child of Imagination and Misery'*, p. 76.

98. See, for example, Bennett, 'Machiavelli's and Mary Shelley's Castruccio'; Blumberg, *Mary Shelley's Early Novels*; Pamela Clemit, *The Godwinian Novel: The Rational Fictions of Godwin, Brockden Brown, Mary Shelley*; Joseph W. Lew, 'God's Sister: History and Ideology in *Valperga*'; and Anne K. Mellor, *Mary Shelley: Her Life, Her Fiction, Her Monsters*.

99. Deidre Lynch, 'Historical Novelist', p. 137.

100. Michael Rossington, 'Future Uncertain: The Republican Tradition and Its Destiny in *Valperga*', p. 103.

101. Rajan, Introduction, in *Valperga*, p. 17.

102. Shelley, *Rambles*, vol. 1, p. xvi.

103. Ibid. vol. 2, p. 261.

Chapter 2

Italian Exiles from Young Italy to 1848: Risorgimento Refugees in Giovanni Ruffini's *Lorenzo Benoni* and *Doctor Antonio*

In 1845, when Italian exile Giuseppe Mazzini had become a household name in Britain,[1] Robert Browning wrote two companion pieces, which appeared in the post-1848 collection *Dramatic Romances and Lyrics* (1849). These poems depict figures representing the opposite sides of the mutually constitutive Anglo-Italian relationship: the exile and the tourist. The disparity between the individual who is expelled from his or her own country and the one who chooses to leave to seek pleasure elsewhere that Browning develops is evident in numerous other Victorian representations of Italy and Italians in the subsequent decades. In contrast to the fruitful luxury of the Sorrento landscape of 'The Englishman in Italy', in 'The Italian in England' a Lombard recalls being 'hunted' and 'hound[ed]' 'From hill to plain, from shore to sea' by Austrian authorities in a menacing setting.[2] For the fugitive, the Italian landscape transforms from a familiar homeland into a trap; he hides for 'six days' in an 'old aqueduct' where he played as a child (6, 7). Despite the speaker's restricted movement (16–110), the short, rhyming lines of iambic tetrametre build momentum and rush the reader from one line to the next. The poem thus illustrates the exile's simultaneous movement away from the state's authority and immobilisation within its borders.

Yet, for Browning, the speaker is not merely a victim of Austrian oppression; he is an active revolutionist and his exile is politically inseparable from his participation in rebellion. His life attains value through his devotion to the cause: he argues,

on me
Rested the hopes of Italy (49–50)

suggesting his Mazzini-like leadership among revolutionists. His political hopes are, furthermore, vengeful and bloodthirsty, as his three wishes indicate. First, he claims,

> I would grasp [Prince Klemens von] Metternich until
> I felt his red wet throat distil
> In blood thro' these two hands. (121–3)

His hatred for the Austrian Chancellor is accentuated by the intimacy of his fantasy of removing Metternich from power face to face and with his bare hands. Second, he wishes that his childhood friend and traitor Charles 'Should die slow of a broken heart' (126). His final wish shows his nostalgia for his lost home and for the moment of kindness he recounts early in the poem, when a generous stranger aids his escape:

> I should wish to stand
> This evening in that dear, lost land,
> Over the sea the thousand miles,
> And know if yet that woman smiles
> With the calm smile. (145–9)

Though the first two wishes comprise a bloody political vendetta, the third constructs a wistful picture of the national solidarity and sense of an Italian homeland that the fugitive aims to build. Telling his story, the speaker becomes a propagandist for his movement. His final words, 'To business now' (162), indicate his continued revolutionary work. Unsurprisingly, Mazzini identified with the speaker's blending of politicised suffering, endorsement of violence, nation-making nostalgia and business-like focus on the cause. He translated the poem for his mother and described it as 'a truly beautiful poem, by one of the best poets of the age'.[3]

This mixed portrayal of a Mazzinian patriot, combining sympathy for the speaker's plight with reluctance to disguise his violence, reflects a mix of support with disaffection that unsettles British portrayals of Risorgimento politics, particularly in works dealing with the combined experiences of exile and insurrection in the mid-Victorian period. While Browning reveals his patriot's bloodlust, he also displaces the exiled speaker's experience from Mazzini's home, Piedmontese-ruled Genoa, to Austrian-governed Lombardy, presenting the reader with a more clear-cut political choice between Italian independence and foreign, imperialist rule. This subtle revision of the conspirator's background allows an opening for international, liberal support for the cause without necessarily endorsing his methods, support like that which eventually developed for Piedmont's constitutional leadership in unification efforts. Pointing to a range of options for British response to the Risorgimento, including sympathy, critique and tentative understanding, Browning initiates a complex literary conversation surrounding Italian exile and rebellion in the mid-nineteenth century that infiltrates numerous canonical Victorian texts, from Charles Dickens's *Pictures from Italy* to George Eliot's *Middlemarch*. As Italian politics became progressively unsettled across the century, Victorian writers such as Dickens, Eliot, Elizabeth Barrett Browning and Anthony Trollope engaged in a literary project of incorporating the effects of displacement and discomfort into their depictions of Italian place.

Yet, the English-language writer most fluent in this conversation – the writer with the greatest investment in Italian insurrection and exile and personal expertise in the Mazzinian years of the early Risorgimento – is the Italian refugee Giovanni Ruffini. Ruffini's early novels, *Lorenzo Benoni* (1853) and *Doctor Antonio* (1855), fictionalise his experiences as a Young Italy activist and those of his revolutionary compatriots in 1848. Focusing on his own conspiratorial history and nightmarish flight in the semi-autobiographical *Lorenzo Benoni* and imagining the life of an internally displaced Sicilian in northern Italy in *Doctor Antonio*, Ruffini transforms Italy into a site of political disaffection, failures of international solidarity and emotional estrangement. Using what Peter Burke describes as the exile's 'power to unsettle others',[4] Ruffini disrupts his British audience's romance with nineteenth-century Italy. Ruffini's Risorgimento novels challenge the concept of a rooted Italian nation by writing Italian place through narratives of displacement and loss. Yet, his plots of forcible expulsion also construct the refugee experience as the fundamental experience of the Risorgimento. In Ruffini's works, displacement constitutes Italian identity, as the process of nation-making also violently disrupts homes, families and communities. Plotting the entanglement of political activism and exile, furthermore, these novels suggest a broadening of the unsettling effects of Risorgimento conflict beyond Italy's borders. The numerous canonical Victorian narratives of homesickness and estrangement in Italy, with which this chapter opens, reflect the reverberations of displacement and discomfort surrounding the Risorgimento's progress that emanated outwards from the politically unsettled peninsula.

'This Stupendous Fragmentariness': Displacement and Homesickness in Victorian Italy

When P. B. Shelley described Italy as a 'Paradise of exiles',[5] he drew a connecting line through literary history from the medieval Florentine exile Dante Alighieri, via the rebellious English poet John Milton, associated with the heavenly Italian setting of Vallombrosa, to his own present. This gesture traces a poetic lineage that would place British Romantics – himself and, more particularly, Byron – within an illustrious literary tradition. The Italy of Romantic exile is a liberating aesthetic space, in which poets explore their perceived exceptionalism, identify with their precursors and publicly project selves modelled through an exilic stance. In *The Artistry of Exile*, Jane Stabler outlines the attractions of Italian exile, arguing that 'Romantic-period writers sought to identify themselves with historical and literary outcasts and aliens to forward political protest, but also to understand their own states of mind and to people their isolation'.[6] They then absorbed and re-filtered the trope of Italian exile for their readership; the writers whom Stabler explores 'informed themselves about Italy through a literature of exile. Their writing, in turn, added to the echo chamber of exiled voices that resounded in literary works from Italy'.[7] Exile, for the Romantic poets, is foremost a literary, not a political, experience.

Childe Harold's Pilgrimage (1812–18), the basis for Byron's dramatic leap into fame, was also the foundation of his identification with Italian exile as an artist, expatriate and celebrity. The poem opens with Harold leaving England for self-chosen exile; his voice first appears in a song of mourning for his homeland with the refrain 'My native Land – Good Night'.[8] Yet, Harold's departure from England is less an escape from something than a flight towards the desolate sea and landscapes he has chosen for himself; after all, his journey is a pilgrimage, a voyage of spiritual self-discovery and renewal, rather than the forced migration of a political refugee:[9]

> Welcome, welcome, ye dark-blue waves!
>   And when you fail my sight,
> Welcome, ye deserts, and ye caves!
>   My native Land – Good Night![10]

'Welcom[ing]' his separateness, Harold embraces exile's spiritual and aesthetic opportunities, so that his outsider status becomes the source of his identity as he travels.

Byron's life as an expatriate in Italy reinforced the glamour associated with *Childe Harold*. As Barbara Schaff argues, 'The stance of the exile was to become the hallmark of his identity, insofar as he disowned Englishness and immersed himself in Italian culture: Italy became the stimulus and setting for his life's performance'.[11]

Furthermore, Harold became a Byronic model for other travellers, 'provid[ing] the tourist with an elitist consciousness of literariness as well as an attractive role model of distanced separateness from the hordes of other tourists'.[12] Byronic exile, then, used the negative experiences of exile – loss, loneliness and lack of community – to produce a sense of exceptionalism, of unique subjective depths, for those who identified with Harold's, and Byron's, Italian travels. Rather than disrupting one's sense of self, Byronic exile confirms one's special status and locates in the tourist or expatriate in Italy a means of identifying with the glamourous poet and his famous creation.

After 1820–1 and as the Risorgimento progressed in the nineteenth century, however, awareness of the forced political exile of Italian democrats and liberals, many of whom ended up in Britain, replaced exile as a chosen aesthetic stance in the Victorian imagination. The letters of Mazzini, the foremost among Italian refugees in Britain, show him to be, in Dante Della Terza's words, 'the exile who has experienced in his flesh and bones the drama of solitude and despair'.[13] Giuseppe Garibaldi, the most famous Risorgimento exile, was rendered stateless in his home territory of Piedmont after 1848–9. Garibaldi's military intervention in the Roman Republic marked him as the defender of a foreign state; Piedmont designated him an 'unlawful immigrant' and he was arrested on re-entry.[14] Despite Piedmont's hostility to its own Risorgimento hero, Piedmontese policy shifted to embrace moderate liberalism and Italian nationalists from across the peninsula, as thousands of Italians from other states arrived in the northern Italian kingdom during this period.[15] Large numbers of Italians began arriving in Britain in the 1820s, followed by Poles in the 1830s and an array of Europeans after 1848, including German and French refugees;[16] London thus became a European capital of refugees after 1848.[17] Britain, then, was exposed to the 'deprovincialization' Burke identifies as the form of knowledge most associated with exile.[18] Consisting of 'mediation', 'detachment' and 'hybridization',[19] the 'deprovincialization' cultivated by exile[20] also contributes to non-exiles' understandings of self, community and identity. '[E]xiles, "unsettled" themselves', Burke argues, 'have the power to unsettle others'.[21] In Victorian literary responses to the Risorgimento, contact with and awareness of the Italian exiles literally unsettled from their homelands translate into an uneasy blend of sympathy and hesitation, often depicted as disaffection from the methods and outcomes of the unification movement or estrangement within an Italian landscape.

Encounters with Italian place in British literature become more disorienting as awareness of Italy's political unsettlement increases in the Victorian public through the middle of the century. Victorian works such as *Pictures from Italy, Aurora Leigh, Little Dorrit, He Knew He Was Right* and *Middlemarch* explore a shift from the Italy of the Grand Tour and Romantic exile to the Italy of rebellion and disaffection that tracks nineteenth-century Italy's political developments: revolution, military occupation and international war. Geographical theorists Tim Cresswell and Peter Merriman argue that

> Rather than think of places or landscapes as settings, surfaces or contained spaces through and across which things move, it is perhaps more useful to think about the ongoing processes of 'spacing', 'placing' and 'landscaping' through which the world is shaped and formed.[22]

'Space, place and landscape', they continue, 'are best approached as "verbs" rather than as "nouns"'.[23] While these well-known Victorian works do not all address the plights of Italian refugees and internally displaced persons directly, they move from representing Italy as a site of pilgrimage and glamourous exile to portraying Italy as an unsettling place, disrupted by conflict. They thus participate in a mid-Victorian imaginative project of 'placing' the emerging nation-state of Italy. The mobility of figures like the tourist and the exile is crucial to this process; attention to mobilities allows for the establishment of an interpretive framework 'in which', John Urry argues, 'movement, potential movement and blocked movement are all conceptualized as constitutive of economic, social and political relations'.[24] Engaging with touristic commonplaces like crossing the Alps, visiting ruins and viewing churches, artwork and museums, Victorian writers track the Risorgimento's unsettling conflicts obliquely and reveal a trend towards increased discomfort with Italian affairs.

Disorientation pervades Charles Dickens's travel book, *Pictures from Italy* (1846). His arrival in Genoa indicates the sense of disruption that infiltrates Victorian representations of Italian place:

> I never, in my life, was so dismayed! The wonderful novelty to everything, the unusual smells, the unaccountable filth ... [T]he disorderly jumbling of dirty houses, one upon the roof of another; the passages more squalid and more close than any in Saint Giles's, or old Paris ... the perfect absence of any resemblance in any dwelling-house, or shop, or wall, or post, or pillar, to anything one had ever seen before; and the disheartening dirt, discomfort, and decay; perfectly confounded me. I fell into

a dismal reverie. I am conscious of a feverish and bewildered vision of saints and virgins' shrines at the street corners – of great numbers of friars, monks, and soldiers – of vast red curtains, waving in the door-ways of the churches – of always going up hill, and yet seeing every other street and passage going higher up – of fruit-stalls, with fresh lemons and oranges hanging in garlands made of vine leaves – of a guard-house, and a draw-bridge – and some gateways – and vendors of iced water, sitting with little trays upon the margin of the kennel – and this is all the consciousness I had, until I was set down in a rank, dull, weedy court-yard, attached to a kind of pink jail; and was told I lived there.[25]

The recurring dashes, shifts in tense, contrast between the 'wonderful' and 'disheartening' and sense of passivity stress the disoriented travel-ler's fragmented and unreceptive mindset. In contrast with the roman-ticised, conventional depiction of Venice as 'this strange Dream upon the water' later in the narrative,[26] Dickens's Genoa, well known by the 1840s as the birthplace of Young Italy and a decades-long site of resis-tance to an expanded Piedmontese state, is a place of confusion.

Disorienting Italian place also features in Dickens's fiction, most notably *Little Dorrit* (1855–7). Descending the Alps into Italy after her father's release from the Marshalsea, Amy Dorrit feels 'quite dis-placed even from the last point of the old standing-ground in life on which her feet had lingered'.[27] Physical displacement intensifies into homesickness in Venice and Rome and Amy comes to identify with Rome's ruins, which suggest the fragmentation of her own history and coherent identity:

Little Dorrit would often ride out in a hired carriage . . . and alight alone and wander among the ruins of old Rome. The ruins of the vast old Amphitheatre, of the old Temples, of the old commemorative Arches, of the old trodden highways, of the old tombs, besides being what they were, to her, were ruins of the old Marshalsea – ruins of her own old life – ruins of the faces and forms that of old peopled it – ruins of its loves, hopes, cares, and joys. Two ruined spheres of action and suffering were before the solitary girl often sitting on some broken fragment; and in the lonely places, under the blue sky, she saw them both together.[28]

Once foundational to Western identity, as in Byron's cry in *Childe Harold*,

> Oh Rome! my country! city of the soul!
> The orphans of the heart must turn to thee,
> Lone mother of dead empires![29]

this Rome of the mid-nineteenth century is intellectually staggering and incomprehensible. Yet, as Amanda Anderson argues, Amy's confrontation with Rome illustrates 'her capacity for a kind of double vision, one that remains true to the experience of cultural otherness as well as to her own psychological past';[30] Amy becomes a version of the deprovincialised exile, unsettled by the multiple expulsions – from her class, from the Marshalsea, from London – that culminate with her travels in Italy.[31]

For Dorothea Casaubon in George Eliot's *Middlemarch* (1871–2), a famous confrontation with Rome's fragmented layers of meaning intensifies the sense of estrangement already emerging within her marriage. Though Andrew Thompson views Dorothea's experience of Rome as a reflection of 'a pre-*Risorgimento* condition', missing the interpretive framework provided by the Risorgimento's 'mythology',[32] alongside these other Victorian texts, Dorothea's Rome appears more characteristic of Risorgimento Italy than exceptional:

> she was beholding Rome, the city of visible history, where the past of a whole hemisphere seems moving in funeral procession with strange ancestral images and trophies gathered from afar.
>
> But this stupendous fragmentariness heightened the dream-like strangeness of her bridal life . . . She had been led through the best galleries, had been taken to the chief points of view, had been shown the grandest ruins and the most glorious churches, and she had ended by oftenest choosing to drive out to the Campagna where she could feel alone with the earth and sky, away from the oppressive masquerade of ages, in which her own life too seemed to become a masque with enigmatical costumes.[33]

Rome's overdetermination, its excess of meaning, disrupts Dorothea's sense of self, rather than enlightening her or expanding her sympathies and intellect. She retreats into isolation, even from her own life, which is, like Rome's history, an 'enigmatical' parade of confusion detached from her inner reality.

Dorothea's experience of Rome more resembles a symptomatology – of fatigue, detachment, flashbacks of dream-like memory and ocular disorder – than an edifying Grand Tour:

> all this vast wreck of ambitious ideals, sensuous and spiritual, mixed confusedly with the signs of breathing forgetfulness and degradation, at first jarred her as with an electric shock, and then urged themselves on her with that ache belonging to a glut of confused ideas which check the

flow of emotion. Forms both pale and glowing took possession of her young sense, and fixed themselves in her memory even when she was not thinking of them, preparing strange associations which remained through her after-years. Our moods are apt to bring with them images which succeed each other like the magic-lantern pictures of a doze; and in certain states of dull forlornness Dorothea all her life continued to see the vastness of St. Peter's, the huge bronze canopy, the excited intention in the attitudes and garments of the prophets and evangelists in the mosaics above, and the red drapery which was being hung for Christmas spreading itself everywhere like a disease of the retina.[34]

Though Rome in these Victorian instances no longer takes the foundational place in identity that it occupies for Byron, for example, Dorothea's Rome, the Rome of intellectual fragmentation and emotional disruption, still lingers in the psyche; however, rather than laying the basis for Dorothea's sense of self, her lifelong unwilling recollection of this moment remains an uncontrollable and incoherent break from the self.[35]

The increasingly unstable protagonist of Anthony Trollope's *He Knew He Was Right* (1868–9), Louis Trevelyan, in fact seeks an Italian experience resembling Amy's and Dorothea's to reinforce his domestic estrangement. Initially imagining a future of familial 'banish[ment]' to Naples as a last effort to save his marriage,[36] he chooses Tuscany for self-imposed exile in response to his wife Emily's rebellion against his authority. This exile is framed as purposeless wandering rather than the aesthetically productive seeking of *Childe Harold* or even the targeted touring imposed on Amy and Dorothea. Crossing into Italy, Trevelyan is 'on his way, – he knew not whither' (350); he enacts his fantasy of exile at Casalunga, the 'very remote' house 'not . . . on the way to any place' he occupies in Siena (730, 731). Despite Tuscany's fertility and beauty, Casalunga possesses a 'look of desolation' (732); with its windows shuttered, it appears 'as though . . . deserted' and becomes the 'wretched, desolate, comfortless abode which he called his home' (733, 791). For Trevelyan, Italian place mirrors an already confused, lonely mental state.

Even Victorian characters for whom travel to Italy should feel like a homecoming, like Elizabeth Barrett Browning's Anglo-Italian poet Aurora Leigh, can be unsettled by encounters with Italy. *Aurora Leigh* initially confirms Romantic notions of Italy, like those associated with Germaine de Staël's *Corinne*; in Maura O'Connor's words, 'The idea . . . that Italy is a land where one could be free to be oneself is an integral part of the Romantic writer's understanding of the place'.[37] Indeed, arriving in England from Italy as an orphan, Aurora encounters the same overwhelming estrangement that Amy and Dorothea feel in Italy:

> All new and strange;
> The universe turned stranger, for a child.[38]

Nonetheless, Aurora's long-awaited return to Italy is initially a homecoming experienced as exile. Rather than restoring her lost mother's love,[39] Italy unsettlingly reminds Aurora of her father's absence:

> I did not think, 'my Italy,'
> I thought, 'my father!' O my father's house,
> Without his presence! (VII, 490–2)

She continues,

> 'Tis only good to be or here or there,
> Because we had a dream on such a stone,
> Or this or that, – but, once being wholly waked
> And come back to the stone without the dream,
> We trip upon't, – alas, and hurt ourselves;
> Or else it falls on us and grinds us flat,
> The heaviest grave-stone on this burying earth. (VII, 497–503)

The 'dream' of homecoming cannot survive against the heavy, palpable reality of loss that Aurora confronts in her return to Italy. Italy is the land of her father's grave and the emotional weight that his 'grave-stone' carries.[40]

For Aurora, then, Italy is a land of graves, but not the graves towards which Harold directs his cultural pilgrimage; instead, Italian graves connote an irreparable personal loss and Aurora's seemingly permanent emotional displacement from the land of her birth. Recounting a visit to her Tuscan childhood home, Aurora recognises that her sense of disruption inflects place with temporal dislocation:

> O land of all men's past! for me alone,
> It would not mix its tenses. I was past,
> It seemed, like others, – only not in heaven.
> And many a Tuscan eve I wandered down
> The cypress alley like a restless ghost. (VII, 1157–61)

Aurora's uncanny ghostliness in Italy's present haunts her homecoming and translates into a parallel feeling of Florence's 'foreign[ness]' (VII, 1194), despite the city's familiarity. Aurora's 'disembodiment'

(VII, 1209) when wandering the native city that is no longer her home is yet another stage of displacement for her, one that contrasts her arrival in her now 'foreign' (VII, 1194) homeland with the 'urgency and yearning' of her earlier hopes to return (V, 1269). Italy, then, leads Aurora further along the path of emotional displacement that she faced in England by rendering her 'foreign to myself' (VII, 1215). Her out-of-body experience erases her personal history with the cityscape she explores and the Tuscan community she should be part of, making her an exile in her own home.

Though the above works do not directly address the Risorgimento, they feature several reminders of the conflicts that shaped nineteenth-century Italy that help to contextualise the shift from Byron's pilgrimage to Dorothea's ordeal or Aurora's ghostly un-belonging. *Little Dorrit*'s Genoese exile Cavalletto, for example, is imprisoned in Marseilles for smuggling other exiles beyond the Piedmontese border to France during the repressive 1820s,[41] while *Middlemarch*'s Will Ladislaw, though of Polish extraction, tempts questions from other characters about his radical politics and mixed national origins that draw attention to the international networks of nineteenth-century Italian revolutionaries like Mazzini.[42] Will is described as that quintessentially foreign type, a Fosco-like 'Italian with white mice',[43] and draws speculation about his national origins, including possible Italian origins.[44] *He Knew He Was Right*, set contemporaneously to its publication in the late 1860s, includes the most direct Risorgimento references. Trevelyan's claim that 'England was my home once ... Italy is now my nation, and Casalunga is my home' (869) reveals both a consciousness of the Italian cause and a disruption of any straightforward kind of national belonging, given Casalunga's desolation. In addition, Trevelyan gives his young son Louey a patriotic 'regiment of Garibaldian soldiers, all with red shirts, and a drum to give the regiment martial spirit' to play with (786). Yet, in the bleak atmosphere of Louey's unhappy home, the child cannot bring himself to engage with games of Risorgimento heroism. Instead, 'the toys remained where the father had placed them, almost unheeded, and the child sat looking out the window, melancholy, silent, and repressed. Even the drum did not tempt him to be noisy' (786). Trollope explicitly links Trevelyan's isolated exile with the heroic Garibaldian soldiers, unsettling his identification with the Italian nation and, by extension, confidence in the Italian state that emerged after unification in the 1860s.[45]

The canonical Victorian works discussed here track a shift in literary imaginings of Italian place as Risorgimento propaganda and conflict intensified in the middle of the nineteenth century. As thousands of Italians were literally unsettled, or expelled, from their home countries, a corresponding discomfort with Italian place registers in British literature about Italy. In contrast to the rich diversity and potential of the Italian peninsula, as presented by Lady Morgan and Mary Shelley in the works examined in Chapter 1, the Victorian writing discussed here records an Italy of overwhelming fragmentation, emotional burden and disaffection.

'Among Strangers': Giovanni Ruffini and Italian Place

The unsettlement in Italy that emerges among British characters in the above works registers an association between Italian place and displacement in the Victorian period. Giovanni Ruffini's first two novels, *Lorenzo Benoni* and *Doctor Antonio*, brought an Italian exile's perspective on the Risorgimento's early stages, from the founding of Young Italy to revolutionary 1848, before the British public. Ruffini's complex portrayal of Italian exile and activism highlights the contested fields of place and displacement in Risorgimento Italy.

As constitutionalists, republicans and secret society members left Italy after 1815, 1820–1 and 1848, exile became central to the Risorgimento. Maurizio Isabella, whose *Risorgimento in Exile* focuses on the early refugees who fled in the aftermath of the failed 1820–1 insurrections in the Two Sicilies and Piedmont, argues that by 1860, 'exile was perceived as a defining feature of Italy's recent history both at home and abroad'.[46] Ruffini's novels are set at similar flashpoints of revolutionary activity and subsequent expulsion. *Lorenzo Benoni* follows the life of a Young Italy propagandist alongside the emerging leadership of a fictionalised Mazzini after the carbonarist failures of 1820–1 and culminates with Lorenzo's escape into exile in the early 1830s. *Doctor Antonio*, a courtship novel following the romance between an English tourist and her Italian doctor in the Italian Riviera, depicts Antonio's participation in the 1848 constitutionalist Sicilian revolution and the subsequent period of counterrevolution in Naples. Both novels track specific sites of resistance to Italian state authority that occurred within the context of other revolutionary outbursts and campaigns, such as the 1831 disturbances in central Italy and the emergence of Young Italy's open propaganda war against the existing Italian states. In particular, the January 1848 Palermo revolution was the first among a series of insurrections that swept Italy and Europe in 1848–9. Temporary republics emerged in Florence, Rome and Venice; uprisings known as the *Cinque Giornate*, or Five Days of Milan, occurred in Lombardy; and Piedmontese King Charles Albert fought an unsuccessful war against Austria that resulted in his abdication after the Battle of Novara. By 1849, counterrevolution had succeeded in Piedmont, Lombardy, Tuscany and Sicily, and French and Austrian forces successfully laid siege to the revolutionary Roman and Venetian republics.[47]

Such turbulence caused new expulsions, especially after 1848. Italian refugees in relatively safe asylums like Britain could continue their political activities; thus, 'The experience of emigration was crucial to the manner in which the Italian national community was imagined, at a time when certain important political discussions could be conducted only outside of Italy'.[48] Despite a temporary Aliens' Act taking force after 1848, which expired in 1858 and did not materially affect refugees in Britain,[49] Britain was a favoured, and sometimes the only, option for European exiles because of its open-door policy and permissiveness of continued political activity. After 1848, 'Britain became the ideal country of asylum in Europe not only because of the liberal attitudes of her politicians, but also because the more attractive alternatives which had hitherto existed disappeared one by one'.[50] Britain thus became a central point for a network of European political exiles who often knew each other, belonged to international political associations and cooperated across borders to effect change in Italy, France, Russia, Poland, Hungary and elsewhere.

Italian exiles, then, could continue their political activities, but at the expense of direct contact with Italy's population and at a distance from the homeland they attempted to bring into being. The exile of the early Risorgimento's leaders meant that political networks formed outside of Italy and away from everyday Italians' lived experiences; Adrian Lyttelton notes, for example, that '[t]he failure of the revolutions of 1820–1 shifted the centre of gravity of the movement for national independence, with the formation of important communities of political exiles'.[51] While these exiles and later refugees like Mazzini fundamentally shaped the emerging discourse of Italian independence that allowed Europeans to imagine a united Italy from outside of its borders, in his 1832 essay 'On the Superiority of Representative Government' Mazzini admits that exiles like himself were unsuited to legislate reform within the peninsula because they could not adequately represent those inhabitants who remained.[52] While exile allowed for greater political freedom, then, it also meant the loss of political insight and direct participation.

The political exile is one among a cluster of migrant figures constructed through the experience of loss entailed by mobility. In *The Figure of the Migrant*, Thomas Nail argues that

> what all migrants . . . share, at some point, is the experience that their *movement* results in a certain degree of expulsion from their territorial, political, juridical, or economic status . . . [T]he *process of migration itself* almost always involves an insecurity of some kind and duration.[53]

The 'insecurity' caused by 'expulsion' characterises much of the mid-Victorian discourse surrounding Italian exile. Yet, as Nail continues, 'The figure of the migrant is not merely an effect of different regimes of social expulsion. It also has its own forms of social motion in riots, revolts, rebellions, and resistances'.[54] The revolutionary Risorgimento exile, like Browning's patriot speaker, is not merely acted upon by the regimes that expel him or her, but is operative in constructing the 'riots, revolts, rebellions, and resistances' that at once counteract those regimes and figure as intrinsic features of the experience of nineteenth-century Italian exile. Many of the volunteers who fought with Giuseppe Garibaldi's Thousand to liberate – or conquer – southern Italy, after all, were exiles themselves. Thus, the Victorian works discussed above reflect an atmosphere of estrangement that is entangled with acts of rebellion or coded references to radicalism.

Yet, no matter how troubled the above travellers' experiences of Italian place might be, none directly confronts the costs of resistance and losses entailed by expulsion as experienced by actual refugees. As British Mazzinian W. J. Linton reminds his readers in his collection of European republican biographies, exile, even in relative comfort in Britain, takes steep emotional and physical tolls. Of his close friend Charles Stolzman, Linton mournfully states, 'The life of an exile has not much variety: inaction alternating with fruitless endeavour, deferred hope, disappointment, poverty, sickness or broken health, premature old age, and death. The history of one of the exiles is the history of all'.[55] In 'Reflections on Exile', Edward W. Said highlights the contrast between romanticised notions of exile and the harsh realities of living as a refugee. Said remarks that

> while it is true that literature and history contain heroic, romantic, glorious, even triumphant episodes in an exile's life, these are no more than efforts meant to overcome the crippling sorrow of estrangement. The achievements of exile are permanently undermined by the loss of something left behind forever.[56]

Exile, he concludes, is 'a condition of terminal loss'.[57] Said identifies the twentieth century as 'the age of the refugee, the displaced person, mass immigration'.[58] Yet, nineteenth-century Italy's international wars, absolute governments and outside military occupations created their own forcible expulsions, mass migrations and internal displacements within the politically fractured peninsula.

To understand the British responses to Risorgimento Italy that infiltrate the canonical texts discussed above, then, we must turn to refugee narratives like Ruffini's, which actively perform the 'placing'[59] of Risorgimento Italy in light of the peninsula's violent ruptures and displacements. Ruffini, who was 'widely known to the British (and French) reading public',[60] published in English with the Edinburgh-based Thomas Constable. His work was known to Dickens, who listed Ruffini among potential contributors to his periodical *All the Year Round* alongside Frances and Anthony Trollope, George Eliot and Elizabeth Gaskell when he launched the project in 1859.[61] Ruffini's novels were also specifically framed as political interventions in British print culture: he modelled his work on the Victorian novel,[62] referred to British events such as the 1844 Post Office Espionage Scandal, the subject of Chapter 3, and cited British writing on Italian affairs, like William Gladstone's *Two Letters to the Earl of Aberdeen, on the State Prosecutions of the Neapolitan Government* (1851).[63] Lorenzo is imprisoned as a schoolboy for reading the fundamental text of British liberty, Milton's *Paradise Lost*, which is banned by the Pope (44–8), and his friend, the Mazzini-like Fantasio, is arrested while reading Byron (214).[64] Antonio, a Sicilian, draws on Britain's historical sympathies with Sicilian constitutionalism, dating from Lord Bentinck's garrison of the Napoleonic period and culminating with Gladstone's *Two Letters*. Ruffini, moreover, established a reputation for writing Italian place for British audiences, as his 1872 autobiographical sketch 'Sanremo Revisited' illustrates. 'Sanremo Revisited' self-deprecatingly recounts two visits Ruffini made to his favourite childhood holiday spot after *Doctor Antonio* appeared. During the first visit of 1857, Ruffini's Sanremo acquaintances are hurt by the stereotypical descriptions of the town voiced by a prejudiced British character in the novel, but by the time of his second visit in 1864, the town's inhabitants credit *Doctor Antonio* with helping establish Sanremo as a destination for English tourists. Ruffini is met by a delegation from the town council and toured through Sanremo's new, Anglophile hotels; he promises the residents to 'keep my eyes wide open, and afterwards write down my impressions of all I have seen there, and then do my best to have them published' to help the local economy.[65]

Ruffini's work, however, is about displacement as much as Italian place. The textual history of his first two novels indicates the 'multiple displacements' for which his work was known.[66] These novels, set in Italy, were written in Paris under the Second Empire – Ruffini left London in 1841 – but published in English in Edinburgh, where Ruffini's brother Agostino lived in exile in the 1840s.[67] Though Ruffini's decision to write in English rather than Italian suggests his 'alienation from the Italian cultural context and his corresponding immersion in the British milieu',[68] his embrace of Parisian life complicates this choice. *Lorenzo Benoni*, which Ruffini initially sketched out in English, was completed partly in French and translated into English by Ruffini's companion, Cornelia Turner; *Doctor Antonio* was drafted in English with occasional French words, corrected with Turner's help. Both drafts were further corrected by Henrietta Jenkin, romantic partner to Agostino, and later Giovanni, who lived for long periods with Ruffini and Turner.[69] In addition to positioning himself as a 'cultural mediator'[70] targeting a British audience, then, Ruffini exploits the 'liminal space where different cultures, languages and literary genres intersect'[71] of Risorgimento internationalism.

A Mazzinian refugee who fled Piedmont-Sardinia in 1833, Ruffini fictionalised his own youthful participation in Mazzini's revolutionary plots and subsequent escape into exile in *Lorenzo Benoni*.[72] Ruffini was intimately connected with the first phases of the Young Italy movement and its early martyrs; he and two of his brothers, Jacopo and Agostino, became Young Italy's 'most important proselytizers' after Mazzini's 1830 exile.[73] *Lorenzo Benoni* follows its autobiographical protagonist from his childhood and school days in the repressive aftermath of the 1821 Piedmontese uprisings through his initiation into the *Carboneria* alongside his close friend Fantasio and brother Caesar, which results in Fantasio's arrest and exile. The novel reaches its climax when Fantasio, based in Marseilles, recruits the Benonis to establish a new revolutionary network resembling Mazzini's Young Italy (242–5), an organisation founded in 1831 and described by Stefano Recchia and Nadia Urbinati as 'Italy's first political party';[74] Caesar is arrested and Lorenzo escapes dramatically into exile. The novel follows the lives of the real Ruffini brothers closely: Jacopo, Mazzini's closest friend, ended his own life in prison after interrogators presented him with a false denunciation bearing Mazzini's forged signature.[75] Giovanni and Agostino followed Mazzini into exile and lived with him in France, Switzerland and England for eight years, until Agostino relocated to Edinburgh and Giovanni to Paris.[76] Mazzini appears in *Lorenzo Benoni* as the conspiratorial Fantasio[77] and Jacopo features as Caesar, whose fate is revealed in the novel's final sentences, when Lorenzo joins Fantasio in Marseilles.

The foundational Risorgimento myth of Jacopo Ruffini's martyrdom for Young Italy becomes the novel's shocking emotional centre:

> But my joy was soon damped at the sight of the dreadful change that had come over Fantasio's appearance. He looked so pale, so careworn, so haggard – the shadow of himself.
>
> 'What is the matter with you?' said I; 'you look very ill.'
>
> 'Oh! nothing at all,' stammered out Fantasio; 'I have been very uneasy about you, and – .' He stopped. I hesitated also to speak.
>
> At last I said, 'Any bad news from home?' Fantasio attempted to reply, but could not, and turned away.
>
> 'For Heaven's sake,' I cried, 'do not try to deceive me; – tell me what has happened. What – of – Caesar?'
>
> Fantasio hid his face and sobbed aloud.
>
> I understood it all. Merciful God! Caesar was no more! (325)

This abrupt ending to Ruffini's narrative of youthful rebellion and expulsion from home, family and country speaks to Said's description of exile as 'terminal loss'.[78] The 'heroic, romantic, glorious, even triumphant episodes in an exile's life' that Said recognises in literature and history[79] are pre-empted for Ruffini by the personal loss that denies Lorenzo even one moment of 'joy' (325) in his newfound personal safety and reunion with his friend.

Instead, unspeakable loss dominates the scene. The inability of the revolutionary propagandists Fantasio and Lorenzo to communicate in this final passage appears in the dashes that disrupt speech, as in Lorenzo's prolonged question, 'What – of – Caesar?', and in the prevalence of non-verbal cues: Fantasio 'stammered out', 'stopped', 'attempted to reply, but could not', 'turned away' and, finally, 'hid his face and sobbed aloud'. Lorenzo, similarly, 'hesitated' to question Fantasio about his family; his final revelation, 'Caesar was no more!' is reserved for the reader, as the friends remain incapable of speech. This inability to articulate the 'terminal loss'[80] that Lorenzo experiences in his first moment of exile extends to the editorial note with which the novel concludes. Though the note confirms Caesar's fate, it adds no further detail about Lorenzo's loss or Caesar's death. Knowledge of Caesar's fate can only come from real-world familiarity with Jacopo Ruffini's history. Instead, the concluding note lists other victims of Piedmontese repression (325–6). Such embedded editorial content alongside the novel's subtitle, *Passages in the Life of an Italian. Edited by a Friend*, indicates Lorenzo's disappearance from the implied future publication context. The editorial apparatus suggests that, as Allan C. Christensen argues, 'Ruffini could not imagine a Lorenzo Benoni that survived a Caesar Benoni in order calmly to compose a reflective narrative of their common life'.[81] The statement of loss with which the narrative ends, 'Caesar was no more!' (325), points to a greater absence at the novel's centre as Lorenzo is displaced from his own text, an absence that speaks to exile as loss. Ruffini refuses the propagandistic value of Caesar's death, instead layering the novel with erasure and dislocation.

Lorenzo Benoni also explores a plot of displacement, casting the migrant as a figure which, as Nail theorises, is both an 'effect of different regimes of social expulsion' and an actor with 'its own forms of social motion in riots, revolts, rebellions, and resistances'.[82] As in Ruffini's own life, activism and expulsion are the two poles of the Italian exile's experience. The dramatic exodus that results from Lorenzo's political activities comprises the novel's final section: four of the five closing chapters are titled 'The Fugitive' (288–317). Though the novel appeared in 1853, in early 1839, Christensen notes, 'Ruffini was obsessively drafting . . . an account of his nearly fatal adventure'.[83] The long narrative of Lorenzo's flight into exile, written first but placed last to subvert the text's apparently linear movement, culminating in the shocking news of Caesar's death and illustrating the 'nightmare'[84] of exile's dominance over the remainder of the text, is the heart of Ruffini's autobiographical novel. What Nicoletta Pireddu refers to in *Doctor Antonio* as 'the pathos of distance from one's homeland for which Ruffini was remembered for decades'[85] also features in *Lorenzo Benoni*. Expulsion from the familiarity of Genoese place symbolises Lorenzo's emotional estrangement in his new life. This displacement centres on the Lanterna, a landmark designed to allow travellers to find their bearings; when he loses sight of the Lanterna, he states, 'It was then that I felt in its full entireness that I was a fugitive. So long as I saw that well-known object, I certainly had not realized the idea that I was absolutely and utterly without either home or country; that perhaps I should never again behold my mother's face' (284). Lorenzo's exhaustive language – 'entireness', 'absolutely', 'utterly' – combined with negative diction like 'without' and 'never' indicates the depth of his loss as he leaves Genoa behind. Landing in France and parting from the human smugglers who ferried him beyond the border, he is again stricken with homesickness; he claims, 'I turned away with my heart quite full; they were my countrymen: henceforth I should be among strangers' (312). Without the familiar landmarks and people that place Lorenzo within a community, he loses his bearings.

Ruffini also emphasises the liminality that accompanies Lorenzo's escape from Piedmont. Like Browning's exile, Lorenzo hovers near the border; Ruffini thus stresses the process of expulsion through which Lorenzo's home state displaces him, rather than his new life elsewhere. Rather than decisively crossing the border into France to mark the transition from fugitive to refugee, the newly stateless Lorenzo returns twice to the margins of Liguria, first at the command of a *guarda-costa* looking for smugglers (282–3) and once when Lorenzo feverishly demands to be placed on shore when he is overwhelmed by suspicion of the men hired to take him over the border (292–5), which delays his final departure for several days. A fugitive, able neither to cross to safety nor to claim citizenship in Piedmont, upon his first return to the coast Lorenzo is shocked by the stresses of internal displacement:

> Thick-coming thoughts coursed through my brain, graven still on my memory, but incapable of being rendered into words . . . Home, country, friends, all so dear and yet so distant! The soil that I trode once more, and which I thought I had left for ever, burned my feet. There was no repose, no rest for me, as I lay stretched on the bosom of my native land; there was only a voice of woe echoing through my soul, like the wind as it sighs and wails through the forest on its errand of desolation. (284)

Neither at home nor yet an exile, Lorenzo feels the 'desolation' and estrangement of occupying his 'native land' without any of the comforts of 'Home, country, friends' that root him to his birthplace. Piedmont can never again be Lorenzo's home.

The disguise Lorenzo adopts in his flight and his stress-induced paranoia further accentuate the estrangement of exile. Before embarking with the smugglers, he dresses as 'an English gentleman bent on a fishing excursion' (277) and is warned, 'Always speak Italian, never Genoese' (282). During the voyage, Lorenzo pretends he is 'a stranger, almost altogether ignorant of the language of the country' (283). As the journey progresses, Lorenzo is subject to delusions brought on by anxiety and exhaustion, which highlight his liminal mental state as he wavers between reason and madness. Seeing a large stone in the boat, Lorenzo believes the hired smugglers intend to use it as a weapon against him:

As my eye chanced to alight on it, I thought – that stone round my neck – a hole in the water, followed by a gurgling hollow sound, and then silence – a dead mournful silence – horrible, horrible! all looks as it did – there is nothing to bear witness that crime has been busy here. A day comes at last – a week, nay, perhaps, a month hence – and some wave washes on the beach a swollen corpse, not to be recognised even by the tender mother herself. A crowd gathers, looking with horror and disgust, at what? – for that frightful object has almost lost all traces of humanity. I saw the whole scene from beginning to end enacted before me with all the vividness of reality. I did not spare myself one detail; there was a gloomy fascination in it. (290)

Lorenzo's expulsion from Italian place transforms into a monstrous fantasy of abjection. Even his mother will not recognise him; no longer Genoese and trafficked across the border like smuggled goods, he loses his sense of human dignity, imagining himself as 'that frightful object', a 'swollen corpse', which has 'almost lost all traces of humanity'. The dashes that litter Ruffini's transcription of these panicked imaginings stress the incoherence of Lorenzo's thoughts, emphasising confusion in a manner that prefigures the Italian experiences of later fictional tourists like Amy Dorrit and Dorothea Casaubon. Lorenzo finally embraces the in-betweenness of marginality under this delusion, leaping into the sea to escape the smugglers and forcing a return to shore (292).

Most horrifically, Ruffini highlights Lorenzo's inability to find his bearings during his flight when he finally disembarks at the river Var, marking the border between Piedmont and France, where he learns that the smugglers have left him on an island in the middle of the torrential river from which he will have to swim to safety (311–17). Unsure whether the island is French or Piedmontese territory, Lorenzo is truly trapped in the margins between the homeland where he can no longer remain and the host land he attempts to reach. He is swept away by the river in 'a state of half unconsciousness' and awakens from a trance-like acceptance that he will drift out to sea when he approaches a whirlpool, which spurs him to swim to safety (317). This final ordeal reaffirms Lorenzo's liminality as a new exile. In fictionalising his horrific personal refugee experience for the British public, Ruffini inscribes Italian place with the unsettling marks of damage incurred through Risorgimento conflict. Focusing on displacement, the marginality of the borderland and the violent wrenching apart of families and communities, Ruffini presents a Risorgimento constituted by personal loss, not national gain.

Doctor Antonio reverses *Lorenzo Benoni*'s trajectory of activism–rebellion–exile, opening with Antonio already living in exile in Liguria, having fled Sicily after defending a cholera patient[86] against soldiers sent to arrest him (257–9). Antonio is internally displaced within the Italian peninsula; Ruffini thus points towards Italy's divisions and Antonio's complicated political commitments. Christensen reads the novel as a timeless narrative associated more with psychological than political loss, arguing that it

> transcends all national, political, and public contexts. Like other great treatments of the myth of exile, it may finally imply that the soul's private and lost homeland – whether associated with Sicily, Liguria, or the English Lake District – can never be regained in this world.[87]

However, Ruffini's choice of Sicily for the novel's political content allows him to explore the distinctiveness of Italy's diverse regions and respond to the particular atrocities of Bourbon rule in southern Italy; though Antonio's nationalism seems rooted in his concept of a 'lost' Italian 'homeland', his exile is demonstrably and concretely political, and within the novel's volatile political setting, that 'homeland' cannot be unproblematically defined.

Ruffini destabilises *Doctor Antonio* by fracturing the novel's setting both temporally and geographically. The novel is divided between northern and southern Italy and the period of Antonio's exile on the Riviera in 1840 and his subsequent return home to the Two Sicilies and participation in the 1848 revolution. By placing Antonio in internal exile, Ruffini exposes the disjunctures across Italian jurisdictions that pose barriers to the nationalist movement and draws attention to the meridianist discourse that hinders the growth of cultural unity between north and south. Antonio resists these divisions by binding himself to a sense of Italian place: he chooses Sardinian territory for his exile (123–9) partly because it mitigates the distance from his southern homeland. He states, for example, 'to have left Italy would have been utter despair to me' (124) and rejects the idea of moving to London, like many of his real-world counterparts (212–3); he claims he 'cannot do without' the features of the southern landscape, adding, 'they are my life' (129). Piedmont thus becomes a kind of emotional lifeline connecting Antonio to Sicily.

Yet, the Riviera's inhabitants see Antonio as an outsider rather than a compatriot. He exclaims in surprise, 'yes, a man born in the south was called a foreigner in the north of Italy!' (124), indicating a degree of political and cultural fragmentation across the peninsula that Antonio had not thought possible. The geopolitical fact that Antonio relocates, across borders, from the southern, Bourbon Two Sicilies to the northern, Savoyard Piedmont-Sardinia outweighs pan-Italian commonality. This complicates his presence in the narrative as a figure of Italianness who represents and speaks for the Italian population to the English tourists, Sir John Davenne and his daughter Lucy, the novel's other primary characters. As Pireddu argues, 'the narrator's recurring definition of Antonio as "the Italian" hence sounds like a speech act, positing his nationness through linguistic performance in the absence of a political reality'.[88] In fact, Ruffini points throughout the novel to multiple, concurrent relationships between Antonio and place, culture and state. A subject of the Two Sicilies living as a refugee in the host country of Piedmont, he does not straightforwardly represent Italy, but, rather, mediates between Sicily and the Riviera. Moreover, his lessons on Sicilian politics for the Davennes are mediated by the Ligurian landscape and community of Bordighera in which he interacts with the English tourists, but he also interprets northern Italy for the Davennes as a resident 'foreigner' (124) who views the Riviera with a combination of familiarity and distance. He is further hybridised by his fluency in English, acquired through his upbringing and education alongside Anglo-Italian cousins whose father was an English officer stationed in Sicily during the Napoleonic period (36). Antonio thus represents the process of deprovincialisation[89] and 'power to unsettle others' Burke associates with exile.[90] Finally, Antonio is a fictional Sicilian as mediated by the Ligurian Ruffini, who projects his own ideological interest in Italian unity onto his southern character.

Further problematising Antonio's internal displacement in 1840s Sardinia is the fact that Charles Albert's repressive kingdom is no more a safe haven for political activists than the Two Sicilies. Pireddu claims that 'Antonio . . . considers himself a stranger and an exile on what should be his own homeland because . . . being born in Sicily he comes from a different state, still in the oppressor's hands'.[91] Ruffini, however, stresses that Antonio's host land is also a repressive, lost homeland for Piedmontese political exiles like Ruffini himself. Ruffini refers to his own family through the character of Signora Eleonora, whose two sons are exiled from Liguria (302–3) but return in 1848 (377), as did Ruffini and Agostino; Eleonora Ruffini, for whom Mazzini coined the name 'La Madre Santa' was, like her sons, a well-known figure in Mazzinian Risorgimento mythology.[92]

Moreover, Antonio's host country never becomes a permanent home. When Antonio's beloved Lucy returns to England to marry, Antonio experiences renewed emotional exile in the Riviera, as his surroundings remind him of her loss:

> there was the dear face looking at him out of every corner, haunting him at every turn. The little library . . . the flute and guitar . . . the map of Sicily he had taken to her when her interest in his country was first awakened, the flowers she had given him . . . all around him was full of her. All seemed to ask, 'Where is she?' . . .
>
> . . . Not a foot of ground but was hallowed by some recollection of her. There, past that sharp descent of the road, he had seen her for the first time . . . There she had smiled on him so sweetly . . . there, on the first fold of the hill behind the house, one day, at dusk, she had discovered the first fireflies of the season . . . Not a path but they had trodden it together . . . not one of the thousand hues of sea, or earth, or sky, that they had not admired together! (352–3)

Interior spaces are no longer home-like, and the Ligurian landscape is inscribed with signs of Lucy's absence, reminding Antonio, as Lorenzo is reminded by Genoa's Lanterna, of loss. Even the map of Antonio's beloved Sicily is written with Lucy's erasure. Antonio is once more dislocated, as the repetition of 'There', 'There', 'there' marks Lucy's unsettling absence as presence, an uncanny 'haunting' of Italian place.

Lucy's departure signals Antonio's recognition that he is not at home in Liguria: he remains both estranged from the setting and a stranger to his neighbours. His disaffection is heightened by his reflections on Lucy's erasure from his host land: 'It seemed so strange, so unnatural, so impossible, that she should have passed away from a place so full of her' (353). For one who mediates between the English tourists and their northern Italian hosts, occupying the liminal position of an Italian who is not Ligurian, Antonio finds Bordighera altered without the English, 'strange' and 'unnatural', and must navigate his place in the town anew. When Bordighera's priests band against Antonio, targeting him with speeches against 'foreigners' (374), Ruffini shows that Antonio's hopes for pan-Italian unity are weighed down by the divisions sown by party faction and regional bias. Even the sympathetic innkeeper Speranza views Antonio as an outsider; when the widowed Lucy returns to Bordighera in 1848, Speranza declares that 'Doctor Antonio went back to his own country' (372).

Antonio's return to Sicily in 1847–8 indicates that the novel's political focal point is local, not national. Antonio is, it is true, devoted to Italy; when Lucy returns to England, he swears

> to have no other mistress than his country, and to devote to her, and her alone, all the energies of his soul and mind; and, when we say his country, we mean of course Italy, for Antonio's patriotism was not confined to the isle in which he was born, but embraced the whole of the motherland. (393)

Nonetheless, the particularity of Sicily's political situation complicates Antonio's patriotism. Ruffini includes Antonio's long exposition of Sicilian politics for his English friends (236–57), emphasising the importance of regional difference in any attempt to address reform within Italy. Ruffini's attention to Sicilian politics, within the context of the Kingdom of the Two Sicilies' governance from Naples and against the backdrop of Piedmontese King Charles Albert's First War of Independence against Austria, reveals the multi-layered complexities of the Risorgimento in the 1840s. Christensen argues that as an effect of Ruffini's cosmopolitan vision, 'his works treat both the forces of political disintegration – that undermine the unity of the Swiss cantons, of the Hapsburg empire, and of Piedmont-Savoy – and the movements towards integration',[93] and Ruffini's interest in exploring the competing pressures of integration and disintegration is apparent in his choice of Sicily for Antonio's home. A distinct country within a larger Kingdom, Sicily provides a framework for exploring Antonio's conflicting political commitments. Antonio simultaneously desires Sicily's independence from Neapolitan Bourbon rule, pan-Italian unity and King Ferdinand's participation in the Piedmontese war alongside Charles Albert, in hopes of 'furthering the cause of Italian independence . . . [and] another and not less precious advantage . . . of rendering for the present hostilities impossible between Naples and Sicily' (406).[94] Though his multiple allegiances briefly align in 1848, they are most often at odds with each other.

In fact, Sicily's January 1848 constitutional revolution,[95] in which Antonio participates alongside a community of returned exiles (393–5), precipitates the Two Sicilies into civil war and pushes the narrative towards a bleak conclusion that draws on an existing anti-Neapolitan polemic in British print culture. Antonio travels to Naples to conciliate the Bourbons in hopes of avoiding the 'fratricidal war' (398) looming between Naples and Sicily (399–400). Despite his efforts, rebellion and counterrevolution collide in the Neapolitan streets on 15 May: 'civil war, with all its horrors, was raging in beautiful Naples' (412). Antonio, caught up in the street fighting while tending the wounded, is forced to play dead and hide among corpses to escape being killed himself (425): the mobility that enabled his contact with northern Italians and tourists and helped to construct him as a mediator for disparate cultural groups is eliminated in the counterrevolution and his subsequent imprisonment.

Ruffini intentionally places Antonio within this clearly delineated and topical political setting, drawing on its traction in the 1850s British literary market for which he wrote. Gladstone's *Two Letters to the Earl of Aberdeen*, a public critique of the post-1848 Neapolitan justice system, carved out a space in British print culture for such polemical interventions. In his open letters, the then-Peelite Gladstone appealed to his parliamentary colleague Lord Aberdeen to hold the Neapolitan government to account for the 'horrors'[96] the state perpetrated against its people after 1848, which he witnessed as a visitor to Naples. For Gladstone, who pleaded his case to Aberdeen in the press rather than in Parliament, the obligations of shared humanity pre-empt British state or party interest: 'The claims, the interests, which I have in view are not those of England. Either they are wholly null and valueless, or they are broad as the extension of the human race, and long-lived as its duration'.[97] Thus, while appearing to refrain from using his official position to chastise an ally, Gladstone astutely brings the power of public opinion and the press to bear on his own party and government through his apparently personal public intervention.

In *Doctor Antonio*'s final chapters, Ruffini presents his audience with an uneasy blend of the personal narrative, through his courtship plot, and the interventionist political pamphlet. Upon Antonio's capture and imprisonment, Ruffini's narrative shifts into a Gladstonian exposure of the Neapolitan prison and court systems, including the use of torture (431–8). Ruffini's characters reappear in the final pages almost as an afterthought, confirming Bourbon brutality: Antonio is imprisoned on the island of Ischia, from which Lucy unsuccessfully tries to free him (464–8). Like Gladstone, Lucy is transformed from an apolitical tourist into a concerned eyewitness, morally obliged to intervene against an injustice; through Lucy, Ruffini transposes Gladstonian polemic into direct action undertaken by a private individual representative of Britishness throughout the novel. When the prisoners are moved in the aftermath of the escape attempt, however, the infirm Lucy dies from shock (470). The novel's harsh final sentence reads, 'Doctor Antonio still suffers, prays, and hopes for his country'

(471). A novel that opens as an apparent courtship narrative, exploring symbolic contact among representatives of different cultures and seemingly moving towards conciliation and union, *Doctor Antonio* ends with the weight of political oppression and civil war terminating any possibility of alliance or mutual understanding across, and even within, borders.

Ruffini's novels, then, construct the early Risorgimento for a British audience through representations of Italian place and Italian mobilities. Place, as Tim Cresswell defines it, refers to 'locations imbued with meaning and power';[98] in Ruffini's refugee narratives, a struggle emerges between the meanings attributed to Italy as place by patriots like Lorenzo and Antonio and existing state control over Italian territory and its inhabitants. Mobility is, similarly, for Cresswell, 'about the contested world of meaning and power'.[99] Ruffini's exile figures cross borders as activists working to subvert state authority or move beyond its grasp, suggesting an effort to construct a Risorgimento that is not confined by the arbitrary boundaries imposed on the peninsula in 1815. Nonetheless, the state retains the power to deprive subjects of their citizenship, forcibly expel them from their native territories and, in some cases, restrict their movement and confine them to prison. These contests surrounding mobility and place inform Ruffini's representation of Risorgimento Italy and its exiles.

Ruffini's emphasis on these conflicts reflects his own position as a long-time exile as well as his disaffection from his youthful Mazzinian idealism and the Italian political scene for which he sacrificed family, personal safety and his childhood home. As Sardinian politics shifted in the 1840s, the opportunity to return to Italy was open to Ruffini. In fact, in 1848 he was elected to Parliament in Turin but 'nearly refused the post',[100] reluctant to leave Paris. For Rafaella Antinucci, Antonio's position as a conciliator in the Bourbon court re-imagines Ruffini's election, 'when he faced the humiliation of taking an oath of allegiance to the same king who some years earlier had sentenced him to death and forced him to exile'.[101] He was quickly appointed Minister to Paris but resigned from Parliament completely after the March 1849 Battle of Novara, which ended the Piedmontese–Austrian war.[102] Ruffini discovered 'that he now preferred to live outside Italy, and . . . [developed] a particular horror of his native city, Genoa'.[103] In Pireddu's words, 'Paradoxically, it is . . . within the borders of his disappointing nation, rather than abroad, that he experiences the most dramatically reductive aspect of exile', 'alienation' from the community.[104] This feeling of continued displacement was shared by Agostino Ruffini, who returned to Piedmont in 1848 and remained there throughout his final illness; rather than celebrating his homecoming, Agostino wrote to an Edinburgh friend John Hunter, 'I feel a *stranger at home*'.[105] Christensen, furthermore, reads Ruffini's ultimate return to Liguria after Cornelia Turner's 1874 death as a second exile from his chosen home, Paris, rather than a homecoming.[106] In the wake of the early Risorgimento's violent contests over Italian place and citizenship, there is no political or emotional space for a returned exile in Giovanni Ruffini's imagination: what is lost in exile cannot be recovered and a return from exile constitutes further dislocation, not restoration.

Moreover, an element of belatedness to Ruffini's representations of the early Risorgimento from the 1850s adds to the narrative dislocation his novels convey. Though *Doctor Antonio*'s critique of Neapolitan prisons remained topical in 1855, Ruffini's political intervention in *Lorenzo Benoni* was already outdated, as the repressive Piedmont of Charles Felix's reign and Lorenzo's youth had become one of the peninsula's most liberal regimes after Victor Emmanuel II's succession.[107] Ruffini's shift towards criticism of the Bourbon regime with *Doctor Antonio*, then, responds to the increased popularity of the so-called 'Piedmontese solution', which Ruffini, among other republicans and former revolutionaries, also 'embraced'.[108] Like Austria, the Two Sicilies was a palatable target for a British audience, and Antonio's Sicilian constitutionalism resembles British meliorism more than Lorenzo's Mazzinian republicanism. By focusing on the Two Sicilies, Ruffini avoids discussing Mazzini's more radical Roman Republic and its sister, the revolutionary Venetian Republic, in this moderate packaging of 1848 for British readers. However, the Sicilian focal point also allows Ruffini to minimise Charles Albert's Piedmontese leadership in the independence movement; similarly, the critique of Piedmont offered through Eleonora in *Doctor Antonio* draws on a lingering sense of grievance that contests the direction of Italian politics after 1848. Thus, though Ruffini moderates his depiction of the Risorgimento's early stages for an 1850s British audience, he refuses to fully exonerate Piedmont for its absorption of independent Liguria or overtly endorse a state-driven, Piedmontese Risorgimento. This belated return to 1830s and 1840s Risorgimento conflict, then, indicates a sustained engagement with the political struggles of the past, despite Piedmont's gradual assumption of leadership within 1850s Italy. Disaffection with the Risorgimento's process and outcomes in Ruffini's novels points to a continuing uncertainty about what unification efforts and the future Italian state might stand for and whether Risorgimento promise could truly be fulfilled.

Victorian narratives of unsettlement in Italy participate in a process of placing Italy in reaction to the violent displacements that occurred as a result of the collision of activist agendas and repressive regimes as Risorgimento conflict intensified across the nineteenth century. Giovanni Ruffini, a revolutionary and a refugee, is a vital voice in this project. Though an early convert to Mazzini's Young Italy movement, Ruffini reflects back on the years between the emergence of the Mazzinian Risorgimento and the radical climax of Risorgimento revolution in 1848 from the 1850s with a mixture of sympathy and disaffection that stems from his novels' emphasis on the real stakes of the Risorgimento for those who, like himself, were expelled from Italy while acting to bring Italy into geopolitical being. Though initiated through nationalist sentiments rooted in place, like the historically republican Genoa that resisted Piedmontese territorial expansion or the constitutionalist Sicily prepared to fight a civil war with Naples for its independence, Ruffini's Risorgimento Italy is constituted through such stories of displacement.

Notes

1. See Chapter 3 for more on the spy scandal that made Mazzini famous. For a discussion of 'The Italian in England' in relation to the scandal, see Marjorie Stone, 'Joseph Mazzini, English Writers, and the Post Office Espionage Scandal: Politics, Privacy, and Twenty-First Century Parallels'. Stone notes that 'Mazzini is widely assumed to be the chief model' for the speaker (p. 15). See also Maurizio Masetti, 'Lost in Translation: "The Italian in England"'. For a discussion of Browning's attitudes towards Italians, see Britta Martens, '"Oh, a Day in the City Square, There is no Such Pleasure in Life!": Robert Browning's Portrayal of Contemporary Italians'.
2. Robert Browning, 'The Italian in England', ll. 1, 3, 2. Subsequent citations will appear parenthetically in the text by line number.
3. Quoted in Jessie White Mario, *The Birth of Modern Italy: Posthumous Papers of Jessie White Mario*, p. 97.
4. Peter Burke, *Exiles and Expatriates in the History of Knowledge, 1500–2000*, p. 32.
5. P. B. Shelley, 'Julian and Maddalo: A Conversation', in *Poems of Shelley*, vol. 2, l. 57.
6. Jane Stabler, *The Artistry of Exile: Romantic and Victorian Writers in Italy*, p. 4.
7. Ibid. p. 17.
8. Lord Byron, *Childe Harold's Pilgrimage*, I, 125.

9. 'Pilgrimage' is defined as 'A journey . . . made to a sacred place as an act of religious devotion; the action or practice of making such a journey'. *Oxford English Dictionary*.

10. Byron, *Childe Harold's Pilgrimage*, I, 194–7.

11. Barbara Schaff, 'Italianised Byron – Byronised Italy', p. 103.

12. Ibid. p. 114. See the discussion of Byron's influence over continental travel in James Buzard, *The Beaten Track: European Tourism, Literature, and the Ways to Culture, 1800–1918*, pp. 114–130. Buzard describes Byron as 'the poet who had remade travel in his image' (p. 114).

13. Dante Della Terza, 'Mazzini's Image and the Italian Risorgimento: De Amicis, De Sanctis, Ruffini', p. 123.

14. Lucy Riall, *Garibaldi: Invention of a Hero*, p. 105. Garibaldi's South American exile and guerrilla fighting in Uruguay are well known. After 1849, Garibaldi went into a second exile, mostly in New York (pp. 106–15).

15. Riall estimates that 50,000 refugees arrived in Piedmont in 1849, with 20–30,000 of those remaining (Ibid. p. 117).

16. Bernard Porter, *The Refugee Question in Mid-Victorian Politics*, pp. 13–18.

17. Burke, *Exiles and Expatriates*, p. 131.

18. Ibid. p. 16.

19. Ibid. p. 19.

20. Ibid. p. 16.

21. Ibid. p. 32.

22. Tim Cresswell and Peter Merriman, 'Geographies of Mobilities', p. 7.

23. Ibid.

24. John Urry, *Mobilities*, p. 43.

25. Charles Dickens, *Pictures from Italy*, pp. 63–4.

26. Ibid. p. 127.

27. Charles Dickens, *Little Dorrit*, p. 458.

28. Ibid. p. 600.

29. Byron, *Childe Harold's Pilgrimage*, IV, 694–6.

30. Amanda Anderson, *The Powers of Distance: Cosmopolitanism and the Cultivation of Detachment*, p. 75.

31. For a more detailed discussion of the Dorrits' travels in Italy, see William Burgan, 'Little Dorrit in Italy'. Burgan sees Dickens's portrayal of Italy as a universal, rather than historically particular and political, gesture towards disenchantment:

> The relative absence of hortatory rhetoric (there is not much that Dickens or his readers can *do* about Italy) gives a contemplative, universal quality to this record of disenchantment; . . . the scenes through which they pass are primarily vehicles for a saddened awareness of the contrast between natural beauty and human suffering, cultural magnificence and social failure. (394)

Restoring historical consciousness of Italian refugees, however, allows us to read this 'social failure' in a more explicitly political light.

32. Andrew Thompson, *George Eliot and Italy: Literary, Cultural and Political Influences from Dante to the* Risorgimento, p. 126.
33. George Eliot, *Middlemarch*, pp. 180–1.
34. Ibid. pp. 181–2.
35. See Jill L. Matus's discussion of Eliot's use of the imagery of electric shock in Jill L. Matus, *Shock, Memory and the Unconscious in Victorian Fiction*, pp. 53–4. For more detailed discussions of Italy's role in *Middlemarch*, see Thompson, *George Eliot and Italy* and Joel J. Brattin, '*Middlemarch*: The Novel, the Manuscript, and Italy'.
36. Anthony Trollope, *He Knew He Was Right*, p. 177. Subsequent citations will appear parenthetically in the text.
37. Maura O'Connor, *The Romance of Italy and the English Political Imagination*, p. 29.
38. Elizabeth Barrett Browning, *Aurora Leigh*, I, 249–50. Subsequent citations will appear parenthetically in the text by book and line numbers.
39. For a psychoanalytic reading of Aurora's need to recover maternal love, see Virginia V. Steinmetz, 'Images of "Mother-Want" in Elizabeth Barrett Browning's *Aurora Leigh*'.
40. For a feminist reading of the poem that sees the father's grave as a liberating force suggesting the text's rejection of patriarchy, see Sandra M. Gilbert, 'From *Patria* to *Matria*: Elizabeth Barrett Browning's Risorgimento'. Gilbert argues that 'man as father must be exorcised rather than internalized and that, in a risorgimento of matriarchal law, he must be replaced with man as brother or man as son' (205). Yet, this reading neglects the ways in which Aurora feels burdened and displaced from the land of her birth by these reminders of her father's grave.
41. Rigaud describes Cavalletto as 'a poor little contraband trader, whose papers are wrong, and whom the police lay hold of, besides, for placing his boat (as a means of getting beyond the frontier) at the disposition of other little people whose papers are wrong' (Dickens, *Little Dorrit*, p. 23). For more on Cavalletto's links to Risorgimento discourse, see Vicky Greenaway, 'The Italian, the Risorgimento, and Romanticism in *Little Dorrit* and *The Woman in White*'. Cavalletto is anachronistically drawn as a Garibaldian volunteer, Greenaway notes (44).
42. Eliot, *Middlemarch*, pp. 336–7. For more detail about these European republican networks, see W. J. Linton, *European Republicans: Recollections of Mazzini and His Friends*.
43. Eliot, *Middlemarch*, p. 460.
44. Ibid. pp. 676, 727. For more on Ladislaw and Italian stereotypes, see Thompson, *George Eliot and Italy*, pp. 127–31.
45. The Garibaldi reference also contrasts Garibaldi's romanticised internal exile on the island of Caprera with Trevelyan's jealous, obsessive separation from his family.
46. Maurizio Isabella, *Risorgimento in Exile: Italian Émigrés and the Liberal International in the Post-Napoleonic Era*, p. 1.

47. For a summary of the Risorgimento's main conflicts, see Lucy Riall, *Risorgimento: The History of Italy from Napoleon to Nation-State*, pp. 1–36.
48. Isabella, *Risorgimento in Exile*, p. 1.
49. Sabine Freitag, Introduction, in *Exiles from European Revolutions: Refugees in Mid-Victorian England*, p. 3.
50. Andreas Fahrmeir, 'British Exceptionalism in Perspective: Political Asylum in Continental Europe', p. 33.
51. Adrian Lyttelton, 'The National Question in Italy', p. 79.
52. Giuseppe Mazzini, 'On the Superiority of Representative Government (1832)', in *A Cosmopolitanism of Nations: Giuseppe Mazzini's Writings on Democracy, Nation Building, and International Relations*, pp. 47–8.
53. Thomas Nail, *The Figure of the Migrant*, p. 2.
54. Ibid. p. 7.
55. Linton, *European Republicans*, p. 320.
56. Edward W. Said, 'Reflections on Exile', p. 173.
57. Ibid.
58. Ibid. p. 174.
59. Cresswell and Merriman, 'Geographies of Mobilities', p. 7.
60. Raffaella Antinucci, '"An Italy Independent and One": Giovanni (John) Ruffini, Britain and the Italian Risorgimento', p. 104.
61. Ibid.
62. Ibid. p. 105 and Allan C. Christensen, *A European Version of Victorian Fiction: The Novels of Giovanni Ruffini*.
63. Giovanni Ruffini, *Doctor Antonio*, pp. 431, 433–4. Subsequent citations will appear parenthetically in the text. See Antinucci, 'An Italy Independent and One', p. 114. Antinucci notes that 'Gladstone congratulated Ruffini' on *Doctor Antonio* (113). Lorenzo also describes the Sardinian government of his youth 'in the words of Mr. Gladstone', arguing 'that it "set up as a system the negation of God"'. Giovanni Ruffini, *Lorenzo Benoni, or Passages in the Life of an Italian. Edited by a Friend*, p. 146. Subsequent citations will appear parenthetically in the text.
64. Lorenzo notes that 'Shakspere [sic], Byron, Goethe, Schiller, were as familiar to him [Fantasio] as Dante and Alfieri' (122).
65. Giovanni Ruffini, 'Sanremo Revisited', p. 209.
66. Nicoletta Pireddu, 'Foreignizing the Imagi-Nation: Giovanni Ruffini's Contrapuntal Risorgimento', p. 93. Though Pireddu refers to *Doctor Antonio*, her phrase also applies to *Lorenzo Benoni*.
67. For details about biographical influences on Ruffini's writing, see Christensen, *European Version*, pp. 9–40. Although Ruffini published in English, Christensen sees his move to Paris, his home from 1841 until 1875, as a rejection of England. Christensen, *European Version*, p. 24.

68. Ibid. p. 19.
69. Ibid. pp. 32–3.
70. Antinucci, 'An Italy Independent and One', p. 105.
71. Ibid. p. 104.
72. Christensen notes that Lorenzo's history draws on some events from the lives of Ruffini's brothers Agostino and Jacopo. Christensen, *European Version*, pp. 46–7.
73. Ibid. p. 11.
74. Stefano Recchia and Nadia Urbinati, 'Giuseppe Mazzini's International Political Thought', p. 5.
75. See Linton, *European Republicans*, pp. 171–3 and White Mario, *The Birth of Modern Italy*, pp. 15–17 for detailed nineteenth-century accounts.
76. Christensen, *European Version*, p. 12. Mazzini and the Ruffinis travelled from France to England together in 1837. Agostino eventually continued on to Edinburgh to teach, with letters of introduction from the Carlyles. Giovanni lived with Mazzini until he travelled to Paris with Mazzini's letter of introduction to George Sand in the 1840s. White Mario, *The Birth of Modern Italy*, pp. 25–6, 40, 62.
77. The name 'Fantasio' suggests Ruffini's well-known disillusionment with Mazzini's idealism in the first years of their shared exile. Christensen argues that Mazzini is represented by two characters in the novel, the 'romantic and disturbingly charismatic' Fantasio and Lorenzo's more moderate, 'reasonable and sensible' Uncle John. Christensen, *European Version*, p. 45.
78. Said, 'Reflections on Exile', p. 173.
79. Ibid.
80. Ibid.
81. Christensen, *European Version*, p. 48.
82. Nail, *The Figure of the Migrant*, p. 7.
83. Christensen, *European Version*, p. 43.
84. Ibid.
85. Pireddu, 'Foreignizing the Imagi-Nation', p. 93.
86. For more on the devastating cholera outbreaks in nineteenth-century Italian cities, see Riall: 'In 1837, 13,810 died in Naples and 27,000 people, one-sixth of the total population, died of cholera in Palermo' (Riall, *Risorgimento*, p. 94). Antonio is permitted to settle in Piedmont so he can treat patients during the Riviera's 1837 epidemic (123–4).
87. Allan C. Christensen, 'Giovanni Ruffini and *Doctor Antonio*: Italian and English Contributions to a Myth of Exile', p. 135. Christensen sees Antonio's exile as a kind of universal story of human psychological displacement from an idealised youth, with the early Risorgimento featuring as the object of nostalgia (149). This is the reverse of my argument that the Risorgimento's political dimensions are the source of the displacement that creeps into Victorian narratives of Italy mid-century.

88. Pireddu, 'Foreignizing the Imagi-Nation', p. 99.
89. Burke, *Exiles and Expatriates*, p. 16.
90. Ibid. p. 32. See also Amanda Anderson's discussion of 'a tradition of cosmopolitan critique in Victorian culture' (63).
91. Pireddu, 'Foreignizing the Imagi-Nation', p. 99.
92. Christensen, *European Version*, p. 27. See also Christensen's discussion of Signora Eleonora as a *mater dolorosa* figure based on Eleonora Ruffini (129).
93. Ibid. p. 162.
94. See Christensen on Antonio's conflicting loyalties (86).
95. See Ruffini's description of the revolution and resulting constitution (381–4).
96. W. E. Gladstone, *Two Letters to the Earl of Aberdeen, on the State Prosecutions of the Neapolitan Government*, p. 5.
97. Ibid. p. 41.
98. Tim Cresswell, *On the Move: Mobility in the Modern Western World*, p. 3.
99. Ibid. p. 265.
100. Christensen, *European Version*, p. 13.
101. Antinucci, 'An Italy Independent and One', p. 119.
102. Christensen, *European Version*, pp. 13–14.
103. Ibid. p. 16.
104. Pireddu, 'Foreignizing the Imagi-Nation', p. 111.
105. Quoted in Mary Ambrose, 'An Italian Exile in Edinburgh, 1840–48', p. 323.
106. Christensen, *European Version*, p. 36.
107. Victor Emmanuel II succeeded Charles Albert, who abdicated after the Battle of Novara. See Dante Della Terza's discussion of this belatedness, and particularly of Piedmont's occupation of Liguria after 1815 (132).
108. Antinucci, 'An Italy Independent and One', p. 117.

Chapter 3

Spying in the British Post Office: Letter-Opening, Italy and Wilkie Collins's *The Woman in White*

On 14 June 1844, radical British Member of Parliament Thomas Slingsby Duncombe presented a petition in the House of Commons to reveal that the British government was secretly opening exiled Young Italy leader Giuseppe Mazzini's private letters and sharing information with continental European governments. That the British government could be collaborating with supposedly tyrannical foreign rulers and using as its instrument of espionage that quintessential liberal institution, the newly reformed British Post Office, shocked the Parliament and the public. A Victorian sensation with a long afterlife in British cultural memory,[1] the Post Office Espionage Scandal was a media event that represented the practices of the British government to the public in Gothic terms. Debate over the Post Office Scandal in Parliament and print located violations of privacy in supposedly modern institutions and potentially criminal despotism in government actions against the political exiles who came to Britain to find refuge. The scandal thus tracks an imaginative shift from the geographically or historically distanced early Gothic towards the more contemporary sensation genre, concerned with exposing Victorian Britain's secrets and hypocrisies. Representations of the Post Office Scandal in Victorian print culture predict the revision of the Gothic into the sensation novel that occurred with the publication of Wilkie Collins's *The Woman in White* (1859–60). Reading *The Woman in White* with attention to the fields of Anglo-Italian studies, mid-Victorian print culture – particularly the media sensation produced by Post Office espionage – and the development of narrative form in the mid-nineteenth century illustrates the historical and political implications of letter-opening for the representation of secrecy and authority in Collins's first sensation novel. Together, the letter-opening scandal and *The Woman in White* reveal and help produce a major mid-century shift in British attitudes towards Italy

and Italians that occurred as the Risorgimento came to public prominence as well as an accompanying challenge to myths of British identity and Britain's leadership in European liberalism.

The Post Office Scandal and its long-term reverberations show
how British writers and their literary experiments were shaped by
Risorgimento politics in the nineteenth century. The Risorgimento
was not merely represented by British writers and to British audiences through print; British culture and Italian politics were, in fact,
reciprocally entangled. As the previous chapters have discussed, British and Italian cultural interactions in the nineteenth century were
determined within a web of discourses of otherness, appropriation
and identification. Scholars of Anglo-Italian studies recognise Italy's
resemblance to imperial 'contact zones', which Mary Louise Pratt
defines as 'social spaces where disparate cultures meet, clash, and
grapple with each other, often in highly asymmetrical relations of
dominion and subordination'.[2] Following Pratt, critics note the
ways in which British and Italian identities are mutually constitutive; Manfred Pfister, for example, argues that '"Englishness" or
"Britishness" and *Italianità* . . . are staged both within each culture
and, more importantly, in joint performances of difference across
cultural borders'.[3] A colonised space itself, the Italian peninsula was
seen in the Victorian period as a site of exotic difference from northern Europe, while remaining the historical cradle of European civilisation.[4] Investment in Risorgimento mythology, Maura O'Connor
finds, led to an 'English enterprise of romantically recasting Italy as
a nation'[5] across the nineteenth century.

Yet, the Risorgimento also generated moments of particularly British crisis, scandal and sudden realignment, such as Giuseppe Garibaldi's 1864 visit to England,[6] the 1858 Orsini affair[7] and, above all,
the 1844 letter-opening scandal. Such incidents provocatively shaped
British political and literary cultures. The representational resonances between the media event surrounding the Post Office Scandal
and the emergence of the sensation genre with *The Woman in White*
track the mid-century sea-change that occurred in British thought
about Italy as the Risorgimento assumed a privileged place in public
awareness and sympathy in the 1840s and 1850s. The attention and
sympathy the Post Office Scandal produced for the Italian cause[8]
contributed to increased British interest in the Risorgimento, culminating in the establishment of support networks such as the Society
of the Friends of Italy and Emancipation of Italy Fund Committee[9]
in the decade leading up to *The Woman in White*'s publication. As
the Italian cause rose in public estimation, the mutually constitutive

relationship between Italian and British identities evolved. The Post Office Espionage Scandal and *The Woman in White* share a central place in this mid-century moment of evolution, generating and reflecting a crisis in British identity focused on the secret tyrannies concealed beneath the surface of British liberalism in international affairs and the private sphere.

'The Mysteries Which are at Our Own Doors': Secrecy, Narrative and the Post Office Scandal

The sensation genre and its best-known specimen, *The Woman in White*, are often recognised for bringing the Gothic home to England. Yet, the representational possibilities for a genre in which 'narratives of secrets and guilty pasts are set in respectable town houses and suburban villas'[10] were shaped by a real-life Victorian sensation, one that located violations of privacy in supposedly modern, rational institutions and potentially criminal despotism in the British government's actions against the refugees inside Britain's borders. As a Victorian sensation, the Post Office Espionage Scandal helped to create the imaginative space through which sensation novels like *The Woman in White* could begin to interrogate Gothic national stereotypes and relocate the Gothic plot within modern Britain: in its private homes and its institutions.

Letters, manifested either through the epistolary form or as material objects within texts, profoundly impacted the development of the British novel and often indicated the cultural and historical concerns with which novelists engaged in their work. Literary critics such as Mary A. Favret and Nicola J. Watson, for example, trace the ways in which the Romantic-era epistolary tradition reflects the politics of the revolutionary period.[11] As Kate Thomas argues, however, in the nineteenth century 'the postal took the place of the epistolary in the cultural imagination'.[12] Despite this shift, the form of the Victorian novel remained invested in the figure of the letter. Richard Menke's study of information systems in relation to the Victorian novel indicates the extensive overlap between the principles of postal reform and those of Victorian realism. These include 'Transparency, inclusiveness, regularity, and a certain pragmatism, all bound up with ideas about the power of private communication to express and strengthen the structure of social relations'.[13] Moreover, according to Menke, realist Victorian fiction and information networks like the reformed Post Office share formal concerns: 'a sprawling Victorian triple-decker looks like both a treatment of a world as information, and an affirmation that such a mass of information could be arranged and made meaningful while still remaining true'.[14] In this context, Post Office espionage represented the British government's betrayal of the principles of transparency and inclusiveness as well as the violation of the supposed liberal contract between British institutions and the public; perhaps unsurprisingly, letter-opening plots incorporated this betrayal into the sensation novel, a novel of secrets that critiques Victorian realism.

The sensation novel represents both a rejection of the myth of liberal, British 'Transparency, inclusiveness, regularity, and . . . pragmatism' promoted by realist fiction[15] and a shift from the early Gothic's distancing techniques towards the contemporary, the exposure of the secrecy and hypocrisy underlying the surface of Victorian stability and respectability. Robert Mighall identifies 'historical and/or geographical distancing' as 'key characteristics of the early Gothic';[16] thus, the Gothic typically explores the otherness of supposed exotic locales or benighted pasts. By contrast, the sensation novel is the novel of contemporary, British secrets and their exposure. In *The Maniac in the Cellar*, Winifred Hughes concludes,

> The final import of the sensation novel is that things are not what they seem, even – in fact, especially – in the respectable classes and their respectable institutions. At the climax of the Victorian era, the sensation novels portray a society in which secrets are the rule rather than the exception, in which passion and crime fester beneath the surface of the official ideal.[17]

As a mid-century media event, the Post Office Scandal predicted the ways in which the secrets of 'respectable institutions' came to challenge the primacy of traditional Gothic narratives of otherness in Victorian culture.

Nineteenth-century readers recognised that contemporaneity and immediacy informed sensation fiction. Henry James, for example, noted the ways in which sensation novels like Collins's transformed the Gothic by incorporating Gothic plots into the contemporary novel of domestic realism. His 1865 review of Mary Elizabeth Braddon's work for *The Nation* praises Collins over Braddon, claiming,

> To Mr. Collins belongs the credit of having introduced into fiction those most mysterious of mysteries, the mysteries which are at our own doors . . . Instead of the terrors of [Ann Radcliffe's] 'Udolpho,'

we were treated to the terrors of the cheerful country-house and the busy London lodgings. And there is no doubt that these were infinitely the more terrible . . . [T]he nearer the criminal and the detective are brought home to the reader, the more lively his 'sensation'.[18]

For James, contemporaneity, especially concerning modern technology and communications, attracts readers' attention and establishes the genre's success in the literary market. In Braddon's work,

> The novelty lay in the heroine being, not a picturesque Italian of the fourteenth century, but an English gentlewoman of the current year, familiar with the use of the railway and the telegraph . . . Modern England – the England of to-day's newspaper – crops up at every step.[19]

Familiarity, rather than Gothic otherness, produces the sensation novel's excitement.

More recent literary critics explore the ways in which the genre 'brought' the Gothic 'home' to its readers,[20] dislodging terror from its exotic and historical settings and introducing it into modern, respectable Britain, using various critical lenses. For Lyn Pykett, as for James, sensation fiction imports the Gothic into 'the otherwise prosaic, everyday, domestic setting of a modern middle-class or aristocratic English household'.[21] Similarly, in her reading of Collins's work alongside Victorian psychological discourse, Jenny Bourne Taylor echoes James in arguing that Collins 'transpos[es] the disruptive and disturbing elements of Gothic fiction into the homely setting of the family and the everyday, recognizable world'.[22] Mighall, furthermore, traces the impact of the geographical shifts within the Gothic tradition, arguing, like James, that sensation is 'a Gothic of modernity and anonymity, where appearances of respectability can be deceptive, and where, in place of legends, the burden of the past is recorded in legal documents or memories, to be discovered by blackmailers or detectives'.[23] These critical positions point to two major ways in which representations of government letter-opening in Parliament and the press resemble the sensation genre that emerged in the years after the scandal: sensation fiction's modernisation – and anglicisation – of the Gothic, and the material functions of documents, which are used in sensation plots against private individuals by criminals and police alike. What is 'brought home'[24] to the British public by the Post Office Scandal and its resonance with *The Woman in White* is the possibility of citizens' betrayal by a secretive state, by the clandestine exercise of illegitimate authority against private individuals and by the collaboration of

Cabinet, the reformed Post Office and foreign powers in the practice of government surveillance.

In *The Woman in White*, Collins modernises the Italian criminals and secret organisations that feature in the early Radcliffean Gothic into exiled *carbonari* and continental agents spying on their compatriots, illustrating his engagement with Risorgimento politics and print culture. Lauren M. E. Goodlad reads Collins's fiction in light of what she describes as its 'disallowed histories',[25] identifying Welmingham and Blackwater Park as sites of 'evacuated historical experience' in *The Woman in White*[26] and arguing that Risorgimento Italy is 'emptied of substance' in Collins's later novel, *Armadale*.[27] However, in *The Woman in White*, the points of impact among British and Italian politics and culture are palpable. The novel is set in 1849–52, just after Italy's First War of Independence (1848–9), and was written and published in 1859–60, at the climax of Risorgimento political and military conflict: the Second War of Independence (1859) and Giuseppe Garibaldi's conquest of southern Italy (1860) led to official unification in 1861. The serial novel appeared alongside a number of articles on Italy, revolution and the war between Austria and the allied France and Piedmont in Charles Dickens's magazine, *All the Year Round*. Between *All the Year Round*'s first issue and the final instalment of *The Woman in White*, twenty-six pieces on Italian affairs, blending travel writing, political opinion, religious commentary and eyewitness war reporting, appeared in the magazine, often running next to Collins's novel.[28] The novel is populated with Italian expatriates, Austrian spies and agents of secret societies operating on British soil to further Italian revolutionary projects. Italian expatriates of the 1840s and 1850s furnished a wealth of material for a sensational work of fiction. In fact, Risorgimento scholar Harry W. Rudman describes Mazzini's life in terms of the sensation plot, suggesting he was pursued by 'spies and *agents provocateurs* like the extraordinary villain . . . Count Fosco, whose task it was to keep a watch in England over the Italian expatriates'.[29] In the late 1850s, Italian nationalists and exiles were ubiquitous in the British imagination. In addition to the European military campaigns of 1859–60, two scandals involving refugees in Britain occurred: an Italian with the Fosco-esque name of Foschini stabbed four other Italians, possibly believing them to be spies, in 1856; more famously, Felice Orsini attacked Napoleon III in 1858 using home-made bombs built on British soil.[30]

The Orsini affair generated a British political crisis similar to that created by Post Office spying in 1844. Orsini, exiled to Britain in

1856–7 after a dramatic escape from the window of San Giorgio, an Austrian prison in Mantua, capitalised on his ordeal to garner attention for the independence movement. His English-language memoir *The Austrian Dungeons in Italy* (1856), translated by the Mazzinian Jessie White, sold 35,000 copies in one year[31] and was followed up with *Memoirs and Adventures of Felice Orsini* (1857) and an 1856–7 English and Scottish lecture tour.[32] In addition to being widely recognised as a catalyst for Napoleon III's entry into 'a new interventionist phase in French imperial policy towards the Italian question',[33] Orsini's assassination attempt against Napoleon III created a diplomatic crisis for Britain that led to the fall of the Palmerston government in February 1858 over the Conspiracy to Murder Bill designed in response to France's pressure for action in the case.[34] The event is additionally associated with the creation of the Liberal Party, as Lord John Russell and William Gladstone plotted to bring Palmerston down.[35] A political crisis involving, like the Post Office Scandal, Britain's independence from continental interference, the Orsini affair was also connected to letter-opening: the Derby government's new Home Secretary, Spencer Horatio Walpole, directed the Post Office to open letters in April 1858 for the first time since 1844.[36] Orsini and his Mazzinian associates had already used his fame to remind the British public of the 1844 scandal that made Mazzini a household name, referring to the Post Office Espionage Scandal in *Austrian Dungeons*[37] and *Memoirs and Adventures*.[38]

Although it is not clear that Collins ever knew Mazzini personally, they were part of the same literary community in London and shared some acquaintances. Collins's close friend Dickens certainly knew Mazzini from 1846 on: he met Mazzini after an imposter exploited the scandal's publicity to beg Dickens for money – by letter – in Mazzini's name.[39] Dickens was aware of the letter-opening scandal and

> expressed anti-Graham sentiments [directed at the Home Secretary held responsible] at the time of the incident, writing a letter to Thomas Beard on 28 June 1844 in which he wrote on the envelope flap, 'It is particularly requested that if Sir James Graham should open this, he will not trouble himself to seal it [agai]n.'[40]

This same literary community, furthermore, was highly invested in Risorgimento politics and propaganda when *The Woman in White* was written several years later, as the articles in *All the Year Round* suggest.

Collins was clearly compelled by the narrative possibilities offered by Italian refugees and spies and the British who aligned themselves to one side or the other in Risorgimento conflict. *The Woman in White*'s characters Laura and Sir Percival travel to Italy in the wake of the turbulence of the late 1840s, departing from Limmeridge in December 1849 and returning to Blackwater Park in June 1850. Suspiciously, Count Fosco remains in Vienna rather than meeting the Glydes in Rome, as planned.[41] Marian quickly registers a suspicion of Fosco's activities in her journal, writing that after their first meeting in Rome, Percival and Fosco

> have been perpetually together in London, in Paris, and in Vienna – but never in Italy again; the Count having . . . not crossed the frontiers of his native country for years past. Perhaps, he has been made the victim of some political persecution? At all events, he seems to be patriotically anxious not to lose sight of any of his countrymen who may happen to be in England. On the evening of his arrival, he asked how far we were from the nearest town, and whether we knew of any Italian gentlemen who might happen to be settled there. He is certainly in correspondence with people on the Continent, for his letters have all sorts of odd stamps on them; and I saw one for him . . . with a huge official-looking seal on it. Perhaps he is in correspondence with his government? And yet, that is hardly to be reconciled, either, with my other idea that he may be a political exile. (222–3)

Marian thus questions Fosco's cover and records that his secret activities, spying on Italian refugees in Britain for a continental government, are facilitated by the British Post Office, which enables Fosco's correspondence with his political masters.

The association between continental espionage and British institutions here works against Victorian beliefs about Britain's openness to political exiles. For much of the British public, Britain was a natural ally to the Italian refugees whose liberal aims seemed to replicate mid-Victorian Britain's dominant progressive ideology. As O'Connor explains, 'since liberal England increasingly saw its own mission (as it developed in the nineteenth century) reflected in the Italian past, helping create a new Italy would enhance liberalism's national prestige and profile'.[42] *The Woman in White*'s exiled *Carboneria* member and anglophile Pesca illustrates this supposed affinity and constructs an image of Italy as a less-advanced younger sibling to Britain, growing to achieve a political maturity that mirrors Britain's; he tells Hartright, after all, 'It is the dream of my whole life to be Honourable Pesca, M. P.!' (21). This stereotype of Italian immaturity, at least where constitutional politics are concerned, comically translates into the more emphatic youthful frivolity Gabriel Betteredge identifies as Franklin Blake's 'Italian side' in *The Moonstone*.[43] Blake, raised in Germany, France and Italy, returns to Britain in May 1848[44] as the revolutionary springtime of the peoples sweeps continental Europe, sporting a beard that identifies him as a radical in 1840s fashion politics.[45] He has four distinct personalities that Betteredge readily aligns to stereotypes of European national character. Italian character fares poorly, appearing in Blake at moments of indecisive abdication of responsibility, during which he looks to others to solve his problems: 'the Italian side of him was uppermost, on those occasions when he unexpectedly gave in, and asked you in his nice sweet-tempered way to take his own responsibilities on your shoulders'.[46] To Betteredge, Italians are 'sweet-tempered' children when it comes to decision-making, but children nonetheless. Betteredge is even more critical of Blake's supposedly Italian approach to politics. When a local parliamentarian laments the spread of democracy in 1848 Britain, asking, 'If we once lose our ancient safeguards, Mr Blake, I beg to ask you, what have we got left?', Blake frivolously replies, 'from the Italian point of view: "We have got three things left, sir – Love, Music, and Salad"'.[47] Collins thus comically introduces the ideological myth of Britain's role as a guide to developing constitutional political systems across Europe in his work.

Such images of Italy's political immaturity, however, do not necessarily disadvantage the Italian cause. Mazzini, an expert propagandist who devoted his life to creating a Risorgimento myth intended to convert international liberals to his ideological position,[48] cultivated the British public's sense of fraternity with that supposedly less-advanced Italian sibling, presenting Britain as a mentor to an Italy that was dependent on British support to achieve its political maturity. After the letter-opening scandal, Mazzini exploited his British audience's sense of responsibility towards other European populations in his reprimands of the government in an 1845 open letter to Home Secretary Sir James Graham, the member of Cabinet most clearly implicated in the scandal, titled *Italy, Austria, and the Pope*. Mazzini stresses Young Italy's youthfulness and argues that by opening private correspondence '[Graham] destroyed the *prestige* which in their [young Italians'] eyes attached itself to the respected name of England'.[49] Despite this loss of respect for the elder political sibling, Mazzini continues to argue for an Italian revolution modelled on Britain's own revolutionary history as a necessary step in Italy's path to liberal government, exploiting the sentiment among members of the British public that O'Connor traces, even imitating the voice of the British liberal in doing so: '[Italians] desire to obtain the same liberty which *We* – let it not be forgotten, through a revolution – are now enjoying'.[50] The younger sibling should not be reprimanded by the elder for following in the same footsteps. Mazzini here minimises the reciprocity of his international, democratic networks, including his own influence among British radicals, to fashion a message that might be palatable to the broader British public.[51] His image of Young Italy thus prepares the way for British representations of Italian nationalists like Pesca as enthusiastic anglophiles waiting to be led to liberty by the British, so long as Britain fulfils its fraternal responsibilities.

If in *The Woman in White* 'the Englishman Hartright is Pesca's ideal of adulthood, in the same way that English liberalism is the beacon guiding Italian nationalism',[52] the reformed Post Office seems the perfect institution to symbolise that 'beacon'. The goals of 'transparency, utility, and efficiency' with which Rowland Hill presented the postal reforms of the 1830s[53] could equally describe the optimistic principles of British progress in the liberal Victorian age. However, the 'tradition of nervous confidence' with which Britain accepted its new Post Office after the reforms[54] was disrupted in 1844 when Duncombe presented Mazzini's petition. In the ensuing debates, parliamentarians and the public learned that the power to intercept and open letters by warrant, granted to Secretaries of State under Queen Anne, was retained in the 1837 reforms, although the surprise of most members of both Houses of Parliament and the general public indicates that the government's possession of these powers was little known.[55] The Post Office Scandal was a major event in terms of British public awareness of and evolving sympathies for Risorgimento politics. As historian Denis Mack Smith suggests,

> It would be hard to overestimate the importance of this episode in drawing the Italian question to the notice of politicians and public opinion in Britain. Few British people hitherto had heard of Mazzini, but parliamentary debates on the matter now took up as much as 559 columns of Hansard.[56]

However, the scandal also exposed the repressive practices of a supposedly transparent, constitutional British government to a shocked public. Eventually, parliamentary committees found that forty-four warrants for letters were issued in 1842–4; Duncombe's own letters may have been among those.[57] Far from being transparent, the Post

Office helped to conceal the secret practices of a covert government operation; the uncertainty surrounding the historical question of Duncombe's letters indicates the continued gaps in knowledge about the government's letter-opening even after it was publicly exposed.

The facts of Post Office espionage contradicted both the apparent rationalism of the reforms and Britain's liberal policy of openness to refugees across the Victorian period and undermined the stereotype of Britain's leadership role in promoting European liberty that Collins later presents comically in his novels. As Bernard Porter explains, 'between 1823 and 1906 no refugee who came to Britain was ever denied entry, or expelled; or necessitated any very drastic revision of Britain's free institutions'.[58] The scandal revealed, however, that despite accepting political refugees, the British government was aligned with repressive continental regimes and betrayed its own values by practising what Duncombe labelled 'the odious spy system of foreign countries'.[59] The idea that government surveillance was un-English, or, in Duncombe's words, 'did not suit the free air of this free country',[60] dominated parliamentary debate on this issue. Ministers were accused of becoming 'a tool of other Sovereigns' and studying espionage 'in the school of [Joseph] Fouché', the first Napoleon's Minister of Police.[61] For M. P. John Bowring, letter-opening for an 'honest purpose' was distinct from spying for a 'foreign purpose';[62] Bowring urged Graham to accept a motion for a committee of inquiry, unless he wished 'to be considered as an Italian sbirro'[63] or reinforce the view of the Cabinet as 'a Cabinet Noir'.[64]

This language, demonising 'foreign' intelligence and policing and opposing supposedly authoritarian, Gothic Europe to 'free' Britain,[65] appeared even more forcefully in the print controversy. The 'generally pro-Austrian'[66] *Times* echoed parliamentarians' disgust at the supposedly continental methods and motives that encouraged letter-opening.[67] A 17 June 1844 editorial describes the practice as 'at once unconstitutional, un-English, and ungenerous'.[68] 'Hitherto', the editorialist continues,

> it has been the peculiar boast of England that . . . her citizens are not liable to the same petty persecutions, the same rigorous police, the same insidious and incessant watching, the same dogging of their footsteps, opening of their letters, and prying into cabinets as harass the subjects of continental states. But this boast cannot now be uttered with justice. The national *prestige* has gone . . . No man's correspondence is safe. No man's confidence can be deemed secure; the secrets of no family, of no individual, can be guaranteed from reaching the ear of a Cabinet Minister.[69]

For this writer, Britain's claim to singularity among European states with respect to liberty and justice can no longer be supported: the myth of British freedom, its 'national *prestige*', folds under the pressure of the letter-opening scandal. To enforce this point the editorialist concludes, 'Sir J. GRAHAM must have been studying [French criminal and spy Eugène François] VIDOCQ and FOUCHE [sic]'.[70] In addition to violating the implied contract between the British government and its people, here, Graham also becomes a student and a tool of other states in adopting supposedly continental policing tactics to appease European powers.

Other publications followed the lead of *The Times*. *The Satirist* of 30 June calls the letter-opening law an 'un-English deformity' and condemns its use 'upon the motion or solicitation of any Foreign Power, State, or Potentate, in aid of foreign objects or designs';[71] as late as 22 February 1845 *The Illustrated London News* argues that

> to make it [the letter-opening power] a detective means in the hands of any other country – to convert the noble establishment at St Martin's-le-Grand into a mere department of the police-office of Vienna – is to court the very depth of national disgrace.[72]

The 31 August issue of *Punch* identifies 'the EMPEROR OF RUSSIA and the KING OF NAPLES' as potential beneficiaries of British state spying, linking governments with the reputation for tyranny together regardless of their involvement in this particular case.[73] For *The Satirist*'s 30 June editorialist, not only is the myth of British liberty at stake, but Britain's place as a safe haven for continental refugees is also in question: 'England can no longer be deemed the refuge or sanctuary of the oppressed, if foreigners are to be thus used and degraded'.[74] The 29 June *Illustrated London News* likewise uses the revelation that the British government might behave as 'the assistant spy of foreign states' to challenge the public to 'consider . . . what is the duty of a free country like England towards those who seek a refuge in it from persecution at home'.[75]

Mazzini's friend Thomas Carlyle was among the most outraged members of the Victorian public. He wrote pointedly in *The Times* of 19 June,

> it is a question vital to us that sealed letters in an English post-office be, as we all fancied they were, respected as things sacred; that opening of men's letters, a practice near of kin to picking men's pockets, and to other still viler and far fataler forms of scoundrelism, be not resorted to in England, except in cases of the very last extremity . . . To all Austrian

Kaisers and such like, in their time of trouble, let us answer, as our fathers from of old have answered: – Not by such means is help here for you.[76]

Carlyle characterises spying as despotic, un-English, criminal and, most particularly, continental – in short, Gothic.

After the executions of Attilio and Emilio Bandiera and their followers for their uprising in Calabria, Britain's betrayal of the refugees it claimed to protect became even clearer in the eyes of the public, as the press argued that Mazzini's letters provided information used to entrap the rebels.[77] *Punch* satirically describes the 'good' results of Graham's actions:

> They *do* say that the Italians who were all lately shot in the back, were only found out by the news that was sent of them from the Home Office – news picked out of opened letters to Italians here in London.[78]

A letter to the editor of *The Morning Chronicle*, published 26 February 1845, extends the responsibility for the executions to all those who perpetuated the myth of Britain's freedom from state spying:

> Who is there that has not asserted, again and again, especially in his intercourse with foreigners, that the seals of an English postbag were inviolable? These rash assertions were believed. They have helped to form the general conviction, and Bandiera and his companions have fallen victim to the delusion.[79]

In this view, the very ideology of British liberalism carries blame for its own failings.

As the scandal unfolded, however, Members of Parliament were forced to revise the language associating letter-opening with French, Italian and Austrian practices, as French Foreign Minister François Guizot denied such activities occurred on French soil and even Napoleon Bonaparte was determined by parliamentarians to have believed that private correspondence was inviolable.[80] In July, Duncombe used an apology to France as an excuse to press the British government further:

> It was said before that it was an un-English custom, but it now appeared to be peculiarly English, particularly in the way we carried it out; for . . . in Austria even . . . whenever any letters were opened they were re-sealed with the government seal, by which it was known that they had been opened by authority.[81]

The process by which the scandal brought the threats associated with the Gothic home to Britain, even imagined them as embedded in liberal British institutions, was complete. The British government, it became apparent, practised techniques of state surveillance usually associated, according to public belief, with continental authoritarianism. More importantly, as in the sensation genre, the scandal revealed that 'things are not what they seem'; the secret despotism underlying the 'official ideal' of Victorian liberalism had been exposed.[82]

Parliamentarians also objected to letter-opening on the grounds that it violated the privacy of the sanctified Victorian domestic sphere. The Earl of Radnor argued on 17 June,

> It had ever been the subject of boast on the part of Englishmen . . . that letters in England were sacred – that they went through the Post Office perfectly free and unexamined – that they never were opened, or their contents sought to be extracted.[83]

The 'sacred' letter of Radnor's speech and Carlyle's letter to *The Times* thus resembles the sanctified private space of the home, and should, like the private sphere, remain inviolable, especially to state intrusion. Duncombe explicitly linked private letters to domesticity by suggesting that Graham might gain access to 'family secrets' in his investigations.[84] The government and, by extension, the continental governments with which Graham and his colleagues collaborated, were, like Collins's Fosco, spies concealed in the bosom of the Victorian family.

The press took this rhetoric further, framing privacy as a British institution, the violation of which indicated the government's lack of respect for all free institutions and constitutional liberties. The 25 June *Times* argues that letter-opening is a question 'of personal application, as well as of public importance, – as involving considerations of private comfort and security, not less than of national character and constitutional privileges'.[85] The privilege of privacy is presented as an extension of the freedoms granted by the British constitution. The 23 June *Satirist* argues that in opening letters Graham assumed 'the odious functions of inquisitor, and the violator of the sanctity of the secrecy of private correspondence',[86] deftly folding the violation of privacy into a set of illiberal practices such as unjust imprisonment, forced confession and torture imaginatively identifiable with the Inquisition, a state institution still operating in nineteenth-century Papal Italy. Thus, the two strands of the debate over letter-opening come together in the language that contrasts the supposed British right to privacy with the institution of continental state despotism most hated by the British public. The subversion of domestic privacy and exposure of Victorian hypocrisy that are later highlights of the sensation genre are on full display in the parliamentary and media reactions to this mid-century scandal.

'Letters are Not Safe': Letter-Opening and *The Woman in White*

In Collins's experimental sensation novel, letter-opening takes a privileged place alongside other forms of documentary meddling and eavesdropping in a plot propelled by invasions of privacy and the drive to uncover secrets. In his engagement with letter-opening in *The Woman in White*, Collins establishes a link between the illegitimate espionage practices of state authorities and criminal acts like burglary and assault, drawing on the Post Office Scandal's exposure of liberal, Victorian Britain's concealed hypocrisies. Highlighting the crucial Risorgimento periods of 1848–9 and 1859–60 in its setting and publication contexts, *The Woman in White* also exploits the shocking material presented to the British public during the 1844 letter-opening scandal, using it as fuel for an incendiary new Victorian genre, the sensation novel.

Mazzini's intercepted letters were by no means forgotten when Collins wrote *The Woman in White*. Fiction writers kept the scandal alive in British cultural memory long after the initial media event; versions of Mazzini or the Post Office Scandal appear in novels such as Giovanni Ruffini's *Doctor Antonio* (1855), Benjamin Disraeli's *Lothair* (1870) and Eliza Lynn Linton's *Autobiography of Christopher Kirkland* (1885).[87] *The Woman in White* features numerous violations of privacy, from Marian's eavesdropping to Fosco's appropriation of her journal. Furthermore, *The Woman in White* is replete with letters – letters sent anonymously, intercepted, tampered with or otherwise involved in intrigue. The novel features eighty-eight letters or series of letters in its forty instalments, emphasising the letter's importance in terms of both theme and form for Collins's work. Although *The Woman in White* is not unique among Collins's novels for the number of letters in the plot, his use of letters as material objects in that novel distinguishes it from his other works of the 1860s.[88] With a few notable exceptions, Collins uses letters in *No Name* (1862), *Armadale* (1864–6) and *The Moonstone* (1868) to provide access to alternative points of view and important information or to withhold such information to build suspense, instead of as material objects to be manipulated or violated by his characters, as they function in *The Woman in White*.[89] Nearly 24 per cent of the eighty-eight letters in *The Woman in White* are used by conspirators or investigators: intercepted, copied, kept as evidence, read by audiences other than the intended recipients or protected by extravagant methods indicating suspicion of the usual means of delivery. In the middle section of the novel, dominated by Marian's diary and Fosco's plot against Laura, the proportion of vulnerable letters more than doubles to an extraordinary 52.5 per cent.

The proliferation of texts is a common structural feature of Gothic and sensation novels, and *The Woman in White* is known for its form as a collection of first-hand, eyewitness narratives Walter Hartright edits and assembles as evidence of the conspiracy against Laura. Critics such as Walter M. Kendrick, and Pamela Perkins and Mary Donaghy, discuss Collins's presentation of documentary evidence with varying degrees of suspicion towards Hartright;[90] closer attention to the materiality of Collins's circulating, violated letters adds to this critical conversation over the textual manipulation that is central to Collins's narrative project. As Kristen Johnson rightly argues, 'gothic writers not only capitalized upon the letter as a device of narrative and of plot, but made the precarious nature of its materiality as well as that of its ownership central to the themes of gothic fiction'.[91] The 'precarious . . . materiality' of letters Johnson identifies in the Gothic tradition features in *The Woman in White* to reinforce the novel's themes of violation, detection, surveillance and the abuse of power.

Letter-opening is crucial to the plot for a novel in which characters constantly conspire to invade privacy and discover secrets and in which this same compulsion towards uncovering concealed information drives the reader's experience. Letters in *The Woman in White* are both effective weapons for the protagonists and weaknesses exploited by the 'anti-refugee spy' Fosco[92] and his English minions, Sir Percival and Madame Fosco, who, like Graham, are tools of a continental power. Some literary critics argue that the letter in sensation fiction 'unveil[s] the dangers lurking beneath the apparently safe façade of bourgeois respectability';[93] however, as Laura Rotunno remarks, Anne Catherick, Marian and Hartright also 'write letters that reclaim disdained epistolary forms including the anonymous letter, the begging letter, the effusive female letter, the blank letter, and the letter de cachet. They show how such letters could be used for good'.[94] To this we might add the form letter that Fairlie signs, attesting to Laura's identity (617), which demonstrates the dissolution of boundaries between private and public information that drives the plot: a letter, an ostensibly private communication, is circulated publicly in order to reclaim public visibility for Laura after her identity as mother to the 'Heir of Limmeridge' (627) has been suppressed by those with power over her within the private sphere. The thematic reverse of the violated private letter, this letter must be read publicly for Laura's name and position to be restored.

The kinds of violations of privacy associated with the letter-opening scandal are nonetheless crucial to the plot and to the production of sensational reactions in readers, tracking shifts in momentum and registering the vulnerability of women like Anne, Laura, Marian and Laura's maid, Fanny. As Ann Elizabeth Gaylin notes, Fosco reads and writes in Marian's journal, 'claim[ing] her most private narrative space for himself' at the moment she is most physically exposed.[95] Like the '"Anti-Graham Envelope" and the associated Anti-Graham "Wafers"', seals used to ensure the inviolability of correspondence so-named by *Punch*,[96] the extra seal Marian places on her own letters overtop of the self-adhesive envelopes brought into circulation with the reforms (255) reveals a suspicion of letter-opening that she develops early in her time at Blackwater. She also carries her letters in her bosom, 'afraid . . . even to trust [them] under lock and key' (272), and locks the door to her room to prevent any fraudulent use of her seal (303). She concludes that '[l]etters are not safe in the post-bag at Blackwater Park' (301), a lesson that Laura later imparts to Mrs Michelson (386). Yet, sensation readers are invested in violations of privacy like letter-opening. As D. A. Miller argues, 'We enjoy our privacy in the act of watching privacy being violated, in the act of watching that is already itself a violation of privacy', while nevertheless remaining 'perturbed by what we are watching'.[97] Readers, then, are positioned as Fosco, or Graham: violators of privacy and repositories of family secrets watching a plot of violation unfold. Letter-opening is a key plot device capable of propelling the sensation novel forwards and generating the feelings of excited discomfort that Miller identifies with the genre.

The trope of the opened letter, furthermore, revises the affinity between the text and the female body characteristic of the sentimental, epistolary novel of the eighteenth century as well as the strengthening of social bonds across the nation figured by the reformed Post Office. Letter-opening, then, indicates a betrayal of both the body politic and the Victorian gender ideology that purported to protect women, and the private sphere with which they were identified, from public taint. In the eighteenth-century seduction plot, Watson argues, the letter 'stand[s] metonymically in the place of the figure of the desiring woman'.[98] The stress on letter writing, reading and opening as a sexualised experience indicative of the desiring female body in eighteenth-century and Romantic epistolary traditions was replaced in the early Victorian period by a metaphor in which the state institution of the Post Office stands in for the interconnected body politic. As Menke discusses in *Telegraphic Realism*, 'the connection between the mass of letters and the national body – a representation of society in every postbag – became a Victorian commonplace'.[99] *The Woman in White* and public responses to the Post Office Scandal reflect both of these ways of imagining the letter, presenting letter-opening as an invasive physical violation that amounts to a betrayal of the national body. For *Punch*, the state's interception of letters in 1844 was akin to a physical frisking. In a July article titled '*Punch*'s Complete Letter Writer', the signatory *Punch* writes to Graham,

> I felt assured that my letters ... had all of them been defiled by the eyes of a spy; that all my most domestic secrets had been rumpled and touzled, and pinched here and pinched there – searched by an English Minister as shuddering modesty is searched at a French custom-house![100]

The physical sensation of 'shuddering' against an intrusive state that 'rumpled', 'tousled' and 'pinched' its citizens transforms the epistolary tradition's seduction plot into the unwanted advances of an encroaching government, while the words 'defiled' and 'modesty' indicate the shamefulness of this trespass on the body politic. Having one's 'domestic secrets' laid open to 'the eyes of a spy' is both an infringement of individual liberty by the state and an intimate and shocking physical intrusion. *Punch*'s accompanying image, in which ministerial hands, disconnected from any human body, hold an envelope open for the intruding head and muscular body of a large snake (Figure 3.1), renders the political critique even more menacing, drawing on biblical and phallic imagery to suggest Graham's seduction into political sin.

Collins makes *Punch*'s comic metaphor both literal and sinister in *The Woman in White* when Madame Fosco drugs and assaults Laura's maid Fanny to steal the letters that Fanny carries concealed in her bosom. According to Fosco,

> the letters being in the bosom of the girl's dress, Madame Fosco could only open them, read them, perform her instructions [of copying one and replacing the other with a blank paper], seal them, and put them back again, by scientific assistance – which assistance I rendered in a half-ounce bottle. (603)

MY DEAR SIR JAMES,
HAVING, as I modestly believe, written a Complete Letter-Writer — yes, having penned some fifty models of epistolary correspondence, involving all the affections, interests, rights, wrongs, and courtesies of social life,— I am naturally anxious to obtain for the work the protecting countenance of a high, appropriate name. Your official privilege makes

Figure 3.1 '*Punch*'s Complete Letter Writer. Dedication to Sir James Graham Bart Secretary for the Home Department'. (Source: *Punch*, 6 July 1844, p. 2.)

Madame Fosco's handling of Fanny's body while she is unconscious is even more alarming, since Fanny loses half an hour's time without understanding what has been done to her or suspecting her victimiser, just as Mazzini and his correspondents would never have learned that their letters were opened without their own expert detective work; nonetheless, the violation leaves Fanny severely emotionally distraught (343). Furthermore, this physical intrusion is concealed by the polite social veneer with which Madame Fosco presents herself to Fanny, a subversion of the cross-class social bonds Menke identifies with the metonymy of the Victorian postbag.[101] The interception of a text here is quite literally a physical attack and thus illustrates the connection between text and body, as well as the vulnerability of women and the private sphere to interference from authority figures, more emphatically even than does the violation of Marian's journal.

This assault against Fanny also suggests that letter-opening reflects on character and reveals the criminality of those who commit it. In the 1844–5 press and *The Woman in White*, little distinguishes the state spy from the criminal. *Punch* describes the letter-opening law as one granting permission 'to burglariously break and enter into every package, bundle, letter, note, or billet-doux, sent through the Post-Office' and, using the sexual imagery discussed above, as

> working away with a crow-bar, smashing red and black wax – or; by the more subtle agency of steam, softening wafers, that the letter may open its lips, and yield up the contents of its very heart to the Secretary of the Home Department.[102]

For the press, the collaboration of Graham's Home Office, the Post Office and the Austrian embassy amounts to a state-sanctioned crime resembling a Gothic home invasion or physical assault.

The alliance between the English baronet, Sir Percival Glyde, and an Austrian agent, the spy Count Fosco, is also a partnership of criminals, one that suggests the consequences of Britain allying itself to continental despots. Sir Percival is both a criminal who commits the serious crime of forgery and a representative of British privilege and the status quo, like the Cabinet or Sir James Graham, another baronet. His secret illegitimacy points to Collins's critique of what he presents as the illegitimate aristocratic authority with which the state invests Sir Percival and the illegitimate government powers with which Sir Percival is aligned, like Fosco's state-authorised spying or letter-opening. Fosco, the character most implicated in letter-tampering in the novel, masterminds the illegal conspiracy against Laura and gleefully defends criminal ingenuity, claiming, 'The fool's crime is the crime that is found out; and the wise man's crime is the crime that is *not* found out' (232). Fosco, however, is both criminal and government instrument, a man 'charged with a delicate political mission from abroad' (598) and invested with the privilege and power of the post-1815 restoration states; as Madame Fosco writes in her biography of her late husband at the end of the novel, 'His life was one long assertion of the rights of the aristocracy, and the sacred principles of Order – and he died a Martyr to his cause' (625). Thus, the man who acts for a government and personifies law and order in the novel is also an opportunistic criminal.

Fosco, furthermore, resembles Napoleon Bonaparte (218), a man who embodied state authority during his rule, and whose dynasty was resurrected by his nephew, Napoleon III, in the mid-nineteenth century. Napoleon III rose to power in the aftermath of 1848, at the time in which *The Woman in White* is set, and his intervention in Italy as Piedmont's ally against Austria during the 1859 Second War of Independence occurred just months before the first chapters of the novel appeared in *All the Year Round*.[103] Napoleon III's rule in France had massive ramifications for the Italian independence movement and helped to re-draw Europe's geopolitical boundaries. As President of France and, later, Emperor, Napoleon III had a fraught relationship with both Britain and Italy. Though Britain and France were allies during the 1853–6 Crimean War, cross-Channel tensions remained high during the first decade of Napoleon III's government. In the 1862 pamphlet 'The Three Panics: An Historical Episode', for example, Richard Cobden identifies three peaks of British fear over the invasion threat France posed to Britain, occurring in 1847–8, 1851–3 and 1859–61.[104] In 1859, British public interest in home defence was high enough that the government authorised a volunteer force on 12 May for the first time since the volunteers of the Revolutionary and Napoleonic Wars were disbanded in 1814.[105]

Napoleon III's military intervention on the Italian peninsula also informed the British public's views on the Second French Empire and the Italian cause. Direct literary responses to Napoleon III's collaboration with Piedmont's Victor Emmanuel II against Austria in the 1859 Second War of Independence ranged from Elizabeth Barrett Browning's celebratory 'Napoleon III. in Italy' (1860)[106] to D. G. Rossetti's cynical 'After the French Liberation of Italy' (1859?),[107] as discussed elsewhere in this study. This range of British opinions reflects the complicated geopolitical changes spurred by the war, including France's annexation of Nice and Savoy and Napoleon III's decision to help garrison the Papal States against the threat posed by Giuseppe Garibaldi's guerrilla fighters for the next several years. Thus, as historian Roger Price argues, Napoleon III pursued a strategy that would remove Austria from the peninsula while keeping Italy geopolitically fragmented,[108] reflecting his overall European policy objective of 'ensur[ing] the pacification of Europe by means of its reconstruction on the basis of its major nationalities. These should be assembled in loose (con)-federal structures, too weak to challenge French predominance, rather than as unitary states'.[109] Collins frequently gestures towards French political and military contexts of 1848–52 and 1859–60, as is apparent in Fosco's resemblance to the first Napoleon (218), his death in Paris within the reach of the conspiratorial Brotherhood and exposure to the public gaze in the Morgue (622–4) and Collins's French source, Maurice Méjan's *Recueil des causes célèbres*, which inspired his plot.[110] These gestures, as France's 1859 involvement in creating the Italian state demonstrates, reinforce *The Woman in White*'s connections to the Risorgimento and Collins's critique of government self-interest and authoritarianism. As a criminal and a state-authorised spy who physically resembles a military dictator, Fosco indicates the extensive overlap between government operations and crime in Collins's text.

Of course, Collins's detective characters, especially Marian, appropriate their opponents' techniques in order to expose the conspiracy against Laura and punish her persecutors. Marian is adept at eavesdropping, listening first to Sir Percival and his lawyer Merriman and then climbing onto the roof to hear Fosco outline his plans. In the first instance, she writes in her journal, 'I listened; and, under similar circumstances, I would listen again – yes! with my ear at the keyhole, if I could not possibly manage it in any other way' (225). Given Laura's outbursts against the 'miserable Spy' Fosco (296), such investigations appear hypocritical. This is a risk common to heroes of sensation fiction, a genre in which, Tamara S. Wagner notes,

> detective-figures become implicated in violations that are all too similar, if not identical, to the transgressions they seek to police. They appropriate private letters, read them out loud, hand them around, turn them into evidence, or use them to blackmail the villains.[111]

However, though Marian and Hartright do spy in order to detect their opponents' crimes, Collins ultimately reins in the cycle of interception and tampering that characterises the circulation of letters across the novel by creating closure through the tool that allows Hartright to bring Fosco to account: a sealed letter.

The integrity of this sealed letter, which is eventually destroyed unopened (580–1, 596–7), finally forces the resolution of Collins's plot. Collins emphasises the inviolability of Hartright's letter to Pesca, except under clear, specific conditions:

> I signed and dated these lines, enclosed them in an envelope, and sealed it up. On the outside, I wrote this direction: 'Keep the enclosure unopened, until 9 o'clock to-morrow morning. If you do not hear from me, or see me, before that time, break the seal when the clock strikes, and read the contents.' I added my initials; and protected the whole by enclosing it in a second sealed envelope. (580)

Doubly enclosed and sealed, signed and initialled, and covered with explicit instructions for its proper use, this letter is the opposite of Mazzini's penetrable letters, vulnerable to misuses that violate the understood contract between the letter sender and the Post Office. Thus, while meddling with documents, eavesdropping and other violations of privacy drive the sensation plot forward, just as the interception and dissemination of Mazzini's letters and secrets potentially spurred government action against his allies such as the Bandiera brothers, for Collins, the letter that remains inviolable – and simply suggests the threat of its potential opening – is the most effective weapon to give to Hartright.

The Woman in White, then, ends with the containment of the threat posed by illegitimate authority to the private individual, represented by secret letter-opening. According to Tamar Heller, Collins's novels unleash subversive potential only to contain that energy in their conclusions;[112] in Heller's reading, at the end of *The Woman in White*, Hartright 'acts not to challenge convention but to restore its legitimacy'.[113] Hartright's final letter, however, urges a different reading: Hartright combats the illegitimate power of letter-opening, represented by a government-sanctioned criminal Fosco and the instrument of his power, a notably illegitimate English baronet, by writing a letter that can never be opened and thus exists as a symbol of epistolary impenetrability. Reading *The Woman in White* in the context of the link between Italian and British politics, and specifically letter-opening, reveals that what Collins's plot contains is also the secret that his first sensation novel exposes: the threat of invasive surveillance by the state and those invested with state power, like Collins's villains. While Marian and Hartright begin by following techniques of surveillance similar to those deployed by Fosco and the imperial Austrian espionage machine to which he belongs, the most important letter in the novel must remain sealed. In fact, it can only serve Hartright's purpose of protecting him and inducing Fosco's confession by being used as its author intends and, finally, returning to its sender intact.

Letter-opening in *The Woman in White* highlights three peaks of mid-Victorian British interest in Risorgimento politics: the period of the Post Office Scandal in 1844–5, which brought government letter-opening and the plight of revolutionary Italian refugees like Mazzini to public prominence; the First Italian War of Independence and revolutions of 1848–9 and their aftermath, alongside which the novel is set; and the climax of the Risorgimento with the Second Italian War of Independence in 1859 and Garibaldi's expedition to Sicily and Naples in 1860, when Collins wrote and published the novel. The anti-continental, Gothic national stereotypes and ideological myth of Britain as a leader of European progress that shaped denunciations of letter-opening in Parliament and the press are those with which Collins engages when he repositions Gothic despotism and violations of privacy within modern Britain in *The Woman in White*. The Post Office Espionage Scandal produced a media sensation in the British public and predicted the shift in the British political imagination that occurred with the sensation genre's relocation of the Gothic within Britain, its institutions and the private sphere. The affinities between *The Woman in White* and representations of Post Office spying in 1844–5 help to clarify the connection between violations of privacy like letter-opening and the intrusive, state-sponsored espionage that Fosco practises in the novel. As *The Woman in White*'s emphasis on Italian politics, continental spying and the uses and misuses of the letter illustrates, Collins offers a sustained critique of the exercise of illegitimate power as it appears in the alliance between the criminal and the government spy. Just as the Post Office Scandal challenged the British public to look beyond the surface liberalism of the reformed institution to the clandestine operations of a deceptive government, so Collins points to the secret illegitimacy that lies beneath authority in *The Woman in White*. Together, the scandal surrounding Post Office spying and Collins's *Woman in White* respond to and generate a challenge to Victorian British complacency that emerged out of the collision of mutually constitutive British and Italian politics and culture in the mid-nineteenth century.

Notes

1. Marjorie Stone examines the longer-term resonances between this mid-Victorian scandal and events of the twenty-first century, including the Canadian Maher Arar affair, WikiLeaks and the *News of the World* hacking scandal. 'Joseph Mazzini, English Writers, and the Post Office Espionage Scandal: Politics, Privacy, and Twenty-First Century Parallels', pp. 17–19.

2. Mary Louise Pratt, *Imperial Eyes: Travel Writing and Transculturation*, p. 4.

3. Manfred Pfister, 'Performing National Identity', p. 9.

4. See Pratt, *Imperial Eyes,* p. 10.

5. Maura O'Connor, *The Romance of Italy and the English Political Imagination*, p. 1.

6. For more on Garibaldi's visit to England, see O'Connor, *The Romance of Italy*, pp. 149–85; Derek Beales, 'Garibaldi in England: The Politics of Italian Enthusiasm'; and Lucy Riall, *Garibaldi: Invention of a Hero*, pp. 330–44.

7. I will return to Orsini below.

8. See O'Connor, *The Romance of Italy*, pp. 70–1.

9. See Maurizio Isabella, *Risorgimento in Exile: Italian Émigrés and the Liberal International in the Post-Napoleonic Era*, p. 211.

10. Robert Mighall, *A Geography of Victorian Gothic Fiction: Mapping History's Nightmares*, p. 118.

11. See Mary A. Favret, *Romantic Correspondence: Women, Politics and the Fiction of Letters* and Nicola J. Watson, *Revolution and the Form of the British Novel*.

12. Kate Thomas, *Postal Pleasures: Sex, Scandal, and Victorian Letters*, p. 2.

13. Richard Menke, *Telegraphic Realism: Victorian Fiction and Other Information Systems*, p. 41.

14. Ibid. p. 4.

15. Ibid. p. 41.

16. Mighall, *A Geography of Victorian Gothic Fiction*, p. xii.

17. Winifred Hughes, *The Maniac in the Cellar: Sensation Novels of the 1860s*, p. 190.

18. Henry James, 'Miss Braddon', p. 593.

19. Ibid.

20. Ibid.

21. Lyn Pykett, *The Nineteenth-Century Sensation Novel*, p. 8.

22. Jenny Bourne Taylor, *In the Secret Theatre of Home: Wilkie Collins, Sensation Narrative, and Nineteenth-Century Psychology*, p. 1.

23. Mighall, *A Geography of Victorian Gothic Fiction*, pp. 128–9.

24. James, 'Miss Braddon', p. 593.

25. Lauren M. E. Goodlad, *The Victorian Geopolitical Aesthetic: Realism, Sovereignty, and the Transnational Experience*, p. 111.
26. Ibid. p. 113.
27. Ibid. p. 127.
28. In some cases, instalments of *The Woman in White* quite literally appeared next to articles about Italy. See Henry T. Spicer, 'Real Horrors of War'.
29. Harry W. Rudman, *Italian Nationalism and English Letters: Figures of the Risorgimento and Victorian Men of Letters*, p. 126.
30. See Bernard Porter, *The Refugee Question in Mid-Victorian Politics*, p. 30 and Lucio Sponza, *Italian Immigrants in Nineteenth-Century Britain: Realities and Images*, p. 132.
31. Elena Bacchin, 'Felice Orsini and the Construction of the Pro-Italian Narrative in Britain', p. 83.
32. Ibid. pp. 85–8.
33. Ibid. p. 80.
34. Porter, *The Refugee Question*, p. 183. See Porter's chapter on the Orsini plot (pp. 170–99).
35. Ibid. p. 185.
36. Ibid. p. 189.
37. Felice Orsini, *The Austrian Dungeons in Italy. A Narrative of Fifteen Months' Imprisonment and Final Escape from the Fortress of S. Giorgio*, p. 62.
38. Felice Orsini, *Memoirs and Adventures of Felice Orsini, Written by Himself, Containing Unpublished State Papers of the Roman Court*, p. 56.
39. See Charles Dickens, *The Letters of Charles Dickens*, p. 485.
40. Stone, 'Joseph Mazzini', p. 15. The first set of brackets is mine and the second belongs to the source.
41. Wilkie Collins, *The Woman in White*, p. 201. Subsequent citations will appear parenthetically in the text.
42. O'Connor, *The Romance of Italy*, p. 77.
43. Wilkie Collins, *The Moonstone*, p. 43.
44. Ibid. p. 15.
45. For a discussion of the politics of facial hair, see Christopher Oldstone-Moore, 'The Beard Movement in Victorian Britain'.
46. Collins, *The Moonstone*, p. 43.
47. Ibid. p. 69.
48. See Riall, *Garibaldi*, pp. 19–32.
49. Giuseppe [Joseph] Mazzini, *Italy, Austria, and the Pope. A Letter to Sir James Graham, Bart*, p. 1.
50. Ibid. p. 7.
51. For more on Mazzini's international networks and links with British radicalism, see Marcella Pellegrino Sutcliffe, *Victorian Radicals and Italian Democrats* and Stone, 'Joseph Mazzini', p. 4.

52. Katrien Bollen and Raphael Ingelbien, 'An Intertext that Counts? *Dracula, The Woman in White*, and Victorian Imaginations of the Foreign Other', p. 413.
53. Menke, *Telegraphic Realism*, p. 36.
54. Laura Rotunno, *Postal Plots in British Fiction, 1840–1898: Readdressing Correspondence in Victorian Culture*, p. 15.
55. Howard Robinson, *The British Post Office: A History*, pp. 338–9.
56. Denis Mack Smith, 'Britain and the Italian Risorgimento', pp.17–18.
57. Robinson, *The British Post Office*, pp. 348–51.
58. Porter, *The Refugee Question*, p. 8.
59. *Hansard*, 3rd ser. 75 Parl. Deb., H. C. (1844), p. 895.
60. Ibid. p. 899.
61. Ibid. pp. 904, 900.
62. Ibid. p. 902.
63. A police officer.
64. *Hansard*, 3rd ser. 75 Parl. Deb., H. C. (1844), p. 1270.
65. Ibid. pp. 895, 899.
66. Stone, 'Joseph Mazzini', p. 7.
67. Not all publications expressed anger; some opinions fell predictably along party lines. See Maurizio Masetti, 'The 1844 Post Office Scandal and its Impact on English Public Opinion'.
68. 'The Conversation Which Took Place on Friday', *The Times*, 17 June 1844, p. 4.
69. Ibid.
70. Ibid.
71. 'Sir James Graham and the Spy System', *The Satirist; or, the Censor of the Times*, 30 June 1844, p. 204.
72. 'The Unfortunate Transactions Connected with the Post-Office', *The Illustrated London News*, 22 February 1845, p. 118.
73. 'Sir James Graham's Pupils', *Punch*, 31 August 1844, p. 106. See also Stone's discussion of the press controversy, focused on *Punch*, in 'Joseph Mazzini', pp. 10–13.
74. 'Sir James Graham and the Spy System', p. 204.
75. 'Exiles in England', *The Illustrated London News*, 29 June 1844, p. 409.
76. Thomas Carlyle, 'To the Editor of *The Times*', p. 6.
77. This is another example of the gaps in public knowledge created by state secrecy. The House of Lords' Secret Committee concluded that all communications to continental powers were made 'without the names or details that might expose any individual then residing in the foreign country to which the information was transmitted to danger'. 'Report from the Secret Committee of the House of Lords Relative to the Post Office', p. 465. Articles in the *Westminster Review* and *North British Review* ridiculed this claim: see Antonio Panizzi, 'Post-Office Espionage', pp. 270–4 and W. E. Hickson, 'Mazzini and the Ethics of

Politicians', pp. 237–41. Such failed insurrections were effective public relations tools for Mazzini, shaping his Risorgimento mythology and hagiography. See Riall, *Garibaldi*, p. 31.

78. 'Sir James Graham's Pupils', p. 106.
79. 'The Post-Office Espionage', *The Morning Chronicle*, 26 February 1845, p. 5.
80. *Hansard*, 3rd ser., 76 Parl. Deb., H. C. (1844), pp. 216, 233–4.
81. Ibid. p. 216.
82. Hughes, *The Maniac in the Cellar*, p. 190.
83. *Hansard*, 75 Parl. Deb., H. L., pp. 973–4.
84. *Hansard*, 75 Parl. Deb., H. C., p. 897.
85. 'A Discussion Took Place Last Night', *The Times*, 25 June 1844, p. 5.
86. 'Sir James Graham', *The Satirist; or, the Censor of the Times*, 23 June 1844, p. 195.
87. Lynn Linton's husband, Chartist William James Linton, helped uncover the government's practices against Mazzini. See Thomas, *Postal Pleasures*, p. 124. For Linton's first-hand account of the scandal, see his autobiography, W. J. Linton, *Threescore and Ten Years 1820 to 1890: Recollections*, pp. 50–4. See also Linton's biographical collection, W. J. Linton, *European Republicans: Recollections of Mazzini and His Friends*, pp. v, 57–9. Both Linton and Lynn Linton contributed to *All the Year Round* alongside Collins.
88. See Wilkie Collins, *No Name*; Wilkie Collins, *Armadale*; and Collins, *The Moonstone*. *No Name* includes close to 115 letters, *Armadale* features 145 and *The Moonstone* contains almost seventy. *No Name* and *Armadale* include fully epistolary sections or chapters, which accounts for the larger number of letters compared to *The Woman in White* and *The Moonstone*.
89. These exceptions include *No Name*'s Captain Wragge, who intercepts Magdalen Vanstone's letters and forges a letter recalling Mrs Lecount to Zurich, as well as *Armadale*'s Lydia Gwilt and Mrs Milroy. Miss Gwilt forges a letter from Mr Blanchard to the elder Allan Armadale's mother when Miss Blanchard suppresses her father's letter. Mrs Milroy reads and re-seals a letter to Miss Gwilt from her confidante Mrs Oldershaw. Collins, *No Name*, pp. 317–21; Collins, *Armadale*, pp. 26–7, 306–8.
90. Kendrick argues that Hartright combats Fosco's conspiracy by becoming a 'rhetorical hero, who engages in a long campaign of textual reconstruction, the final achievement of which is the novel itself'. Walter M. Kendrick, 'The Sensationalism of *The Woman in White*', p. 29. Conversely, Perkins and Donaghy suggest that Hartright 'manipulat[es] the narrative for his own ends' ('A Man's Resolution: Narrative Strategies in Wilkie Collins', p. 392).

91. Kristen Johnson, 'When "Letter" Becomes "Litter": The (De)construction of the Message from Ann Radcliffe to Wilkie Collins', p. 153.

92. Porter, *The Refugee Question*, p. 80.

93. Mariaconcetta Costantini et al., Preface, in *Letter(s): Functions and Forms of Letter-Writing in Victorian Art and Literature*, p. 9.

94. Rotunno, *Postal Plots*, p. 71.

95. Ann Elizabeth Gaylin, 'The Madwoman Outside the Attic: Eavesdropping and Narrative Agency in *The Woman in White*', p. 317.

96. Stone, 'Joseph Mazzini', p. 10 (see pp. 10–12).

97. D. A. Miller, '*Cage aux folles*: Sensation and Gender in Wilkie Collins's *The Woman in White*', p. 116.

98. Watson, *Revolution and the Form of the British Novel*, p. 16.

99. Menke, *Telegraphic Realism*, p. 43.

100. '*Punch*'s Complete Letter Writer. Dedication to Sir James Graham Bart Secretary for the Home Department', *Punch*, 6 July 1844, p. 2.

101. Menke, *Telegraphic Realism*, p. 43.

102. '*Punch*'s Complete Letter Writer', p. 2.

103. Louis-Napoleon Bonaparte was elected to the French presidency of the new Second Republic in late 1848. Before his term ended, he seized power in an 1851 coup. His authority was confirmed in a plebiscite of December 1851 and a second plebiscite, in November 1852, re-established the French Empire and named him Emperor Napoleon III. The action of *The Woman in White* occurs between the summers of 1849 and 1852, when the characters return to Limmeridge approximately one year after Fosco's death in summer 1851, corresponding to this period of French history. For details about Napoleon III's rise to power in this period, see Roger Price, *The French Second Empire: An Anatomy of Political Power*, pp. 9–37.

104. Richard Cobden, 'The Three Panics: An Historical Episode'.

105. Hugh Cunningham, *The Volunteer Force: A Social and Political History 1859–1908*, pp. 8, 12.

106. Elizabeth Barret Browning, 'Napoleon III. in Italy', in *Poems Before Congress*, pp. 547–604. For more on British attitudes towards Napoleon III in relation to Barrett Browning, see Denae Dyck and Marjorie Stone, 'The "Sensation" of Elizabeth Barrett Browning's *Poems before Congress* (1860): Events, Politics, Reception', pp. 6–21.

107. D. G. Rossetti, 'After the French Liberation of Italy'.

108. Price, *The French Second Empire*, p. 408.

109. Ibid. p. 406.

110. See Clyde K. Hyder, 'Wilkie Collins and *The Woman in White*', pp. 298–300.
111. Tamara S. Wagner, 'Violating Private Papers: Sensational Epistolary and Violence in Victorian Detective Fiction', p. 35.
112. Tamar Heller, *Dead Secrets: Wilkie Collins and the Female Gothic*, p. 8.
113. Ibid. p. 131.

Chapter 4

Wounded Utterance: Trauma and Italy's Second War of Independence in Elizabeth Barrett Browning's *Poems Before Congress* and *Last Poems*

The bloody battles of Italy's short-lived Second War of Independence (April–July 1859) left permanent marks on nineteenth-century Europe well beyond the Italian peninsula. Their force was felt in the development of international war conventions, the delivery of aid and even the English language; the proper name of Magenta, for the 4 June 1859 Battle of Magenta, came to indicate the bright, blood-red colour whose dye was discovered shortly afterwards.[1] The northern Italian war, which allied France and Piedmont-Sardinia provoked with Austria, led to the first stage of Italian unification with Piedmont's absorption of Lombardy, the eventual annexation of most of the central Italian states and the 1861 creation of the Kingdom of Italy under Piedmontese King Victor Emmanuel II. The conquest of southern Italy followed swiftly upon the 1859 war, with Giuseppe Garibaldi's 1860 expedition to Sicily and Naples. From her position in Tuscany and Rome in the midst of these intense, rapidly unfolding events, fierce Risorgimento supporter Elizabeth Barrett Browning (EBB) maps a collision between poetic expression and history in her final two poetry collections, *Poems Before Congress* (1860) and *Last Poems* (1862). In her description of *Poems Before Congress* as 'political poems – lyrical –' in a private letter,[2] Barrett Browning notes the energising tension her final collections explore as she confronts the uses and limits of lyric utterance in politics.

Through primarily intergenerational familial motifs, Barrett Browning's late Italian poems test how the ideal of patriotic solidarity clashes with the material harm inflicted by the military campaigns that brought Italy into being. *Poems Before Congress* and *Last Poems* bear witness to a traumatic set of military engagements in which the burden of national resurrection is borne by often reluctant individuals and wartime deeds fall short of the aims that EBB helped to mythologise. Barrett Browning framed herself as an international spokesperson of the Risorgimento in her Preface to *Poems Before Congress*. Nonetheless, her poems depicting the Second War of Independence and its aftermath also expose a gap between the mythology of national resurrection and the reality of suffering and disaffection from the new national community, to acknowledge the damage inherent in going to war to forge a new state. The collapse of most of Italy's restoration governments and expansion of Piedmont across the peninsula in 1859–60, Lucy Riall notes, indicates that unification was 'about state-making and state-breaking'[3] as much as nationalist mythology. For Barrett Browning, representing the process of 'state-making and state-breaking' entails recognising the power of language to envision a different political reality, but also noting the silences and erasures imposed through violent, historical change. The transformative utterances of EBB's performative Risorgimento poetry help to make a unified Italy an imaginative – and eventually, a political – possibility. However, EBB also confronts the scars political violence leaves on the body politic in her poems, often unsettling the performative poetic voice in her attempt to articulate the impact of trauma on individuals, families and the new nation. Bearing witness to wartime violence – recognising that violence, transforming it into narrative and sharing it with the world – in *Poems Before Congress* and EBB's posthumously published *Last Poems*, often precludes speech and tests the power of words to produce action.

Poems Before Congress and *Last Poems* navigate an uncomfortable but fertile tension among lyric expression, poetic performance and pain that Barrett Browning pursued across her career. 'Napoleon III. in Italy', 'A Tale of Villafranca Told in Tuscany', 'Died . . .', 'The Forced Recruit' and, especially, 'Mother and Poet' inflect the Risorgimento with the burden of negotiating the performative project of nation-making and the violence of unmaking the existing Italian states. EBB felt an immediate, bodily investment in the unfolding events that culminated in 1859–61, as her oft-quoted 12 September 1859 letter to *Athenaeum* editor Henry Chorley describes: 'I have been living and dying for Italy lately. You don't know how vivid these things are to us, which serve for conversation at London dinner parties'.[4] Though her Preface to *Poems Before Congress* makes a strong claim for the agency of her poetic voice, a manuscript draft of that Preface transcribed in Alison Chapman's *Networking the Nation* identifies the poems with suffering rather than celebration:

After a thirteen years residence in Italy – I have a right to love her people & feel for a cause. If these poems appear to English readers somewhat too passionately felt & ~~uttered~~ sung, I will only say that the blood of my [illegible] kind heart ~~of this singing bird~~ ran red upon those thorns –.[5]

As Chapman argues, EBB's reference to Ovid's Philomela myth 'associates her poetic voice in the poems with personal pain that structures and authenticates the poems'.[6] For Barrett Browning, the lyric inherits violence and pain from these mythological origins. In Catherine Maxwell's reading of the lyric, the 'motif of a beauty produced from sacrifice and loss is one that recurs over and over again in the myths that explore the birth and development of poetry and music'.[7] However, for Virginia Jackson and Yopie Prins, the lyric should be read more for its historicity and conventional self-referentiality than for its efficacy as a conduit for pure self-expression; essentially a performative, rather than expressive mode, they argue, the lyric takes on a 'historical function as vehicle for transporting, and potentially displacing, representative identities'.[8] In her late Risorgimento poems, EBB exploits the gaps and correspondences between a provocatively performative poetry that revels in its dislocations and a deeply felt, immediate and embodied poetry that cannot be dislodged from the historical conflicts that it addresses.

EBB describes the concept of art's 'cost and pain' fundamental to her constantly evolving poetics in, for example, 'A Musical Instrument',[9] first published in the *Cornhill* in 1860 before EBB's death and collected in *Last Poems*. Placed as a 'symbolic hinge'[10] joining and distinguishing between the political and lyrical sections of *Last Poems*, as Chapman notes, the poem 'mediate[s] and oscillate[s] between the poetics of sensibility and politics'.[11] In 'A Musical Instrument', the god Pan creates 'Piercing' (32), 'Blinding' (33) beauty through an act of violence, 'hack[ing] and hew[ing]' a reed (15), associated in mythology with the female figure Syrinx, into the instrument of his artistic creation.[12] The poem's confrontation with violence and the destructiveness of lyrical utterance, then, offers a commentary on the lyric's expressivity and performativity as it draws on and resists poetic convention in a collection whose contents are, like *Poems Before Congress*, 'political poems – lyrical –'.[13]

As EBB's gestures of resistance to the poetics of pain in 'A Musical Instrument' suggest, embodied suffering can preclude utterance just as much as it validates or generates lyric expression, as in the case of Laura Savio, the speaker in Barrett Browning's dramatic monologue, 'Mother and Poet'. In an analysis of Tasso's story of Tancred killing his beloved Clorinda[14] in her classic work *Unclaimed Experience: Trauma, Narrative, and History*, Cathy Caruth posits that trauma

> is always the story of a wound that cries out, that addresses us in the attempt to tell us of a reality or truth that is not otherwise available. This truth, in its delayed appearance and its belated address, cannot be linked only to what is known, but also to what remains unknown in our very actions and our language.[15]

EBB's work explores the intersections between expression and silence as early as the elegiac sonnets she composed on her brother Bro's death in 1840. For Angela Leighton, these poems and EBB's contemporary letters address personal loss circumspectly,[16] as her grief 'drew her ... not into more poetry, but into dumbness'.[17] EBB's poems on the 1859 war and related military campaigns similarly negotiate the connections among grief, silence and expression. The punctured, bleeding heart of EBB's singing bird in the draft Preface to *Poems Before Congress*[18] is an image of Caruth's 'wound that cries out',[19] a wound that utters while signalling what remains unknown and unspeakable: writing and then striking the word 'uttered', and finally abandoning the draft Preface altogether, EBB illustrates her engagement with the representational complexities of writing traumatic violence. The tensions within EBB's work between expressive and performative lyric urges and the violence that forecloses speech, often compelling EBB's speakers to silence, are evident in this early introduction to the final volume of poetry she published in her lifetime and reflect both the horrific battlefield realities of 1859–60 Risorgimento conflict and the reality of political disaffection that accompanied official unification. In charting unfolding history in her late Risorgimento poems, EBB experiments with a poetry that exhibits neither an exhausted overflow of personal, lyrical expression nor an empty, self-referential performance of lyric form. Instead, Barrett Browning attempts a kind of wounded utterance, exploring a poetics of recognition that acknowledges the deep roots of political trauma embedded in the nation-making process while accepting and respecting the wartime experiences of suffering and grief that are beyond the power of poetic convention and speech to convey.

EBB's Intergenerational Risorgimento and the Revitalised Body Politic

On 29 April 1859, the Kingdom of Piedmont-Sardinia, led by King Victor Emmanuel II and Prime Minister Camillo Benso di Cavour and allied to Napoleon III's France, successfully provoked Austria to war. Barrett Browning, who watched Italy's Second War of Independence from Florence and Rome, welcomed the hostilities and celebrated the political leadership of Cavour and Napoleon. Using the motif of intergenerational cooperation to establish a pan-Italian, international solidarity that envisions united Italy as an exertion of popular will, *Poems Before Congress*'s opening ode, 'Napoleon III. in Italy', exhibits a performative poetics in which political speech and acts are aligned and poetic utterance swells up from within the united bodies that compose the resurrected Italian nation and that of their poetic spokeswoman. Yet, even in this powerful opening poem, EBB suggests the discursive limits of prophetic speech that characterise many of the other works in *Poems Before Congress* and *Last Poems*.

For Barrett Browning, war in Italy had long been justifiable and inevitable. In *Casa Guidi Windows* (1851), EBB imagined a violent

> raking of the guns across
>   The world . . .
> . . . the struggle in the slippery fosse
>   Of dying men and horses, and the wave
> Blood-bubbling[20]

as an alternative to an unjust peace. In the weeks leading up to the campaign, EBB wrote to her sister Arabella, 'Yes, I dont see, & nobody here sees very clearly, how it is possible to get on without war', adding that 'the youth drift away to Piedmont, by fifties in the night' to volunteer with the northern Italian forces.[21] As the war entered its crucial phase in June, EBB recorded how her passionate patriotism entailed a bodily investment in the conflict: before the war began, she writes, 'I used to have literal *physical* palpitations over the newspapers – tears in my eyes, sobs in my throat'.[22] For EBB, Italian politics were profoundly personal, deeply felt and translatable into a fervent poetry that combines public utterance with private, familial motifs to cast her civic nationalism in the most intimate, immediate terms.

As the Introduction to this study shows, familial, intergenerational and maternal metaphors run through British writing on the Risorgimento, in keeping with the '"nationalisation" of the private and the familial' Alberto Banti finds in Italian Risorgimento culture.[23] Wartime emphasis on mothering and family structure is not unique to the Risorgimento; as Helen Cooper, Adrienne Munich and Susan Squier argue in their collection, *Arms and the Woman*, '"arms" when juxtaposed to "woman" evokes sexual and maternal love, eclipsing Virgil's masculine military reference'.[24] Women and mothers, moreover, were crucial in forming British national culture after the French Revolution as key participants in a middle-class revolution in the early nineteenth century.[25] For Anne K. Mellor, some women writers deliberately framed themselves as arbiters of British national culture in the public sphere. Such writers, Mellor argues, 'asserted both the right and the duty of women to speak *for* the nation'.[26] In politicising mothers and families in her Risorgimento writing, EBB draws on nineteenth-century British gender discourse as well as Italian Risorgimento mythology.

EBB, furthermore, engages with the politicised figure of the Victorian poetess in her poetic mappings of gender, family and politics across her career. Though Mellor defines the politically engaged female poet figure against a more appropriately feminine Romantic-era poetess,[27] the Victorian poetess is far from the simplified, apolitical writer Mellor's contrast suggests, as more recent work on the poetess indicates. Tricia Lootens, for example, identifies a political poetess figure whose alignment with the Victorian private sphere is a political performance:

> to perform privacy, to perform politics without politics – indeed, to condemn politics altogether – is to perform a deeply patriotic and, in this, deeply political service to the State. The Poetess' symbolic power – the symbolic power of Woman, within this model – is always, by definition, public and patriotic – all the more so, precisely when it is most insistently, even histrionically, privatized.[28]

Yet, for EBB the performance of an apparently apolitical patriotism as 'service to the State' is troubled by her expatriate status, as Chapman notes in her description of an expatriate poetess figure, shaped by Germaine de Staël's *Corinne* and constructed through 'multiple subject positions that allow conflicting loyalties, through which a newly political poetry emerges'.[29] The poetess, Chapman argues, 'is an unstable and transgressive conceit, signifying home and restlessness, stability and flight, the nation and its others. Furthermore, it is the mobility of the figure of the poetess that allows her lyric poetry a political agency'.[30] EBB's poetess performance is further complicated, despite her loyalty to Napoleon III and Cavour, by the absence of a unified Italian state in the 1850s; in other words, 'service' to an Italian state that had yet to exist could also mean resistance to the restoration Italian states and major European powers.

In addition to performing and challenging private, feminine identity in her revisions of the poetess trope, EBB overtly intervenes in the public sphere, participating in what Julia F. Saville describes in *Victorian Soul-Talk* as a 'transnational republican discourse of the civic soul' that 'exploited language's rich aesthetic potential to make . . . readers experience viscerally the complex emotional and spiritual effects of democracy that eluded the public in more explicit forms such as fiction, essays, and newspaper journalism'.[31] For Saville, the silences and displacements in EBB's poetry are not the marks of the essentially empty, self-referential lyric form Jackson and Prins describe as the 'trac[ing]' of a 'cultural pattern',[32] but the consequences of her poetic attempt 'to give full voice to unspeakable injustices experienced by the disenfranchised and unheard, such as child laborers, slaves, or the people of Italy, chafing under foreign occupation'.[33] Saville's argument that 'EBB calls on her readership to attend to significant silences in her printed voices, cultivating active, sympathetic inquiry into others' situated experiences'[34] sheds light on the straddling of public and private spheres that occurs in EBB's works in which gendered and political performance collide with 'situated experiences' that make poetic expression untenable.

Casa Guidi Windows offers an earlier example of the intergenerational motif in EBB's Italian politics that performs privacy while exploring the uses and limits of public utterance, as the speaker addresses politics through the threshold of a private window.[35] This comprehensive poem explores political and cultural material spanning gendered literary depictions of Italy; early modern Florentine history and art; Dante and Florence's republican tradition; Risorgimento martyrs such as Silvio Pellico, the Bandieras and Anita Garibaldi; Austrian occupation and Pius IX's Papal governance; and a message promoting international solidarity directed at England. These public, historical themes are filtered through the private perspective of a maternal speaker and her intergenerational relationships with Florentine children. Despite the difference between Part One's optimism and Part Two's disillusionment, both parts of *Casa Guidi Windows* present children as symbols of Italy's vital future.

Part One opens with an Italian child's voice singing, '*O bella libertà, O bella!*' (I, 3), suggesting unity between the child's words and the 'heart' of the nation (I, 8). The speaker, furthermore, identifies with the child's refreshing confidence, exclaiming,

> hand in hand with that young child, will I
> Go singing . . . '*Bella libertà*'. (I, 165–6)

As Chapman argues, 'Only in the pure denotation of a child's voice can the future of Italy be both represented and enacted'.[36] The maternal speaker is thus led into the future by the child, the physical incarnation of her imminent hope. Despite the sense of lost purpose that permeates Part Two, Barrett Browning returns to a child as a representative of future possibility, closing the poem by beckoning to the speaker's child, 'my own young Florentine' (II, 743), to assume the responsibilities of teacher (II, 750), prophet (II, 757) and witness (II, 761) for the Italian democratic movement. In Part Two, then, hope for Italy lies more firmly with the next generation, as the maternal speaker outlines her peers' failings and bequeaths the movement to her son. Though *Casa Guidi Windows* focuses more on politics than the trauma of war, the failure of the singing voice to bring '*bella libertà*' (I, 3) into being for Italy prefigures the disjuncture between speech and action that structures EBB's later Italian poems.

Barrett Browning revives such intergenerational images in service of Italian patriotism in *Poems Before Congress* and *Last Poems* in her poetic efforts to engage her international, transatlantic audience with the Italian cause. These poems operate within a performative poetics that draws upon the assertions of public, poetic agency of her earlier work, as critics including Esther Schor, Alison Chapman and Katherine Montwieler have amply discussed.[37] In the final decade of her career, EBB frequently frames the pragmatics of her poetry around a combined mission of witnessing events and stimulating further action, enacting a Mazzinian project of 'transform[ing] the idea of Italy expressed so powerfully in literature into an equally powerful political ideology'.[38] She thus inherits the poetic intentions of her predecessors, proto-Mazzinian Romantic poets such as Lord Byron and P. B. Shelley, whose speakers yearn to transform the poetic imagination into revolution, as discussed in Chapter 1. In her February 1860 Preface to *Poems Before Congress*, EBB vehemently asserts the primacy of real-world action, arguing that 'all the virtues are means and uses' as part of her critique of British neutrality and non-interventionalist policy in Risorgimento conflict.[39] Her performative poetics, then, are more than an assertion of her own agency; Barrett Browning's claim for the value of her public utterances is an explicit counter to non-engagement, abdications of world citizenship and passivity in what she views as an essentially moral conflict. Heeding, however reluctantly, the angel's command that she 'Write!' to effect change in *Poems Before Congress*'s concluding work, 'A Curse for a Nation' (1855/1860),[40] Barrett Browning successfully coordinates such a belief in the transformative poetic imagination with the external action occurring around her, enacting the 'unity of "thought and action"'[41] of Mazzinian propaganda.

EBB's efforts to transform Italy through pan-Italian and international solidarity and coordination are framed by familial relationships, and the dominant family image of *Poems Before Congress* and *Last Poems* is intergenerational, like the mother–child relationship of *Casa Guidi Windows*. EBB's emphasis on intergenerational continuity first appears in these volumes in her depiction of Napoleon III, elected by the French to 'renew the line' of the Bonapartes, she argues, in the celebratory, prophetic opening poem, 'Napoleon III. in Italy' (1860).[42] Napoleon III's military gleanings from his uncle's 'open grave' (15), 'a grave that would not close' (16), suggest that he carries Napoleon's legacies forwards into the present, while the sonorous, dactylic refrain of

> Emperor
> Evermore (11–12)[43]

invests Napoleon III with political endurance into the future and support across the body politic. For Saville, 'The ode's first movement (stanzas 1–7) opens sounding the keynote onomatopoeically as the roar of the French crowd, who acclaim Louis their unorthodox leader. As they do so, conventional dactyls become distorted into anapests as "*Emp*eror" becomes "Emp*eror*"'.[44] As the poem progresses, the speaker's voice aligns itself to this 'surging choir' (61) of mass, public acclamation (76–9). Napoleon's endurance, then, is authorised by the people; in voting to accept the Second Empire, the French public

> set the seal
> Of what has been on what shall be. (22–3)

These opening stanzas to *Poems Before Congress* also offer a model for coordinated, intergenerational political action in Italy; like the first Napoleon's open grave, the graves of Italy open to spur a national uprising. The remainder of the poem presents an apocalyptic, personified Italy rising from death 'at the shout of her sons' (129) to, in turn, join with the dead of previous generations to inspire those sons to rise in the national struggle (181–202).

In 'Napoleon III. in Italy', the violence of the past and centuries of political decay inevitably lead to a triumphant moment of resurrection; the colossal Napoleon III strides across the Alps, met by the speaker and the Italian people she represents (71–81), while the military action of the present is sown by past sacrifices. The speaker asks,

> [I]f it were not for the beat and bray
> Of drum and trump of martial men,
> Should we feel the underground heave and strain,
> Where heroes left their dust as a seed
> Sure to emerge one day? (149–51)

This Shelleyan image suggests that present action and past inspiration are mutually constitutive: the forces marching in unison in the present awaken the dead, whose own past acts motivate present military heroism. In EBB's model for Risorgimento action, unity does not just mean coordination across the peninsula or between word and deed, but unity across the generations, including with the dead:

> Piedmontese, Neapolitan,
> Lombard, Tuscan, Romagnole,
> Each man's body having a soul, –
> Count how many they stand,
> All of them sons of the land,
> Every live man there
> Allied to a dead man below,
> And the deadest with blood to spare
> To quicken a living hand
> In case it should ever be slow. (188–97)

The resurrected Italian body politic is also an army of bodies rising up against oppression and merging with the dead, whose spirits 'quicken' the living to heroic achievement. The image of the 'blood' of the dead speaks both to the revitalising principle of the Risorgimento and to the biological ties between the living and their ancestors. Prophecy, in this poem, transforms utterance into reality; uniting the peninsula as one revitalised body politic that is also a national family, Barrett Browning makes a unified Italian nation a viable political possibility.

Yet, while this apocalyptic call for the dead to revive suggests the possibility of political continuity, coordinated action and unified purpose, the ghostly imagery also indicates an unsettlement that underlies *Poems Before Congress* and *Last Poems*. After all, the current generation is possessed by the past, invaded by the dead who spring up to occupy their living bodies. As Chapman argues, EBB's 'risen Italy [is] disturbingly gothic and grotesque'.[45] Just as the current generation is possessed or haunted by Italy's history of violence, the Italian national body that rises to military conflict must also be scarred by traumatic violence in the present. EBB subtly hints at the striking contrast of what war reporter Ferdinand Eber describes as the campaign's unsettling movement 'from Magenta, the field of death, to Milan, the town of joy'[46] in another intergenerational image, when she addresses General Macmahon, who lifts a child into his saddle:

> Take up the child, Macmahon, though
> Thy hand be red
> From Magenta's dead,
> And riding on, in front of the troop,
>   In the dust of the whirlwind of war
> Through the gate of the city of Milan, stoop
> And take up the child to thy saddle-bow. (242–8)

Though framed as a moment of intergenerational sympathy and military triumph, this scene also recalls the campaign's disturbing, bloody battlefields.

Furthermore, the powerful and prophetic poetic voice in 'Napoleon III' contains the suggestion of its own discursive boundaries. Though Katherine Montwieler argues that 'Napoleon III' 'explicitly outlines the power of performative speech acts – to produce potent, transcendent utterances, to anoint leaders, and to move others into action', she also notes that the poem 'acknowledges their limitations' by recognising that the prophetic poet has the power to speak but not to act directly.[47] One such acknowledgement occurs when the speaker 'warns' (84) Napoleon III to stay true to the cause (84–7), in recognition that the power to act, to be 'Found worthy of the deed thou art come to do' (95), lies with the Emperor alone, and not the poet. Discussing *Aurora Leigh*, Marjorie Stone argues that such disruptions of discursive authority are a central feature of EBB's feminist re-writing of the Victorian sage tradition:

> As a work of prophetic sage discourse, it subverts the phallocentric tradition it energetically enters both by destabilizing the infallible authority

typically assumed by the Victorian sage, and by comprehensively deploying the gynocentric emancipatory strategies developed in Barrett Browning's earlier works.[48]

Several of the poems in *Poems Before Congress* and *Last Poems* outline this tension between prophetic, performative utterances and the discursive limits of speech acts, as bearing witness to wartime violence unsettles the performative poetic voice, even precluding speech and testing the power of words to produce action. Though trauma theorists such as Susan J. Brison and Cathy Caruth argue that 'bearing witness' to a traumatic experience, or mediating trauma through language, is essential to recovery,[49] they also recognise such mediation can entail the loss of trauma's 'force' and 'precision'.[50] In other words, 'the transformation of the trauma into a narrative memory'[51] illustrates the limits of language to fully capture the trauma it attempts to convey. In *Poems Before Congress* and *Last Poems*, Barrett Browning confronts these limits.

Trauma and Dissent in *Poems Before Congress* and *Last Poems*

In addition to projecting a celebratory Italian patriotism, as in 'Napoleon III', images of familial relationship and the national body politic in EBB's war poetry explore the unsettling loss that accompanies efforts to mediate Risorgimento trauma, as the voices of the wounded cry out and dissent is expressed through silence. Though an embodied poetics can be an impassioned source of lyrical utterance, the trauma the Second War of Independence, revolution and reprisal in central Italy and the 1860 southern campaign inflicted upon individuals, families and communities could also preclude speech. In 'Mother and Poet', EBB explores a poet's right to refuse patriotic speech as a respectful mode of bearing witness to pain and grief and offers instead expression that resembles a 'wound that cries out'.[52] This poem, along with 'Died . . . ', 'The Forced Recruit' and 'A Tale of Villafranca', shows how trauma and loss shape the new Italy.

The French-Piedmontese military victories of the Second War of Independence were problematised by the war's unsatisfactory geopolitical results and the question of the political will to unify, concealed beneath the Risorgimento mythology promoted by nationalists and the politicians and monarchs who benefitted territorially from unification. Riall argues that

Unification . . . was in fact a contingent response to a grave and much longer-term political and social crisis. Events between 1848 and 1860 had simply made more visible the deep social and political divisions which had long destabilised the Italian peninsula, and these had at last exploded in 1859–60 into a bitter, and in many ways unresolved, struggle for power.[53]

The 1859 war, Garibaldi's 1860 expedition to southern Italy and the new Kingdom of Italy's military consolidation of power could be interpreted in a range of ways, from the liberation of colonised and oppressed territories through a war of nationality, to an opportunistic land-grab, enacting the French policy of establishing a buffer state between France and the Austrian Empire and growing Piedmontese possessions in Italy, to a civil war.

For its supporters, the Risorgimento constituted the shared ideas about an emergent Italian nation that legitimised revolutionary political action, especially patriotic uprising among *il popolo*. Like other nineteenth-century nationalist movements, the Italian movement 'relied on a "foundation story" for the purposes of self-legitimation';[54] Risorgimento mythology, Riall argues, 'creat[ed] a heroic narrative of events which would make nation-state creation seem the inevitable, and morally correct, outcome of what was, in reality, a political struggle for power'.[55] Though EBB fervently supported Piedmont and the 1859 war's political leaders, Napoleon III and Cavour, dissenting voices like Alberto Mario's reveal that the will to unify under a constitutional monarchy was far from universal on the peninsula and disaffection from the imposed government weakened the new Italian nation-state. The process and outcome of the Risorgimento play out concretely what Matthew Reynolds describes as nationalism's 'two opposing connotations': nationalism both 'brings people together, extends sympathies, creates community' and 'holds people apart, creates prejudice, and initiates conflict'.[56] The representational by-products of foundation myths and inclusive, cooperative familial metaphors include voices of dissent and disaffection, as well as purposeful exclusions, like those of Nice and Savoy, which were annexed to France as part of the international negotiations that made Italian unification under Piedmont possible. The disillusioned included British Risorgimento supporters who did not subscribe to meliorist constitutionalism. As Marcella Pellegrino Sutcliffe illustrates, internationalist British republicans, like the Mazzinian W. J. Linton,[57] were disappointed by the political outcome in Italy: 'the "losers" of the "popular Risorgimento" maintained their cross-Channel connections, sharing flickering hopes, as well as feelings of dismay, resentment, disappointment and, finally, nostalgia across borders'.[58] Supporters of Austria and the Pope and conservatives in Britain, furthermore, did not believe an Italian nation-state was inevitable or desirable and opposed Napoleon III's intervention in Italy.[59] Risorgimento politics were contested in Britain as well as in Italy, even after the nation-state was formed, defying the finality and inevitability of unification implied by its 'self-legitimat[ing]' 'foundation story'.[60]

Furthermore, the limited unification that did take place in 1861 was made possible through the traumatic violence of the 1859–60 military campaigns, violence that challenged narratives of soldierly heroism and Risorgimento glory. The high-cost battles of the Second War of Independence are important precursors to those of the First World War, the extreme, traumatic violence of which compelled Sigmund Freud to address trauma in *Beyond the Pleasure Principle* (1920).[61] According to historian Jonathan Marwil, 'this brief conflict jolted consciousness as did no other European war between 1815 and 1914 and in some of the same ways World War I would, despite their differences in scale and duration'.[62] At the Battle of Magenta, in which the French army narrowly defeated Austrian forces, enabling Napoleon III and Victor Emmanuel II to enter Austrian-governed Milan, more than 2,000 were killed and 8,000 wounded.[63] Twenty days later, at the Battle of Solferino, there were 40,000 casualties in one day of fighting;[64] this brutality hastened the armistice at Villafranca that ended the war on 11 July 1859. Unmatched in its horrors by any other military event in nineteenth-century Europe, including in the Crimea and the Napoleonic Wars,[65] the bloody engagement at Solferino led to first Nobel Peace Prize (1901) winner Henri Dunant's creation of the Red Cross and the first Geneva Convention (1864). Dunant, an eyewitness during the battle and its aftermath of prolonged suffering, describes it in *A Memory of Solferino* (1862):

> Here is a hand-to-hand struggle in all its horror and frightfulness; Austrians and Allies trampling each other under foot, killing one another on piles of bleeding corpses, felling their enemies with their rifle butts, crushing skulls, ripping bellies open with sabre and bayonet. No quarter is given; it is a sheer butchery; a struggle between savage beasts, maddened with blood and fury. Even the wounded fight to the last gasp. When they have no weapon left, they seize their enemies by the throat and tear them with their teeth.[66]

When the battle ended, wounded soldiers were left with no food, water[67] or organised aid: some wounded, Dunant writes, were mistakenly buried alive, while the dead were placed in shallow graves, sometimes with limbs protruding, vulnerable to battlefield scavengers.[68]

The Lombardy campaign was not the only violent event of the period. Theodosia Garrow Trollope describes the 20 June 1859 sack of Perugia by Papal troops as the emergence of 'the red right hand gleaming out of the priestly frock'.[69] Her depiction of the rumours of that event reaching Florence is equally grotesque; the circulating news 'glid[ed] about the city, like blood-stained ghosts ever throng-ing thicker and ghastlier, first rumours, then affirmations, at last hor-rible details of a deed that may rank for enormity and foulness with any the world has ever seen'.[70] An American family named Perkins of EBB's acquaintance was caught up in the Papal retaliation in Perugia, as she writes to Arabella:

> they have escaped barely with their lives. The pope's Swiss troops attacked the hotel where they were, & prepared to bayonet them all . . . They got away with the clothes on their backs simply . . . Women & children killed in the streets – & *worse*.[71]

Civilians also perpetrated vengeful acts against their former oppres-sors. Garibaldi recounts with disgust the ferocious reprisals Sicilians committed against the Bourbon troops that retreated as the *Mille* advanced towards Palermo in 1860:

> The local people set upon them with fury, killing as many as they could and chasing the others on to Palermo. It was a wretched sight: we found their corpses lying in the streets being eaten by dogs – the corpses of Ital-ian men slaughtered by their fellow Italians. If they had been brought up as free citizens, then they could have fought for their oppressed country; as it was, and as a result of the hatred in which their masters were held, they had been torn apart by their own brothers, with a frenzy which would make hyenas recoil.[72]

The 1859–60 campaigns, then, combined the violence of interna-tional war with the atrocities of revolution, government repression and civil war.

Barrett Browning did not personally witness the battles of the Sec-ond War of Independence, the sack of Perugia or Garibaldi's cam-paign first-hand; nor was Dunant's account of Solferino available to her, as it remained unpublished until after her death. Nonetheless, EBB was highly invested in Risorgimento political activity and reporting. Chapman shows that 'the Brownings were always concerned, when in Italy, with receiving the latest newspapers – including *Galignani's Messenger, The Athenaeum*, the *Nazione*, the *Monitore, The Spiritual Magazine* . . . and the *Corriere Mercantile*';[73] their engagement with expatriate, international and Italian print culture 'effectively culminated in their winter residence in Rome in 1859–60 . . . [when they] receiv[ed] patriotic Tuscan newspapers and journals that were banned in Rome through [Isa] Blagden and the diplomat Odo Russell'.[74] Though not an eyewitness to the battlefield, then, EBB was an expert navigator and synthesiser of the news that circulated as events unfolded.

Eyewitness descriptions of the 1859 campaign were widely available in newspapers around Europe and even in North America while it occurred, as war reporting had reached an elevated status in newspapers following William Howard Russell's success for *The Times* in Crimea. Napoleon-friendly journalists from the *Moniteur, Constitutionnel* and *Morning Chronicle* were allowed to follow the French army and Italy's Second War of Independence was the first non-American war to be covered by a paper in the United States, as *New York Times* editor and co-founder Henry Jarvis Raymond travelled to Italy to report on the campaign.[75] London's *Times* of 27 June 1859, for example, extracts a letter from a soldier dated four days before Solferino, describing the engagement at Melegnano:

> after a few cannon shots, we rushed on without any orders, uttering shouts and cries loud enough to wake the dead! It was then indeed that a veritable butchery commenced; every one that appeared before us was killed with the bayonet . . . I have seen piles of French and Austrian carcasses encumbering the streets. The best notion I can give you of this affair is, that in the space of 2 ½ [hours] . . . the regiment lost 600 men, including 33 officers, killed and wounded – and the Austrian loss was greater.[76]

Details of Solferino appeared in *The Times* in early July; the correspondent with the allied armies, Ferdinand Eber, states, for example, that the field of battle 'looked like a human butchery after the fight'.[77] Eber's full narrative of the war from the allies' camp was published alongside artist Carlo Bossoli's drawings from the front in an 1859 collection, *The War in Italy* (Figure 4.1).

Figure 4.1 *Battle of Solferino – Attack of S Martino by the Piedmontese.* (Source: *The War in Italy*, Carlo Bossoli [London, 1859].)

Though EBB disliked and distrusted *The Times* for its pro-Austrian stance,[78] her repeated references to its contents in her letters indicates her familiarity with its accounts of the war; moreover, Eber, a Hungarian nationalist who abandoned his position as *Times* correspondent during the campaign in Sicily to fight with Garibaldi the following summer,[79] could scarcely be called pro-Austrian. Eber's graphic account of the horrific aftermath following Magenta, the war's 'first great shock',[80] rivals Dunant's famed description of Solferino:

> Several square miles of carnage, well-nigh 2,000 dead and dying lying about, in some places in heaps, in others dotted all over the ground in every attitude; some with that placid countenance which indicates a well-aimed bullet in the heart or in the head, stiffened in the very position in which they were when the fatal lead struck them; here one with his right arm close to the hip, and with his fists clenched as if he was still holding the musket ready for the charge; there, another, with his hand to his mouth and showing his white teeth, as if ready to bite off the end of the cartridge; the next man as calm as though he were reposing; another near him with his features distorted, and his limbs cramped, exhibiting all the horrors of the death-struggle from a bayonet-wound; further on, one with his head off; another with his limbs shattered; a third reduced by a cannon-ball to a formless heap in a pool of blood; and so on, in all the endless varieties and forms of death. It was a study for an anatomist, or a gloomy painter of horrors.
>
> And all around, mixed up with the dead were the wounded, some only just breathing, and too helpless to crawl under the shade of the next vine, or to chase away the flies feasting on the sweat of death; others cowering down in a ball, shivering under the scorching sun; others looking up imploringly and craving a mouthful of water; from one burst a sob, from another a sigh. It reminded one of Dante's 'Inferno'.[81]

With such reports available, the French government's orders that the Paris newspapers suppress '"details" about Magenta'[82] are unsurprising. EBB, an avid consumer of Risorgimento news and participant in print culture, absorbed this material and mediated the trauma of these brutal military realities for poetry readers in turn.

EBB's patriotism is inflected with her interest in a poetics rooted in pain, and her personal experience of self-imposed exile from Britain informs her representation of the disaffection and shock caused by the 1859 campaign. Writing to her friend Anna Jameson from Paris in 1851, EBB exclaims,

> Oh, England! – I love & hate it at once! – Or rather, where love of coun-
> try ought to be in the heart, there is the mark of the burning iron in mine,
> and the depth of the scar shows the depth of the root of it.[83]

What Chapman describes as the 'startling metaphor of the mark of
one's country as a deep scar, a site of terrible loss and pain'[84] points
to EBB's embodied poetics, as her attention to the 'wound that cries
out'[85] in her image of the bleeding, singing bird discussed above suggests. Such embodied emotion is central to Victorian understandings
of pain and suffering. As Jill L. Matus argues in *Shock, Memory and
the Unconscious in Victorian Fiction*, trauma theory emphasises a
twentieth-century concept of 'a "wound culture"' in which 'evidence
of wounding and its perpetrators is found in the unwitting witnessing, inaccessible to memory except through hypnosis and therapeutic
recovery'.[86] By contrast, Victorian discourses around shock focus on
the connections between consciousness and the emotions.[87] Overwhelming emotions are often embodied; in her reading of shock in
Victorian fiction, Matus finds that the emotions 'offer the nineteenth-
century novelist a way of articulating what is known but not thought.
The shocked somatic body also necessarily implicates the psyche and
may indeed be deputized to "speak" for it'.[88] EBB's 'scar',[89] representing her deeply felt but conflicted patriotism, is such an image for
'what is known but not thought':[90] an articulation of a profoundly
corporeal emotional experience imagined as a physical wound that
leaves its traces on the body.

EBB's dramatic monologue 'Mother and Poet' (1861/1862) in
particular grapples with the bodily suffering overlooked in more
enthusiastic poems like 'Napoleon III. in Italy'. The speaker, poet
Laura Savio,[91] embodies a kind of agonising motherhood that
is analogous to the physical damage incurred through the patriotic fighting she initially supports, which gives birth to Italy as a
nation-state; her reproductive female body, and especially the pain
of maternity, is paradoxically the origin and destroyer of her artistic voice. 'Mother and Poet' presents Savio's voice as a mediated
'double poem', which Isobel Armstrong describes as 'a representation of representation'[92] that addresses 'utterance both as subject
and object'.[93] Savio asks,

> What art can a woman be good at? Oh, vain!
> What art *is* she good at, but hurting her breast
> With the milk-teeth of babes, and a smile at the pain?[94]

The poem, set after both of her sons are killed fighting for independence, stresses that intense physical suffering is inherent in motherhood. The speaker describes how the boys'

> arms round her throat,
> Cling, strangle a little! (17–18)

before moving on to the emotional 'sting[ing]' (21) she feels as the person responsible for their deaths in service of Italian liberty (21–5).

Savio thus embodies maternal pangs originating in the mother–child bond and in the loss of that bond. Her sons' deaths extinguish the maternal identity that Savio believes fuels her poetry and patriotic hope for Italy's future. She laments,

> Ah, ah, 'his,' 'their' mother, – not 'mine,'
> No voice says '*My* mother' again to me (58–9)

and refuses to write patriotic songs in Italy's name, relinquishing her poetic and political agency in her grief (98–100). Though her maternal body is the source of her artistic identity, her suffering as a mother eventually destroys her ability to participate in public discourse; in Christopher M. Keirstead's words, 'Savio's recognition of the inescapably political status of her body – as a poet and as a mother – . . . causes her to reassess the public impact of her poetry'.[95] Her poetess performance, a patriotic performance of privacy,[96] in other words, is disrupted by public history. While in 'Napoleon III. in Italy' graves open to resurrect fallen patriots, stirring the living to concrete political action, in 'Mother and Poet' new graves swallow Italy's youth, severing the motivational, intergenerational blood ties that bind the nation and rendering patriotic martyrdom politically useless. As Savio hopelessly asks,

> And when Italy's made, for what end is it done
> If we have not a son? (74–5)

In fact, Savio's experience of maternal agony resembles the national struggle through which the nation-state of Italy emerges. She states,

> Forgive me. Some women bear children in strength,
> And bite back the cry of their pain in self-scorn;
> But the birth-pangs of nations will wring us at length
> Into wail such as this – and we sit on forlorn
> When the man-child is born. (91–5)

Italy's horrible 'birth-pangs' (93) ultimately disrupt her political commitment to her new nation and the community that benefits from its creation; she describes Italy as '*you*[r] . . . country' (83), while identifying her own otherworldly national home in the heavens, with her sons (86–90). Yet, Savio's 'wring[ing]' (93) pain and 'wail' (94) of suffering are necessary by-products of the very process of nation-building. The violent, traumatic struggle that creates Italy also engenders disaffection like Savio's, and the patriotic poetry Savio formerly produced gives way to the 'wound that cries out'[97] in EBB's mediation of traumatic pain. This dramatic monologue thus acts as a testimony to unglorified violence, violence that unsettles the war effort, disrupts the historical continuity and cooperation 'Napoleon III' works to establish and excludes participants from the new Italy that emerges through war, fracturing instead of generating national commitment.

Bearing witness to both the success of what she believes to be a just cause and to the real pain and suffering that occur in pursuit of that outcome, then, EBB illustrates the ways in which violence becomes fundamental to the emerging Italian nation while respecting diverse responses to the state. Her poems present readers with the 'empathic unsettlement, and the discursive inscription of that unsettlement' that Dominick LaCapra claims is central to trauma writing,[98] an affective response to trauma which 'poses a barrier to closure in discourse and places in jeopardy harmonizing or spiritually uplifting accounts of extreme events from which we attempt to derive reassurance or a benefit'.[99] Barrett Browning suggests this 'barrier to closure' by representing the emotional and rhetorical loop in which Savio is trapped by violence and loss. Savio describes the psychological state that now informs her inability to focus her poetic voice in the third person, indicating a mental dissociation between her conscious voice and her traumatic experience:

> – The east sea and west sea rhyme on in her head
> For ever instead. (9–10)

In addition to suggesting that Savio becomes an object to herself, this statement reveals both the challenge this loss poses to her art, as her rhymes fix on the one topic of her sons, and her circular thought process, as she is unable or unwilling to achieve emotional closure after her sons' deaths. Barrett Browning replicates this mental loop in her own circular form: the first and final stanzas are nearly identical (1–5, 96–100). Savio's refusal to write about the nation is a form of 'empathic unsettlement'[100] as well; she rejects a simplifying resolution that would exploit her sons' deaths for a political purpose. She thus respectfully bears witness to those deaths through her silence.

Barrett Browning also experiments with the dramatic monologue and lyric forms in this effort to bring 'empathic unsettlement'[101] to 'Mother and Poet'. Robert Langbaum influentially argues that the dramatic monologue creates 'tension between sympathy and moral judgment',[102] which allows readers to temporarily occupy a point of view, taken up by the speaker, that they would not normally adhere to.[103] The suspension of critical distance extends readers' sympathies in unlikely directions; however, in 'Mother and Poet', the 'empathic unsettlement'[104] that underlies the poem's affect heightens this tension, which lies within the body of the speaker herself, as she is unable to fully occupy her own position, having experienced a traumatic disruption of the self that her speech cannot accommodate. Neither sympathy nor judgement are possible for readers, as the poem's 'discursive inscription of . . . unsettlement'[105] precludes the production of a stable position for the speaker. Ultimately, the voice of Risorgimento poetry that emerges in 'Mother and Poet' is displaced from the patriot Savio to another poet, the transnational expatriate, EBB. This displacement corresponds to the kind of 'belated address' Caruth identifies with traumatised expression; Savio's 'wound . . . cries out'[106] only through EBB's poetic intervention.

Savio's silence also places strain on the cultural work of the Victorian print lyric, which Matthew Rowlinson identifies with a totalising incorporation of the historical forms it supersedes and the pre-modern cultures they represent that nonetheless leaves traces of that cultural work in the form of 'innumerable omissions and forgettings'.[107] These can be figured as a 'silent other', often a woman, who appears in a poem 'to complete, modify or subvert an utterance dialectically'.[108] In Victorian women's poetry, the silent woman figure is often internalised as muteness within poetic utterance.[109] Savio's paradoxical position as a poem's speaker who is also a poet refusing to speak dramatises such an incorporation of silence into speech. What distinguishes Savio so crucially from, for example, Alfred Tennyson's mute Lady of Shalott, however, is that her silenced voice is not 'align[ed] . . . with forces . . . suffering major historical defeats', such as the landowning classes and artisans associated with the Lady of Shalott.[110] Instead, Savio's silence emerges from historical triumph, allegorised in the poem's birth imagery. Savio is indeed rendered mute by historical movement, but that movement is the traumatically violent emergence of a new nation, in which she has gladly participated, rather than the defeat of an archaic culture. Silence, in 'Mother and Poet', mediates the victorious future rather than the vanquished past, indicating that disaffection can strike the Risorgimento's winners as well as its historical losers.

Savio's testimony of non-testimony is one among many variations of what it means to bear witness to the complexity of political violence in *Poems Before Congress* and *Last Poems*. 'Died . . .', 'The Forced Recruit' and 'A Tale of Villafranca' also navigate the costs of Italian unification. Transforming trauma into narrative, Caruth argues, entails writing 'a history constituted by the erasure of its traces'.[111] Absences and erasures such as Savio's silence are the representational signs of trauma. In 'Died . . .' (1862), published with the Italian poems in *Last Poems* but written before the war,[112] Barrett Browning explores a speaker's inability to communicate a traumatic encounter with death. Although the poem does not identify a particular wartime event or context, it struggles with the problem of representing bodily violence in poetry. The ellipsis of the poem's title points to the gap between the subject matter and the language that is incapable of fully expressing its realities. EBB's ellipsis enacts trauma as a '*history of disappearance*',[113] which sees repetition compulsion as 'the unexpected encounter with an event that the mind misses and then repeatedly attempts to grasp'.[114] The ellipsis in the title is thus the representational equivalent of the gunshot wound EBB describes as a 'deep black hole in the curls' of a dying soldier in *Poems Before Congress*'s 'A Court Lady' (1860).[115] The impact of violence manifests itself as an absence. The emphasis in 'Died . . .' on unanswerable questions and repeated one-word, inadequate responses signals the kind of repeated 'originary departure'[116] from psychological content that the speaker's mind does not grasp theorised by Caruth. The first line confirms this representational dilemma, asking, 'What shall we add now? He is dead'.[117] The 'wash of words across his name' (3) that attempts to find meaning in the unnamed subject's life are no longer applicable against his sudden, absolute death (4–5). The speaker and addressee abruptly end their dialogue about the deceased figure, unable to find language to suit the new circumstance. For example, the speaker claims that she 'Stopped short in praising' (10), while the addressee 'stood restrained' (15). Questions and single-word answers such as 'Where *is* he? Gone' (20), 'Dead' (21), seem to be all the speaker can process. Such answers, moreover, preclude further speech, as the speaker insists:

> Dead. There's an answer to arrest
> All carping. (26–7)

Language becomes macabre, represented as 'flies buzz[ing] round his face' (28), an image that resonates with Dunant's description of the wounded and dead soldiers at Solferino; here, language only achieves meaning by becoming material, like the mortal remains it grotesquely fails to grasp.[118]

EBB confronts wartime death more directly in 'The Forced Recruit', which depicts an Italian conscripted into Austrian forces to fight at Solferino. The eponymous figure is found dead on the battlefield by Italian soldiers, who respectfully bury the youth, although he died fighting against his countrymen. His body is marked by the contradictory position imposed upon him by occupation and war:

> III.
> No stranger, and yet not a traitor,
>   Though alien the cloth on his breast,
> Underneath it how seldom a greater
>   Young heart, has a shot sent to rest!
> IV.
> By your enemy tortured and goaded
>   To march with them, stand in their file,
> His musket (see) never was loaded,
>   He facing your guns with that smile![119]

Though the forced recruit refuses to fire on his Italian brothers, he is nonetheless killed by Italian patriots. As the speaker notes at the poem's opening, 'He died with his face to you all' (2). His recruitment into the Austrian forces severs the ties of brotherhood and national unity that the war attempts to bring into being across the Italian peninsula. Barrett Browning, for example, describes him equally as an orphan yearning for his mother (17) and as a brother-at-arms wishing to die for Italy, but as a 'passive' (36) victim rather than an active, heroic participant (19–20). Though the forced recruit chooses death rather than fire upon his fellow Italians, that death fails to reincorporate him into the Italian community from which Austrian occupation has excluded him. Instead, this soldier dies

> without witness or honour,
> Mixed, shamed in his country's regard, (33–4)

'Cut off' from the brotherhood of Italian patriots who fight for the mother country (38). The alternation between feminine endings – 'traitor' (9), 'greater' (11), 'goaded' (13), 'loaded' (15) – and masculine endings – 'breast' (10), 'rest' (12), 'file' (14), 'smile' (16) – further suggests the soldier's contradictory status, the tension between his feminine preclusion from active participation in the national war and desire for maternal comfort and his fraternal, stoic strength of purpose in sacrificing himself for Italy. The speaker's attempt to bear witness to this unwitnessed, militarily insignificant and isolating death ultimately admits that the forced recruit's fate cannot be represented as an instance of military 'glory' (44) in the kind of language deployed in 'Napoleon III. in Italy'. Instead, bearing witness to this Venetian soldier's story is both material and transient: the speaker concludes, 'let *him* have a tear' (44).

EBB's commitment to representing a range of violent wartime experiences sheds light on those among her Risorgimento poems that express lack of confidence in the performative poetic voice, poems such as the disaffected 'Tale of Villafranca Told in Tuscany' (1859/1860), which responds to Napoleon III's hasty peace with Austria to conclude the 1859 campaign. The poem, originally published in the *Athenaeum* in September of 1859, provides a counterpoint to the optimistic 'rose-water' Tuscan revolution that appeared in Garrow Trollope's Florentine correspondence for the *Athenaeum* of that period.[120] The speaker, addressing her young child, frames narrative as a flawed vehicle for representing wartime politics. She purports to 'tell' the child a tale[121] in a variation of ballad stanza, an accessible poetic form usually conducive to narrative, and uses simple, straightforward diction in the opening stanzas to complement this accessibility: 'A great man' (8); 'a great Deed' (9); 'cloud and clay' (10); 'heart and brain' (12). This presents the Italian question in terms of clear, uncomplicated political stakes that a young child like the addressee can understand. However, the speaker also immediately questions language as her medium: the 'sign' (3) of Italy's nascent independence '[h]as faded' (5), she argues, against the Villafranca peace. Actions, here, disrupt words, breaking the link between signifier and signified and belying the poem's simplistic form. In addition, words – the political arguments of European monarchs and statesmen – arise to overwhelm action with excess language (22–63); their empty words and curses (54) bury the 'great Deed' of liberation and unification (9) in language. The 'Tale', then, reveals the failure of words to spur action and language's convoluted investment in passivity, as words in the poem, including protests (24), mutterings (36), calls for explanation (57) and incitements to violence (61–3), are mired in 'red tape' (53). The speaker concludes the story of mourning she tells her young child with an expression of hopelessness similar to Savio's in 'Mother and Poet':

> In this low world, where great Deeds die,
> What matter if we live? (83–4)

National resurgence is impossible; life is no longer even desirable. An intergenerational communication, this poem gives up on coordinated action and, including the child she addresses in her 'we' (84), the speaker fails even to locate future hope in the next generation. As 'great Deeds die' (83), so too do words falter. The speaker hesitates to articulate further intention, and claims, like Savio, to give up speech, stating,

> I cannot say
> A word more. (78–9)

In this poem, language frustrates action and disrupts the power of speech by burdening it with pointless excess.

Though Barrett Browning's performative promotion of the Italian cause for an international readership does motivate her political poetry, the principle of unsettlement that competes with her more propagandistic poems is equally important to her overall pragmatics in representing the Risorgimento in *Poems Before Congress* and *Last Poems*. Her poems use familial and intergenerational imagery to recognise the range of ways in which the Risorgimento's political violence disrupts language and challenges narratives of heroic engagement in the national cause; however, by incorporating the scars of the Risorgimento into her work, EBB shows how trauma constitutes Italian identity and experience. Italy's 'foundation story'[122] might also be imagined as what LaCapra calls a 'founding trauma',[123] a story of historical suffering and violent emergence as a new state that ideologically underlies the new, post-Risorgimento, pan-Italian identity. While that identity encompasses stories of loss, disaffection, exclusion from the national family and violence, this range of affective experiences of the Risorgimento uncovers and authenticates the diversity and internal tensions inherent in the new Italy. EBB's performative explorations of intergenerational and familial relationships envision an Italian nation that cooperates in solidarity; yet, utterance has its limits and silence has a place in a poetics that bears witness to the 1859–60 campaigns' profound shocks. EBB's work in presenting these tensions in *Poems Before Congress* and *Last Poems* is ultimately a fruitful enterprise, as lyric convention, poetess performance and the poetics of pain are revised into a poetics of recognition that allows for a wounded utterance to emerge to truthfully reflect the newly created Italy.

Notes

1. 'Magenta', in *Oxford English Dictionary*.
2. Elizabeth Barrett Browning, *The Letters of Elizabeth Barrett Browning to Her Sister Arabella*, p. 444.
3. Lucy Riall, *Risorgimento: The History of Italy from Napoleon to Nation-State*, p. 69.
4. Elizabeth Barrett Browning, *Letters of Elizabeth Barrett Browning*, vol. 2, ed. Frederic G. Kenyon, p. 334.
5. Quoted in Alison Chapman, *Networking the Nation: British and American Women's Poetry and Italy, 1840–1870*, p. 218.
6. Ibid.
7. Catherine Maxwell, *The Female Sublime from Milton to Swinburne: Bearing Blindness*, p. 12. See also Maxwell on the Philomela myth (22).
8. Virginia Jackson and Yopie Prins, 'Lyrical Studies', p. 529.
9. Elizabeth Barrett Browning, 'A Musical Instrument', in *Last Poems*, l. 40. Subsequent citations will appear parenthetically in the text by line number.
10. Chapman, *Networking the Nation*, p. 247.
11. Ibid. p. 251.
12. For another detailed analysis of this poem see Dorothy Mermin, *Elizabeth Barrett Browning: The Origins of a New Poetry*, pp. 241–5. Mermin concludes that '"A Musical Instrument" is a reluctant acknowledgment that great poetry might . . . come . . . not from participation in male superiority and cultural dominance, but from exclusion and pain' (245).
13. Barrett Browning, *The Letters of Elizabeth Barrett Browning to Her Sister Arabella*, p. 444.
14. Torquato Tasso, *The Liberation of Jerusalem (Gerusalemme liberata)* [1581].
15. Cathy Caruth, *Unclaimed Experience: Trauma, Narrative, and History*, p. 4. Caruth discusses Sigmund Freud's presentation of Tasso's story from *Gerusalemme Liberata* in *Beyond the Pleasure Principle*. Tancred unknowingly kills Clorinda in battle, then wounds her again by cutting a tree in which her soul is imprisoned; blood pours from the

wound, and Clorinda's voice cries out from within the tree. Caruth, *Unclaimed Experience*, pp. 1–4.

16. Angela Leighton, *Elizabeth Barrett Browning*, pp. 79–90.
17. Ibid. p. 80.
18. Chapman, *Networking the Nation*, p. 218.
19. Caruth, *Unclaimed Experience*, p. 4.
20. Elizabeth Barrett Browning, *Casa Guidi Windows*, II, 401–5. Subsequent citations will appear parenthetically in the text by part and line numbers.
21. Barrett Browning, *The Letters of Elizabeth Barrett Browning to Her Sister Arabella*, p. 400.
22. Ibid. p. 409.
23. Alberto Mario Banti, 'Sacrality and the Aesthetics of Politics: Mazzini's Concept of the Nation', p. 73.
24. Helen Cooper et al., 'Arms and the Woman: The Con(tra)ception of the War Text', p. 9.
25. Gary Kelly argues that 'women were increasingly defined as the ideological and cultural foundation of society, state, nation, and empire' (*Women, Writing, and Revolution 1790–1827*, p. 174).
26. Anne K. Mellor, *Mothers of the Nation: Women's Political Writing in England, 1780–1830*, p. 9.
27. Ibid. p. 70.
28. Tricia Lootens, *The Political Poetess: Victorian Femininity, Race, and the Legacy of Separate Spheres*, p. 14.
29. Chapman, *Networking the Nation*, p. 94.
30. Ibid. p. 99.
31. Julia F. Saville, *Victorian Soul-Talk: Poetry, Democracy, and the Body Politic*, p. 2.
32. Jackson and Prins, 'Lyrical Studies', p. 529.
33. Saville, *Victorian Soul-Talk*, p. 18.
34. Ibid. p. 39.
35. For discussions of the poem interested in the window as a site of liminality and mediation, see Helen Groth, 'A Different Look – Visual Technologies and the Making of History in Elizabeth Barrett Browning's *Casa Guidi Windows*' and Leigh Coral Harris, 'From *Mythos* to *Logos*: Political Aesthetics and Liminal Poetics in Elizabeth Barrett Browning's *Casa Guidi Windows*'.
36. Alison Chapman, '"In Our Own Blood Drenched the Pen": Italy and Sensibility in Elizabeth Barrett Browning's *Last Poems* (1862)', p. 272.
37. *Casa Guidi Windows*, Schor argues, 'addresses an urgent need to claim political agency . . . by meditating on the resonance between poem making and nation making' ('The Poetics of Politics: Barrett Browning's *Casa Guidi Windows*', p. 309). Chapman argues that

> The ending of *Aurora Leigh* refigures the Risorgimento within a radically new sense of poetic writing as a resurgence, renaissance, and resurrection, whose transformative power is located in the body of the expatriate woman poet, the problematic yet exhilarating medium of spiritual, poetical, and political agency.

Alison Chapman, 'Poetry, Network, Nation: Elizabeth Barrett Browning and Expatriate Women's Poetry', p. 283. In *Poems Before Congress*, as Montwieler argues, Barrett Browning intervenes in revolutionary, political action as it unfolds, framing herself 'through imperative speech acts as the director of action and participation' ('Domestic Politics: Gender, Protest, and Elizabeth Barrett Browning's *Poems before Congress*', p. 300).

38. Lucy Riall, *Garibaldi: Invention of a Hero*, p. 29.
39. Elizabeth Barrett Browning, 'Preface', in *Poems Before Congress*, p. 553.
40. Elizabeth Barrett Browning, 'A Curse for a Nation', in *Poems Before Congress*, l. 2.
41. Riall, *Garibaldi*, p. 29.
42. Elizabeth Barrett Browning, 'Napoleon III. in Italy', in *Poems Before Congress*, l. 7. Subsequent citations will appear parenthetically in the text by line number.
43. Compare *Casa Guidi Windows*:

> But never say 'no more'
> To Italy's life! Her memories undismayed
> Still argue 'evermore'. (I, 212–14)

44. Saville, *Victorian Soul-Talk*, p. 68.
45. Alison Chapman, 'Risorgimenti: Spiritualism, Politics and Elizabeth Barrett Browning', p. 87.
46. Carlo Bossoli and Ferdinand Eber, *The War in Italy*, p. 38.
47. Montwieler, 'Domestic Politics', p. 301.
48. Marjorie Stone, *Elizabeth Barrett Browning*, p. 13.
49. Susan J. Brison, *Aftermath: Violence and the Remaking of a Self*, p. xi.
50. Cathy Caruth, 'Recapturing the Past', p. 153.
51. Ibid.
52. Caruth, *Unclaimed Experience*, p. 4.
53. Riall, *Risorgimento*, p. 35.
54. Ibid. p. 39.
55. Ibid. p. 40.
56. Matthew Reynolds, *The Realms of Verse 1830–1870: English Poetry in a Time of Nation-Building*, p. 31.
57. See Linton's hagiography of Mazzini and his international allies, *European Republicans: Recollections of Mazzini and His Friends*.

58. Marcella Pellegrino Sutcliffe, *Victorian Radicals and Italian Democrats*, pp. 4–5.
59. For a detailed discussion of how a range of British political attitudes towards Napoleon III influenced the reviews of *Poems Before Congress*, see Denae Dyck and Marjorie Stone, 'The "Sensation" of Elizabeth Barrett Browning's *Poems before Congress* (1860): Events, Politics, Reception', pp. 6–21. On divisions in British public opinion of the Risorgimento more broadly, see Nick Carter, 'Introduction: Britain, Ireland and the Italian Risorgimento', pp. 15–22.
60. Riall, *Risorgimento*, p. 39.
61. Sigmund Freud, *Beyond the Pleasure Principle*.
62. Jonathan Marwil, *Visiting Modern War in Risorgimento Italy*, p. 3.
63. Ibid. p. 72; for more details about the Battle of Magenta, see pp. 71–4.
64. Ibid. p. 2. The 40,000 plus casualties at Solferino amount to 'more than on any one day of the American Civil War' (2).
65. Ibid. p. 180.
66. Henri Dunant, *A Memory of Solferino*, p. 19.
67. Ibid. p. 40.
68. Ibid. p. 49.
69. Theodosia Garrow Trollope, *Social Aspects of the Italian Revolution, in a Series of Letters from Florence, Reprinted from the* Athenaeum; *with a Sketch of Subsequent Events up to the Present Time*, p. 4.
70. Ibid. pp. 39–40.
71. Barrett Browning, *The Letters of Elizabeth Barrett Browning to Her Sister Arabella*, p. 416.
72. Giuseppe Garibaldi, *My Life*, p. 97.
73. Chapman, *Networking the Nation*, p. 79.
74. Ibid. p. 73.
75. Marwil, *Visiting Modern War*, pp. 22–4, 54–5. Marwil narrates the war through the eyes of the visitors, mostly journalists, painters and photographers, who witnessed events.
76. 'Express from Paris', *The Times*, 27 June 1859, p. 9.
77. Ferdinand Eber, 'The Allied Armies: The Battle of Solferino', *The Times*, 4 July 1859, p. 6. For more on Eber's work for *The Times* in 1859–60, see Marwil, *Visiting Modern War*.
78. Dyck and Stone, 'The "Sensation" of Elizabeth Barrett Browning's *Poems Before Congress*', p. 8.
79. Marwil, *Visiting Modern War*, pp. 168–70.
80. Bossoli and Eber, *The War in Italy*, p. 35.
81. Ibid. pp. 35–6.
82. Marwil, *Visiting Modern War*, p. 74.
83. Elizabeth Barrett Browning and Robert Browning, *The Brownings' Correspondence*, p. 147.
84. Chapman, *Networking the Nation*, p. 91.
85. Caruth, *Unclaimed Experience*, p. 4.

86. Jill L. Matus, *Shock, Memory and the Unconscious in Victorian Fiction*, p. 7.
87. Ibid. p. 43.
88. Ibid. p. 184.
89. Barrett Browning, *The Brownings' Correspondence*, p. 147.
90. Matus, *Shock, Memory and the Unconscious*, p. 184.
91. For more information about the historical Savio and the poem, see the headnote in Elizabeth Barrett Browning, *Works of Elizabeth Barrett Browning* [*WEBB*], gen. ed. Sandra Donaldson, vol. 5, pp. 103–4. Savio's sons died fighting in 1860–1, after the Second War of Independence.
92. Isobel Armstrong, *Victorian Poetry: Poetry, Poetics and Politics*, p. 17.
93. Ibid. p. 13.
94. Elizabeth Barrett Browning, 'Mother and Poet', in *Last Poems*, ll. 11–13. Subsequent citations will appear parenthetically in the text by line number.
95. Christopher M. Keirstead, *Victorian Poetry, Europe, and the Challenge of Cosmopolitanism*, p. 87.
96. Lootens, *The Political Poetess*, p. 14.
97. Caruth, *Unclaimed Experience*, p. 4.
98. Dominick LaCapra, *Writing History, Writing Trauma*, p. xi.
99. Ibid. pp. 41–2.
100. Ibid. p. xi.
101. Ibid.
102. Robert Langbaum, *The Poetry of Experience: The Dramatic Monologue in Modern Literary Tradition*, p. 85.
103. Ibid. p. 105.
104. LaCapra, *Writing History, Writing Trauma*, p. xi.
105. Ibid.
106. Caruth, *Unclaimed Experience*, p. 4.
107. Matthew Rowlinson, 'Lyric', p. 77.
108. Ibid. p. 61.
109. Ibid. pp. 73–4.
110. Ibid. p. 64.
111. Cathy Caruth, *Literature in the Ashes of History*, pp. 78–9.
112. Barrett Browning, *WEBB*, vol. 5, p. 78.
113. Caruth, *Literature in the Ashes of History*, p. x.
114. Ibid. p. 15.
115. Elizabeth Barrett Browning, 'A Court Lady', in *Poems Before Congress*, l. 30.
116. Caruth, *Literature in the Ashes of History*, p. 15.
117. Elizabeth Barrett Browning, 'Died . . .', in *Last Poems*, l. 1. Subsequent citations will appear parenthetically in the text by line number.
118. See Chapman's similar discussion of *Last Poems*' 'Where's Agnes?' (*Networking the Nation*, pp. 211–12).

119. Elizabeth Barrett Browning, 'The Forced Recruit', in *Last Poems*, ll. 9–16. Subsequent citations will appear parenthetically in the text by line number.
120. Garrow Trollope, *Social Aspects of the Italian Revolution*, p. 1.
121. Elizabeth Barrett Browning, 'A Tale of Villafranca Told in Tuscany', in *Poems Before Congress*, l. 3. Subsequent citations will appear parenthetically in the text by line number.
122. Riall, *Risorgimento*, p. 39.
123. LaCapra, *Writing History, Writing Trauma*, p. 81.

Conclusion

In Henry James's 'The Aspern Papers' (1888), an unnamed scholar goes to Venice to ingratiate himself with the elderly Juliana Bordereau, a relic of a bygone era prized by the first-person narrator for her intimacy with the long-dead American poet, Jeffrey Aspern. Seeking the 'faint reverberation' of Aspern's voice in Bordereau's Venetian *palazzo*,[1] the narrator finds close acquaintance with Bordereau and her niece, Tita, 'disenchanting' (71): they are unwelcoming and untidy, and grasp at any chance to earn money. The ageing Bordereau is an uncanny and horrible remnant of the figure that haunts Aspern's youthful poetry; wearing a shade across her face to protect her eyes from the light, she presents the narrator with a vision of 'The divine Juliana as a grinning skull' (65). Though the narrator's disenchantment is primarily with Bordereau herself and the failure of Aspern's poetic permanence she represents, James subtly reinforces his sense of estrangement from the past by resurrecting the Risorgimento trope of decay–death–rebirth for his late-century story. In fact, Bordereau's seeming revivification from decades past is what most unsettles the editor; he claims, 'She was too strange, too literally resurgent' (65). Although Risorgimento politics by 1888 belong, like Aspern, to history, an unsettling quality of resurgence, or *risorgimento*, lingers among the decaying Venetian *palazzi* and *piazze*. By the end of the nineteenth century, writers like James and Vernon Lee step back from the political debates of the Risorgimento period to depoliticise Italy, returning it to the aesthetic domain familiar from pre-Risorgimento discourse on Italy, and particularly the eighteenth-century and Romantic tropes discussed in Chapter 1. Yet, the delicate balance between investment in Italy and disenchantment with unification that characterises the Risorgimento writing discussed above remains, like the ashes of Aspern's papers, the vestiges of his lifetime in decaying Venice, or the skeletal Juliana Bordereau herself.

Italy after the incorporation of Rome (1870) remains resurgent, but that resurgence is grotesque and uncanny and the peninsula is populated by the undead and revived corpses, like Medea da Carpi in Lee's 'Amour Dure' (1887/1890). Like James's editor, Lee's narrator, Spiridion Trepka, is a scholar who seeks to 'come in spirit into the presence of the Past' in Italy.[2] Though cognisant of contemporary Italian politics – the Italians of the story celebrate the anniversary of the incorporation of Rome (50–1) – Trepka disavows modern Italy, instead rejoicing when, in his voyage along the Apennines, he can gladly declare, 'Ah, that was Italy, it was the Past!' (42). Over the course of the story, Trepka's investment in early modern Italy becomes horrifically real, as time collapses with his discovery of a portrait of the femme fatale and object of his academic and sexual fascination, Medea da Carpi, a portrait reminiscent of the famous Bronzino painting that later figures as a symbol of mortality in James's *The Wings of the Dove* (1902).[3] Confronted with this portrait, a relic of Medea's lifetime, Trepka's sense of the barrier between past and present dissolves; Medea makes contact with him through a series of ghastly visitations in a decrepit church, suggesting the threat posed by Trepka's desire to revive the past and live among ghosts. He writes in his diary, 'Those pedants say that the dead are dead, the past is past. For them, yes; but why for me?' (69). Divested of its immediate political content, resurgence in this story becomes obsessive and unsettling: Trepka is possessed by a past that he has summoned into being. The story concludes with Medea pacing forth from out of history to wreak destruction on Trepka, whom she has used as an instrument of revenge against those who wronged her during her lifetime. His ecstasy at her approach is heightened by her bodily incarnation as her revived corpse strides into the present: 'A step on the staircase! It is she! it is she! At last, Medea, Medea! AMOUR DURE – DURE AMOUR!' (76).

These late-century stories empty the concept of *risorgimento* of its political content so that decay and resurgence feature as primarily aesthetic categories; however, such discomfort with the 'literally resurgent' (James 65) can be traced back to the concept of decline fundamental to *risorgimento* and the political writing that expressed hesitation about the Risorgimento's progress and outcome. In George Meredith's *Vittoria* (1866), the revolutionary events of 1847–9 are presented from a post-unification position, making the characters' negotiation of radical republicanism and liberal meliorism uncomfortably belated. *Vittoria*'s perspective on what Meredith described as 'the main historical fact of the 19th Century'[4] combines distance with urgency. While the novel was written after official unification in 1861, Risorgimento conflict flared up continually in the decade between 1861 and the 1870 incorporation of Rome, including with Giuseppe Garibaldi's unsuccessful campaigns to take Rome in 1862 and 1867, which pitted him against Italian and French governments. In June 1866, the Third War of Independence, part of the broader Austro-Prussian war, began as *Vittoria* appeared in *The Fortnightly Review*.[5] Meredith became sympathetic to the Risorgimento through his close relationships with D. G. and William Rossetti, the enthusiastic supporter Algernon Charles Swinburne, who dedicated *Songs Before Sunrise* (1871) to the Italian cause, and Mazzinian Emilie Ashurst Venturi.[6] Meredith's interest in Italy in 1866 was not limited to this romantic novel on the ill-fated Milanese revolution and First War of Independence; on 21 June, having left England as soon as he completed *Vittoria* and the day after war was declared,[7] Meredith arrived in Bologna to cover the conflict as a special correspondent for *The Morning Post*.[8]

Vittoria dramatises the unsettlements of Risorgimento discourse and history through the voice of the Anglo-Italian prima donna Vittoria Campi, who translates ideology into culture from the Milanese stage for the Mazzinian leader known as the Chief. The allegorical opera in which Vittoria performs,[9] written by the conspirator Agostino to incite a Milanese revolution, contains signs of hesitation that suggest Risorgimento discourse's tension between death and resurgence. On the surface, the opera straightforwardly presents Vittoria as Camilla, a Young Italy figure, who plans to marry her lover Camillo against the wishes of the tyrannical Count Orso, who intends Camillo for his daughter, Michiella.[10] The audience understands the political allegory at once: '"Count Orso" [is] Austria; "Michiella" is Austria's spirit of intrigue; "Camillo" is indolent Italy, amorous Italy, Italy aimless; "Camilla" is YOUNG ITALY!' (173). Camilla enters singing of a vision of her lost mother appearing to bless her on the eve of her wedding. The mother figures as sainted, dead Italy, awaiting resurrection through Camilla's agency:

> Her mother was folded in a black shroud, looking formless as death, like very death, save that death sheds no tears . . . She threw apart the shroud: her breasts and her limbs were smooth and firm as those of an immortal Goddess: but breasts and limbs showed the cruel handwriting of base men upon the body of a martyred saint. The blood from those deep gashes sprang out at intervals, mingling with her tears. (176–7)

The scene culminates in Camilla's sacramental consumption of the Mazzinian *Madre Santa*'s blood and tears (177) to the frenzied calls of '*Evviva la Vittoria e l'Italia!*' throughout the house (178). Much like Vittoria herself after opening night, Camilla is forced into exile in the opera's second act (187) but returns to reunite with Camillo before she is killed by her rival, Michiella, in the final scene. Like the unsettlingly grotesque, bleeding mother, on her deathbed Camilla embodies the competing concepts of resurgence and destruction. Vittoria voices the opera's triumphant political refrain, excluded from the libretto to deceive the censors, '*Italia, Italia shall be free!*' (202); yet, she does so with 'exhaustion' (202) while Camilla is in her death-throes.

The imagery of decay and revival that haunts the opera recurs throughout the novel, often with reference to such suffering maternal figures as Camilla's sainted mother. Countess Ammiani is one such suffering mother, as the narrator notes: 'In such mothers Italy revived. The pangs and the martyrdom were theirs . . . Italy revived in these mothers. Their torture was that of the reanimation of her frame from the death-trance' (148). Like Laura Savio in Elizabeth Barrett Browning's 'Mother and Poet' (*Last Poems*, 1862), Countess Ammiani absorbs the shuddering losses emanating outwards from the violence through which the new nation is born. Yet, the reverberations of this violence are also, according to the Chief, signals of life, of Italy's beating heart. He writes to Vittoria before the opera, 'Remember that these uprisings are the manifested pulsations of the heart of your country, so that none shall say she is a corpse, and knowing that she lives, none shall say that she deserves not freedom' (149). The narrator, however, is more hesitant about reading the signs of Italy's metaphorical living body, describing the Chief as one attending a corpse:

> Watching over his Italy; her wrist in his meditative clasp year by year; he stood like a mystic leech by the couch of a fair and hopeless frame, pledged to revive it by the inspired assurance, shared by none, that life had not forsaken it. A body given over to death and vultures – he stood by it in the desert. (159–60)

Even from the narrator's position in 1866, then, it remains unclear whether the shudders of violence pulsing across Italy are those of death, birth or a strengthening, beating heart.[11]

This hesitation between optimism and hopelessness also speaks to the confusing historical moment of 1848, when the distinction between friend and enemy becomes blurred. Austrian rule in

Lombardy is essentially, the narrator argues, a military occupation, since 'The army of Austria was in those days the Austrian Empire' (68). Furthermore, the occupiers willingly abuse their power; one officer, pushing back against Vienna's calls for mild rule, for example, disturbingly

> declared that Italians were like women, and wanted – yes, *wanted* – (their instinct called for it) a beating, a real beating . . . A thundering thrashing, once a month or so, to these unruly Italians, because they are like women! (69–70)

Yet, despite such disconcerting moments, the novel also stresses the heterogeneous personal relationships that grow up in Milanese society even within the political crucible of occupation and insurgency. Even melodramatic villains like Austrians Captain Weisspriess and the von Lenkenstein sisters ultimately align with Meredith's protagonists, Vittoria and Carlo; throughout the novel, these villains are motivated more by personal concerns,[12] including jealousy, desire and repentance, than by political or national allegiances.

Furthermore, though Austrian rule is untenable and intolerable, Meredith's patriots are plagued by petty infighting, political disputes and suspicion. Vittoria and her compatriots are borne away by a revolution that is fated to fail, but so fated because of their own shortcomings as historical actors. In Lionel Stevenson's words, *Vittoria*'s central focus is 'the psychology of revolution'; Meredith 'reproduced with cruel clarity the futility and discord that prevailed in Italy as in all the other abortive revolutions that convulsed Europe in 1848'.[13] The concerted revolutionary action that the Chief plans is undermined by seeming allies, like the conspiratorial Barto Rizzo, who denounces Vittoria before the opera can be performed, thereby postponing the planned uprising. Vittoria's dangerous utterance of '*Italia, Italia shall be free!*' (202) at La Scala is thus a trigger without a resulting explosion. From a life-breathing political action, Vittoria's role in the rebellion diminishes into a futile, grotesque exercise in self-incrimination:

> The feeling that it was she to whom it was given to lift the torch and plant the standard of Italy, had swept her as through the strings of a harp . . . [The denunciation] '*Sei sospetta,*' now made her duty seem dry and miserably fleshless, imaging itself to her as if a skeleton had been told to arise and walk: – say, the thing obeys, and fills a ghastly distension of men's eyelids for a space, and again lies down, and men

get their breath: but who is the rosier for it? where is the glory of it? what is the good? This Milan, and Verona, Padua, Vicenza, Brescia, Venice, Florence, the whole Venetian, Tuscan, and Lombardic lands, down to far Sicily, and that Rome which always lay under the crown of a dead sunset in her idea – they too might rise; but she thought of them as skeletons likewise. Even the shadowy vision of Italy Free had no bloom on it, and stood fronting the blown trumpets of resurrection Lazarus-like.

At these moments young hearts, though full of sap and fire, cannot do common nursing labour for the little suckling sentiments and hopes, the dreams, the languors and the energies hanging about them for nourishment. (121–2)

The already troubling resurrection motif of the opera becomes, with the underlying futility of its coded signals, a ghastly haunting by a revived, skeletal corpse, 'dry and miserably fleshless'. Without the 'nourishment' of Vittoria's patriotic commitment and powerful voice, resurrected Italy cannot arise in full, embodied strength and 'bloom', but, rather, appears as a walking skeleton, a 'thing' that is destined to fall again among the dead to which it properly belongs.

Moreover, the revolution, begun in an atmosphere of wasted energy and distrust, spawns further divisions among patriots and friends. Meredith indicates the seismic dislocations instigated by Milan's rebellion and the war through earthquake imagery that suggests the ways in which political and personal bonds are rent asunder in the course of the narrative, mirroring the Risorgimento's process of 'state-making and state-breaking'.[14] When the *Cinque Giornate* rebellion begins, 'barricades were up everywhere, like a convulsion of the earth' (308); church bells

clanged like souls shrieking across the black gulfs of an earthquake; they swam aloft with mournful delirium, tumbled together, were scattered in spray, dissolved, renewed, died, as a last worn wave casts itself on an unfooted shore, and rang again as through rent doorways, became a clamorous host, an iron body, a pressure as of a down-drawn firmament, and once more a hollow vast, as if the abysses of the Circles were sounded through and through. (309)

As resurgence transforms into insurgence, the 'pulsations' of Italy's beating heart to which the Chief refers in his letter to Vittoria (149) become the convulsions of an earth-shattering, tsunami-generating, sky-collapsing event.

Though Vittoria and Carlo marry in this time of upheaval, their love plot moves towards estrangement, mimicking the gradual disintegration of 1848's revolutionary hopes. At the core of their mutual disaffection are Vittoria's respect for King Charles Albert, so discordant to the republican Carlo, and Carlo's subsequent subjection to the political manipulations of his opportunistic former lover, Violetta D'Isorella, who knowingly pushes Carlo towards his doom at Brescia. For John A. Huzzard, Vittoria and Carlo represent competing strands of Risorgimento politics:

> Vittoria is a symbol of Italy divided against itself, earnest in its desire to free itself from bondage but powerless to effect a means of attaining that freedom; Carlo, on the other hand, is a symbol of the uncompromising Italian who, like Mazzini himself, could see only one path leading to Italy's salvation and who was determined to follow that path in spite of the consequences to himself or his fellow countrymen.[15]

Unable and unwilling to bridge the divisions between them, Vittoria and Carlo allow themselves to be destroyed through their own actions.

The novel's fatalistic conclusion reflects a drawn-out awareness of 1848's inevitable outcome, applied particularly to Carlo, who knows he is being led into a trap at Brescia. For Vittoria's friend Merthyr Powys, a British ally, Carlo is both 'living and dead' (469), having decided to take the fatal step in Brescia despite this knowledge. Merthyr knows, Meredith tells us, 'that the Fates are within us. Those which are the forces of the outer world are as shadows to the power we have created within us' (469). When the revolt in Brescia fails, Carlo and his fellow conspirators wander in the wintry mountains, trapped between Austrian territory, where they are fugitives, and the safety of Switzerland, which they cannot reach:

> Austria here, Switzerland yonder, and but one depth between to bound across and win calm breathing. But mountain might call to mountain, peak shine to peak; a girdle of steel drove the hunted men back to frosty heights and clouds, the shifting bosom of snows and lightnings. They saw nothing of hands stretched out to succour. They saw a sun that did not warm them, a home of exile inaccessible, crags like an earth gone to skeleton in hungry air; and below, the land of their birth, beautiful, and sown everywhere for them with torture and captivity, or death, the sweetest.
> . . . The mountain befriended them, and gave them safety, as truth is given by a bitter friend. Among icy crags and mists, where the touch of life grows dull as the nail of a forefinger, the features of the mountain were stamped on them, and with hunger they lost pride, and with solitude laughter; with endless fleeing they lost the aim of flight. (490–1)

Contrasted to Carlo's 'beautiful' Italian home, the 'skeleton' of the rebels' mountainous death-trap revives Vittoria's earlier conflation of resurrected Italy with the skeletal remains of her lost hope for national resurgence when the opera plot is foiled (121–2). The fated return to the mountains at the end of the novel also recalls the conspiratorial meeting with the Chief on Motterone, with which the novel opens (1–31), heightening the reader's awareness of the nationalists' failure.

Meredith's final gesture towards loss and disaffection in the novel appears in the Epilogue, which confirms Carlo Ammiani's death in the mountains, despite the efforts of three Austrian soldiers, Captain Weisspriess, Karl von Lenkenstein and Wilfrid Pierson, Vittoria's British former lover,[16] to prevent it. In the agony of her loss, Vittoria gives up singing, except for one final performance, ten years later, when Napoleon III and Victor Emmanuel II enter Milan during the 1859 Second War of Independence (500). This ending points to the ultimate success of Italian unification under Piedmontese leadership, of which Meredith's retrospective narrator has knowledge. Yet, this celebration of Lombardy's liberation from Austrian rule by Napoleon III and Victor Emmanuel II is qualified by the symbolic loss of Vittoria's powerful voice, the voice of Mazzinian republicanism, the ideals for which Carlo fought and died, which no longer have a place in the Italian nation-state that existed by the 1860s.

The continuities between the post-unification *Vittoria* and the disturbing, 'literally resurgent' (James, 'The Aspern Papers', 65) Italy that emerges late in the nineteenth century in figures like James's Bordereau or Lee's Medea demonstrate the extent to which politics infiltrated post-Risorgimento, aestheticised Italy and particularly point towards the conflicts that the creation of the Italian nation-state failed to resolve. However, as this study has shown, the Risorgimento's cultural remains were more than the skeletons of political feuds and failed insurrections. Italian politics played an invigorating, energising role for nineteenth-century British literature and culture. Indeed, the very contests over the Risorgimento's process and results demonstrate that its oppositionalist character enlivened political discourse, cultural production and literary experimentation. In Britain, Italian political debates and events spurred reconsiderations of Britain's role as a member of a European family and the public's understanding of British institutions and nationalist myths. The Risorgimento inspired experiments with and re-workings of major literary forms such as travel writing, historical narrative and the lyric; its events and figures even helped to generate a new Victorian genre, the sensation novel. Contentious and exhilarating, the Risorgimento created a fertile range and depth of affective responses that permeate nineteenth-century British culture. Thus, while her silence connotes loss, dissent and struggle, Vittoria's raised, resurgent voice in 1859 reminds readers of the patriotism that inspires her song and the political and emotional complexities that enrich it:

> on the day, ten years later, when an Emperor and a King stood beneath the vault of the grand Duomo, and the organ and a peal of voices rendered thanks to Heaven for liberty, [she] could show the fruit of her devotion in the dark-eyed boy, Carlo Merthyr Ammiani, standing between Merthyr and her, with old blind Agostino's hands upon his head. And then once more, and but for once, her voice was heard in Milan. (500)

A figure for intergenerational and international collaboration and the power of stirring, public utterance to move a mass of people, Vittoria's uplifted singing voice also symbolises the Risorgimento's potential to beget song.

Notes

1. Henry James, 'The Aspern Papers', p. 54. Subsequent citations will appear parenthetically in the text.
2. Vernon Lee, 'Amour Dure: Passages from the Diary of Spiridion Trepka', p. 42. Subsequent citations will appear parenthetically in the text.
3. Henry James, *The Wings of the Dove*, pp. 61–2. Agnolo Bronzino's portrait of Lucrezia di Panciatichi (c. 1450) hangs in the Uffizi.
4. Quoted in Ioan Williams, 'Emilia in England and Italy', p. 155.
5. *Vittoria* was serialised in *The Fortnightly Review* between 15 January and 1 December 1866.
6. Natalie Bell Cole, 'The "Foreign Eye" Outside and Within: Meredith's *Sandra Belloni*', p. 134. Elizabeth Adams Daniels notes that Meredith read Ashurst Venturi's translation of Mazzini's works and 'made use of them and of Emilie's knowledge' for *Vittoria* (*Jessie White Mario: Risorgimento Revolutionary*, p. 104). Ashurst Venturi was one among an influential circle of British Mazzinians, including her sister Caroline Stansfeld and Caroline's husband, Liberal Cabinet Minister James Stansfeld. The Stansfelds named their only child for Mazzini (*Jessie White Mario*, p. 36).
7. George Meredith, *The Letters of George Meredith*, p. 338.
8. Lionel Stevenson, *The Ordeal of George Meredith*, p. 154.

9. John A. Huzzard argues that Meredith's opera is inspired by Verdi's *Attila* ('George Meredith and the Risorgimento', pp. 246–7).
10. See Meredith's long summary of the opera (*Vittoria*, pp. 172–202). Subsequent citations will appear parenthetically in the text.
11. Though Meredith completed the novel before the 1866 war began, Italy's catastrophic campaign, which Lucy Riall describes as a 'dramatic failure' and a 'national disaster' seemed to confirm its struggle to achieve independent nationhood (*Garibaldi: Invention of a Hero*, p. 347).
12. Several critics have noted this point. For Stevenson, the novel displays 'the social and personal affiliations which cut across the partisan lines' (*The Ordeal of George Meredith*, p. 161). Williams argues that Meredith treats the Italian nation 'as a corporate body, subject to the laws that govern individual life' ('Emilia in England and Italy', p. 155).
13. Stevenson, *The Ordeal of George Meredith*, p. 160.
14. Lucy Riall, *Risorgimento: The History of Italy from Napoleon to Nation-State*, p. 69.
15. Huzzard, 'George Meredith and the Risorgimento', p. 249.
16. Wilfrid appears in Meredith's *Sandra Belloni*.

Bibliography

Primary Sources

Barrett Browning, Elizabeth, *Aurora Leigh* [1856], in vol. 3, Sandra Donaldson (ed.), *Works of Elizabeth Barrett Browning* [*WEBB*], gen. ed. Sandra Donaldson (London: Pickering & Chatto, 2010).

Barrett Browning, Elizabeth, *Casa Guidi Windows* [1851], in vol. 2, Marjorie Stone and Beverly Taylor (eds), *WEBB*, gen. ed. Sandra Donaldson (London: Pickering & Chatto, 2010), pp. 481–566.

Barrett Browning, Elizabeth, *Last Poems* [1862], in vol. 5, Sandra Donaldson, Rita Patteson, Marjorie Stone and Beverly Taylor (eds), *WEBB*, gen. ed. Sandra Donaldson (London: Pickering & Chatto, 2010), pp. 1–157.

Barrett Browning, Elizabeth, *Letters of Elizabeth Barrett Browning*, vol. 2, ed. Frederic G. Kenyon (London, 1897), <http://www.gale.com/primary-sources/nineteenth-century-collections-online> (last accessed 3 August 2018).

Barrett Browning, Elizabeth, *Letters of Elizabeth Barrett Browning to Her Sister Arabella*, vol. 2, ed. Scott Lewis (Waco, TX: Wedgestone Press, 2002).

Barrett Browning, Elizabeth, *Poems Before Congress* [1860], in vol. 4, Sandra Donaldson (ed.), *WEBB*, gen. ed. Sandra Donaldson (London: Pickering & Chatto, 2010), pp. 547–604.

Barrett Browning, Elizabeth, *Works of Elizabeth Barrett Browning* [*WEBB*], gen. ed. Sandra Donaldson (London: Pickering & Chatto, 2010).

Barrett Browning, Elizabeth and Robert Browning, *The Brownings' Correspondence*, vol. 17, ed. Philip Kelley, Scott Lewis and Edward Hagan (Winfield, KS: Wedgewood Press, 2010).

Bossoli, Carlo and Ferdinand Eber, *The War in Italy* (London, 1859).

Browning, Robert, 'The Italian in England' [1849], in vol. 4, Ian Jack, Rowena Fowler and Margaret Smith (eds), *The Poetical Works of Robert Browning* (Oxford: Clarendon, 1991), pp. 31–8.

Byron, George Gordon, *Byron's Letters and Journals*, 12 vols, ed. Leslie A. Marchand (Cambridge, MA: Harvard University Press, 1973–94).

Byron, George Gordon, *Childe Harold's Pilgrimage* [1812–18], in Jerome J. McGann (ed.), *Byron* (Oxford and New York: Oxford University Press, 1986), pp. 19–206.

Byron, George Gordon, *Lord Byron: The Complete Poetical Works*, vol. 4, ed. Jerome J. McGann (Oxford: Clarendon, 1986).

Carlyle, Thomas, 'To the Editor of *The Times*', *The Times*, 19 June 1844, p. 6, <http://gale.cengage.co.uk/times.aspx> (last accessed 25 June 2012).

Clough, Arthur Hugh, *Amours de Voyage* [1858], ed. Patrick Scott (St Lucia: University of Queensland Press, 1974).

Cobden, Richard, 'The Three Panics: An Historical Episode' [1862] (London: Cassell, 1970).

Collins, Wilkie, *Armadale* [1864–6], ed. Catherine Peters (Oxford: Oxford University Press, 1989).

Collins, Wilkie, *The Moonstone* [1868], ed. John Sutherland (Oxford: Oxford University Press, 2008).

Collins, Wilkie, *No Name* [1862], ed. Virginia Blain (Oxford: Oxford University Press, 1986).

Collins, Wilkie, *The Woman in White* [1859–60], ed. Matthew Sweet (London: Penguin, 2003).

Dickens, Charles, *The Letters of Charles Dickens*, vol. 4, ed. Kathleen Tillotson, gen. ed. Madeline House, Graham Storey and Kathleen Tillotson (Oxford: Clarendon, 1977), <http://www.nlx.com/home> (last accessed 30 November 2015).

Dickens, Charles, *Little Dorrit* [1855–7], ed. Harvey Peter Sucksmith (Oxford: Oxford University Press, 2012).

Dickens, Charles. *Pictures from Italy* [1846], ed. David Paroissien (New York: Coward, McCann & Geoghegan, 1974).

Disraeli, Benjamin, *Lothair* [1870] (London, 1878).

Dunant, Henri, *A Memory of Solferino* [1862] (Geneva: American Red Cross, 1959), <https://www.icrc.org/en/publication/0361-memory-solferino> (last accessed 25 October 2016).

Eber, Ferdinand, 'The Allied Armies: The Battle of Solferino', *The Times*, 4 July 1859, pp. 6–7, <http://gale.cengage.co.uk/times.aspx> (last accessed 23 June 2017).

Eliot, George, *Middlemarch* [1871–2], ed. David Carroll (Oxford: Oxford University Press, 1998).

Freud, Sigmund, *Beyond the Pleasure Principle* [1920], ed. Todd Dufresne, trans. Gregory C. Richter (Peterborough, ON: Broadview Press, 2011).

Garibaldi, Giuseppe, *My Life* [1849–72], trans. Stephen Parkin (London: Hesperus, 2004).

Garrow Trollope, Theodosia, *Social Aspects of the Italian Revolution, in a Series of Letters from Florence, Reprinted from the* Athenaeum*; with a Sketch of Subsequent Events up to the Present Time* [1861] (New York: AMS, 1975).

Gladstone, W. E, *Two Letters to the Earl of Aberdeen, on the State Prosecutions of the Neapolitan Government*, 3rd edn (London, 1851), <https://www.gale.com/primary-sources/nineteenth-century-collections-online> (last accessed 16 September 2014).

Godwin, William, *Enquiry Concerning Political Justice and its Influence on Modern Morals and Happiness* [1793], ed. Isaac Kramnick (London: Penguin, 1976).

Hansard, <http://hansard.millbanksystems.com> (last accessed 22 May 2015).

Hemans, Felicia, *Felicia Hemans: Selected Poems, Prose, and Letters*, ed. Gary Kelly (Peterborough, ON: Broadview Press, 2002).

Hickson, W. E., 'Mazzini and the Ethics of Politicians', *Westminster Review* 42 (1844), pp. 225–51, <http://www.proquest.com/products-services/british_periodicals.html> (last accessed 29 October 2015).

Illustrated London News Historical Archive 1842–2003, <http://www.gale.com/c/illustrated- london-news-historical-archive> (last accessed 29 October 2015).

James, Henry, 'The Aspern Papers' [1888], in Christof Wegelin and Henry B. Wonham (eds), *Tales of Henry James*, 2nd edn (New York and London: W. W. Norton, 2003), pp. 53–131.

James, Henry, 'Miss Braddon', *The Nation*, 1.19 (1865), pp. 593–4.

James, Henry, *The Wings of the Dove* [1902], ed. J. Donald Crowley and Richard A. Hocks, 2nd edn (New York and London: W. W. Norton, 2003).

Jenkin, Henrietta, *"Who Breaks – Pays." (Italian Proverb.)*, 2 vols (London, 1861), <https://archive.org> (last accessed 12 June 2017).

Lee, Vernon, 'Amour Dure: Passages from the Diary of Spiridion Trepka' [1887/1890], in Catherine Maxwell (ed.), *Hauntings and Other Fantastic Tales* (Peterborough, ON: Broadview Press, 2006), pp. 41–76, <http://ebookcentral.proquest.com> (last accessed 25 November 2016).

Linton, W. J., *European Republicans: Recollections of Mazzini and His Friends* (London, 1892), <https://archive.org> (last accessed 5 December 2016).

Linton, W. J., *Threescore and Ten Years 1820 to 1890: Recollections* (New York, 1894), <https://archive.org> (last accessed 13 October 2015).

Lynn Linton, Eliza, *The Autobiography of Christopher Kirkland* [1885] (New York: Garland, 1976).

Mario, Alberto, *The Red Shirt. Episodes* (London, 1865), <https://archive.org> (last accessed 25 May 2017).

Mazzini, Giuseppe, *A Cosmopolitanism of Nations: Giuseppe Mazzini's Writings on Democracy, Nation Building, and International Relations*, ed. Stefano Recchia and Nadia Urbinati, trans. Stefano Recchia (Princeton and Oxford: Princeton University Press, 2009).

Mazzini, Giuseppe, 'Europe: Its Condition and Prospects', *Westminster Review* (April 1852), pp. 236–50.

Mazzini, Giuseppe, *Italy, Austria, and the Pope. A Letter to Sir James Graham, Bart* (London, 1845), <https://www.hathitrust.org> (last accessed 16 April 2015).

Meredith, George, *The Letters of George Meredith*, vol. 1, ed. C. L. Cline (Oxford: Clarendon, 1970).

Meredith, George, *Sandra Belloni; Originally Emilia in England* [1864] (London, 1889).

Meredith, George, *Vittoria* [1866] (Boston, 1888).

Morgan, Sydney [Sydney Owenson], *Italy* (London, 1821), <https://www.gale.com/primary- sources/nineteenth-century-collections-online> (last accessed 8 October 2015).

Morgan, Sydney. *Letter to the Reviewers of Italy* (Paris, 1821), <https://archive.org> (last accessed 6 May 2018).

The Morning Chronicle, <http://www.britishnewspaperarchive.co.uk> (last accessed 3 November 2015).

Orsini, Felice, *The Austrian Dungeons in Italy. A Narrative of Fifteen Months' Imprisonment and Final Escape from the Fortress of S. Giorgio*, trans. J. Meriton White (London, 1856), <https://babel.hathitrust.org> (last accessed 27 June 2018).

Orsini, Felice, *Memoirs and Adventures of Felice Orsini, Written by Himself, Containing Unpublished State Papers of the Roman Court*, trans. George Carbonel (Edinburgh, 1857), <https://archive.org> (last accessed 15 May 2018).

Oxford English Dictionary, <http://www.oed.com> (last accessed 24 October 2016).

Panizzi, Antonio, 'Post-Office Espionage', *North British Review* 3 (1844), pp. 257–95, <http://www.proquest.com/products-services/british_periodicals.html> (last accessed 29 October 2015).

Punch, <http://www.gale.com/19th-century-uk-periodicals-series-1> (last accessed 3 November 2015).

'Report from the Secret Committee of the House of Lords Relative to the Post Office', *Annual Register, or a View of the History and Politics of the Year 1844*, 86 (London, 1845), pp. 463–6, <https://www.hathitrust.org> (last accessed 18 January 2017).

Review of *Italy*, *Quarterly Review* 25.50, July 1821, pp. 529–34, <http://www.proquest.com/products-services/british_periodicals.html> (last accessed 17 April 2018).

Rossetti, D. G., 'After the French Liberation of Italy', [1859?] in *Rossetti Archive*, <http://www.rossettiarchive.org> (last accessed 7 September 2016).

Ruffini, Giovanni, *Doctor Antonio* (Edinburgh, 1855), <http://archive.org> (last accessed 6 May 2018).

Ruffini, Giovanni, *Lorenzo Benoni, or Passages in the Life of an Italian. Edited by a Friend* (Edinburgh, 1853), <http://archive.org> (last accessed 20 July 2017).

Ruffini, Giovanni, 'Sanremo Revisited', in *Carlino and Other Stories* (Leipzig, 1872), pp. 187–226, <http://archive.org> (last accessed 7 June 2017).

The Satirist; or, the Censor of the Times, <http://www.gale.com/19th-century-uk-periodicals- series-1> (last accessed 3 November 2015).

Shelley, Mary, *Frankenstein or the Modern Prometheus* [1818], ed. Marilyn Butler (Oxford: Oxford University Press, 2008).

Shelley, Mary, *The Journals of Mary Shelley*, vol. 1, ed. Paula R. Feldman and Diana Scott-Kilvert (Oxford: Clarendon, 1987), <http://www.nlx.com/home> (last accessed 1 May 2018).

Shelley, Mary, *The Letters of Mary Wollstonecraft Shelley*, 3 vols, ed. Betty T. Bennett (Baltimore and London: Johns Hopkins University Press, 1980–8).

Shelley, Mary, *Mary Shelley: Collected Tales and Stories*, ed. Charles E. Robinson (Baltimore and London: Johns Hopkins University Press, 1976).

Shelley, Mary, *Rambles in Germany and Italy, in 1840, 1842, and 1843*, 2 vols (London, 1844), <https://www.gale.com/primary-sources/nineteenth-century-collections-online> (last accessed 8 October 2015).

Shelley, Mary, *Valperga: or, the Life and Adventures of Castruccio, Prince of Lucca* [1823], ed. Michael Rossington (Oxford: Oxford University Press, 2000).

Shelley, P. B., *Poems of Shelley*, vol. 2, ed. Kelvin Everest and Geoffrey Matthews (Harlow, Essex: Pearson, 2000).

Shelley, P. B., *Poems of Shelley*, vol. 3, ed. Jack Donovan, Cian Duffy, Kelvin Everest and Michael Rossington (Harlow, Essex: Pearson, 2011).

Shelley, P. B., *Shelley's* Prometheus Unbound*: The Text and the Drafts* [1820], ed. Lawrence John Zillman (New Haven and London: Yale University Press, 1986).

Spicer, Henry T., 'Real Horrors of War', *All the Year Round* 2.32 (1859), pp. 123–5, <http://www.djo.org.uk/all-the-year-round/volume-ii/page-123.html> (last accessed 2 December 2015).

Staël, Germaine de, *Corinne, or Italy* [1807], trans. Avriel H. Goldberger (New Brunswick, NJ, and London: Rutgers University Press, 1987).

Swinburne, Algernon Charles, *Songs Before Sunrise* (London, 1871).

Tasso, Torquato, *The Liberation of Jerusalem (Gerusalemme Liberata)* [1581], trans. Max Wickert (Oxford and New York: Oxford University Press, 2009).

Times Digital Archive, <http://gale.cengage.co.uk/times.aspx>, (last accessed 23 June 2017).

Trollope, Anthony, *He Knew He Was Right* [1868–9], ed. John Sutherland (Oxford: Oxford University Press, 2008).

Trollope, Anthony, 'The Last Austrian Who Left Venice' [1867], in John Sutherland (ed.), *Later Short Stories* (Oxford: Oxford University Press, 1995), pp. 56–74.

Trollope, Thomas Adolphus, *What I Remember* [1888], ed. Herbert Van Thal (London: William Kimber, 1973).

White Mario, Jessie, *The Birth of Modern Italy: Posthumous Papers of Jessie White Mario* (London, 1909), <http://hdl.handle.net> (last accessed 8 September 2016).

Williams, Helen Maria, *Letters Written in France* [1790], ed. Neil Fraisat and Susan S. Lancer (Peterborough, ON: Broadview Press, 2001).

Wordsworth, William, 'On the Extinction of the Venetian Republic', in vol. 1, John O. Hayden (ed.), *Poems* (Harmondsworth, Middlesex: Penguin, 1977), pp. 571–2.

Secondary Sources

Adams Daniels, Elizabeth, *Jessie White Mario: Risorgimento Revolutionary* (Athens: Ohio University Press, 1972).

Ambrose, Mary, 'An Italian Exile in Edinburgh, 1840–48', in Peter Melville Brown and Eileen A. Millar (eds), *Renaissance and Other Studies: Essays Presented to Peter M. Brown* (Glasgow: University of Glasgow Press, 1988), pp. 300–31.

Anderson, Amanda, *The Powers of Distance: Cosmopolitanism and the Cultivation of Detachment* (Princeton: Princeton University Press, 2001).

Anderson, Benedict, *Imagined Communities: Reflections on the Origin and Spread of Nationalism*, 2nd edn (London: Verso, 1991).

Antinucci, Raffaella, '"An Italy Independent and One": Giovanni (John) Ruffini, Britain and the Italian Risorgimento', in Nick Carter (ed.), *Britain, Ireland and the Italian Risorgimento* (Basingstoke: Palgrave Macmillan, 2015), pp. 104–26, <http://ebookcentral.proquest.com> (last accessed 10 May 2018).

Armstrong, Isobel, *Victorian Poetry: Poetry, Poetics and Politics* (London and New York: Routledge, 1993).

Bacchin, Elena, 'Felice Orsini and the Construction of the Pro-Italian Narrative in Britain', in Nick Carter (ed.), *Britain, Ireland and the Italian Risorgimento* (Basingstoke: Palgrave Macmillan, 2015), pp. 80–103, <http://ebookcentral.proquest.com> (last accessed 10 May 2018).

Badin, Donatella Abbate, *Lady Morgan's Italy: Anglo-Irish Sensibilities and Italian Realities* (Bethesda, MD: Academica, 2007).

Banti, Alberto Mario, 'Sacrality and the Aesthetics of Politics: Mazzini's Concept of the Nation', *Proceedings of the British Academy* 152 (2008), pp. 59–74.

Beales, Derek, 'Garibaldi in England: The Politics of Italian Enthusiasm', in John A. Davis and Paul Ginsborg (eds), *Society and Politics in the Age of the Risorgimento: Essays in Honour of Denis Mack Smith* (Cambridge: Cambridge University Press, 2002), pp. 184–216.

Beales, Derek, *The Risorgimento and the Unification of Italy* (London: George Allen & Unwin, 1971).

Bennett, Betty T., 'Machiavelli's and Mary Shelley's Castruccio: Biography as Metaphor', *Romanticism* 3.2 (1997), pp. 139–51.

Blumberg, Jane, *Mary Shelley's Early Novels: 'This Child of Imagination and Misery'* (Basingstoke and London: Macmillan, 1993).

Bollen, Katrien and Raphael Ingelbien, 'An Intertext that Counts? *Dracula, The Woman in White*, and Victorian Imaginations of the Foreign Other', *English Studies* 90.4 (2009), pp. 403–20, <http://www.tandfonline.com/loi/nest20> (last accessed 26 June 2014).

Bourne Taylor, Jenny, *In the Secret Theatre of Home: Wilkie Collins, Sensation Narrative, and Nineteenth-Century Psychology* (London and New York: Routledge, 1988).

Brattin, Joel. J., '*Middlemarch*: The Novel, the Manuscript, and Italy', in Alessandro Vescovi, Luisa Villa and Paul Vita (eds), *The Victorians and Italy: Literature, Travel, Politics and Art* (Monza, Italy: Polimetrica, 2009), pp. 291–300.

Brison, Susan J., *Aftermath: Violence and the Remaking of a Self* (Princeton: Princeton University Press, 2002).

Burgan, William, 'Little Dorrit in Italy', *Nineteenth-Century Fiction* 29.4 (1975), <https://www.jstor.org/stable/2933367> (last accessed 12 June 2016), pp. 393–411.

Burke, Peter, *Exiles and Expatriates in the History of Knowledge, 1500–2000* (Waltham, MA: Brandeis University Press, 2017).

Buzard, James, *The Beaten Track: European Tourism, Literature, and the Ways to Culture, 1800–1918* (Oxford: Oxford University Press, 1993).

Carter, Nick, 'Introduction: Britain, Ireland and the Italian Risorgimento', in Nick Carter (ed.), *Britain, Ireland and the Italian Risorgimento* (Basingstoke: Palgrave Macmillan, 2015), pp. 1–32, <http://ebookcentral.proquest.com> (last accessed 10 May 2018).

Caruth, Cathy, *Literature in the Ashes of History* (Baltimore: Johns Hopkins University Press, 2013).

Caruth, Cathy, 'Recapturing the Past', in Cathy Caruth (ed.), *Trauma: Explorations in Memory* (Baltimore: Johns Hopkins University Press, 1995), pp. 151–7.

Caruth, Cathy, *Unclaimed Experience: Trauma, Narrative, and History* (Baltimore and London: Johns Hopkins University Press, 1996).

Cavaliero, Roderick, *Italia Romantica: English Romantics and Italian Freedom* (London and New York: I. B. Tauris, 2005).

Chapman, Alison, '"In Our Own Blood Drenched the Pen": Italy and Sensibility in Elizabeth Barrett Browning's *Last Poems* (1862)', *Women's Writing* 10.2 (2003), pp. 269–86, <https://www.tandfonline.com> (last accessed 6 September 2014).

Chapman, Alison, *Networking the Nation: British and American Women's Poetry and Italy, 1840–1870* (Oxford: Oxford University Press, 2015).

Chapman, Alison, 'On *Il Risorgimento*', in Dino Franco Felluga (ed.), *BRANCH: Britain, Representation and Nineteenth-Century History*, <http://www.branchcollective.org> (last accessed 20 May 2014).

Chapman, Alison, 'Poetry, Network, Nation: Elizabeth Barrett Browning and Expatriate Women's Poetry', *Victorian Studies* 55.2 (2013), pp. 275–85, <https://muse.jhu.edu> (last accessed 6 September 2014).

Chapman, Alison, 'Risorgimenti: Spiritualism, Politics and Elizabeth Barrett Browning', in Alison Chapman and Jane Stabler (eds), *Unfolding the South: Nineteenth-Century British Women Writers and Artists in Italy* (Manchester and New York: Manchester University Press, 2003), pp. 70–89.

Christensen, Allan C., *A European Version of Victorian Fiction: The Novels of Giovanni Ruffini* (Amsterdam and Atlanta: Rodopi, 1996).

Christensen, Allan C., 'Giovanni Ruffini and *Doctor Antonio*: Italian and English Contributions to a Myth of Exile', *Browning Institute Studies* 12 (1984), pp. 133–54, <http://www.jstor.org/stable/25057758> (last accessed 8 June 2017).

Clemit, Pamela, *The Godwinian Novel: The Rational Fictions of Godwin, Brockden Brown, Mary Shelley* (Oxford: Clarendon, 1993).

Cole, Natalie Bell, 'The "Foreign Eye" Outside and Within: Meredith's *Sandra Belloni*', *Victorians Institute Journal* 25 (1997), pp. 133–57.

Cooper, Helen, Adrienne Munich and Susan Squier, 'Arms and the Woman: The Con(tra)ception of the War Text', in Helen M. Cooper, Adrienne Auslander Munich and Susan Merrill Squier (eds), *Arms and the Woman: War, Gender, and Literary Representation* (Chapel Hill and London: University of North Carolina Press, 1989), pp. 9–24.

Costantini, Mariaconcetta, Francesco Marroni and Anna Enrichetta Soccio, Preface, in Mariaconcetta Costantini, Francesco Marroni and Anna Enrichetta Soccio (eds), *Letter(s): Functions and Forms of Letter-Writing in Victorian Art and Literature* (Rome: Aracne, 2009), pp. 7–10.

Cox, Jeffrey N., 'Re-Visioning Rimini: Dante in the Cockney School', in Frederick Burwick and Paul Douglass (eds), *Dante and Italy in British Romanticism* (New York: Palgrave Macmillan, 2011), pp. 183–203, e-book, DOI: 10.1057/9780230119970 (last accessed 14 April 2016).

Cresswell, Tim. *On the Move: Mobility in the Modern Western World* (New York and London: Routledge, 2006).

Cresswell, Tim and Peter Merriman, 'Geographies of Mobilities – Practices, Spaces, Subjects', in Tim Cresswell and Peter Merriman (eds), *Geographies of Mobilities: Practices, Spaces, Subjects* (Farnham: Ashgate, 2011), pp. 1–15.

Crook, Nora, '"Meek and Bold": Mary Shelley's Support for the Risorgimento', in Lilla Maria Crisafulli and Giovanna Silvani (eds), *Mary versus Mary* (Naples: Liguori, 2001), pp. 73–88.

Cunningham, Hugh, *The Volunteer Force: A Social and Political History 1859–1908* (Hamden, CT: Archon, 1975).

Curran, Stuart, 'Reproductions of Italy in Post-Waterloo Britain', in Lilla Maria Crisafulli (ed.), *Imagining Italy: Literary Itineraries in British Romanticism* (Bologna: CLUEB, 2002), pp. 135–51.

Curran, Stuart, '*Valperga*', in Esther Schor (ed.), *Cambridge Companion to Mary Shelley* (Cambridge: Cambridge University Press, 2003), pp. 103–15.

D'Agnillo, Renzo, '"Now in Happier Air": Arthur Hugh Clough's "Amours de Voyage" and Italian Republicanism', in Alessandro Vescovi, Luisa Villa and Paul Vita (eds), *The Victorians and Italy: Literature, Travel, Politics and Art* (Monza, Italy: Polimetrica, 2009), pp. 99–111.

Della Terza, Dante, 'Mazzini's Image and the Italian Risorgimento: De Amicis, De Sanctis, Ruffini', *Yearbook of Italian Studies* 3 (1973), pp. 107–37.

Döring, Tobias, 'Imaginary Homelands? D. G. Rossetti and his Father between Italy and England', in Barbara Schaff (ed.), *Exiles, Emigrés and Intermediaries: Anglo-Italian Cultural Transactions* (Amsterdam and New York: Rodopi, 2010), pp. 271–88.

Dyck, Denae and Marjorie Stone, 'The "Sensation" of Elizabeth Barrett Browning's *Poems before Congress* (1860): Events, Politics, Reception', in Dino Franco Felluga (ed.), *BRANCH: Britain, Representation and Nineteenth-Century History*, <http://www.branchcollective.org> (last accessed 6 July 2018).

Esposito, Roberto, *Living Thought: The Origins and Actuality of Italian Philosophy*, trans. Zakiya Hanafi (Stanford: Stanford University Press, 2012).

Fahrmeir, Andreas, 'British Exceptionalism in Perspective: Political Asylum in Continental Europe', in Sabine Freitag (ed.), *Exiles from European Revolutions: Refugees in Mid-Victorian England* (New York and Oxford: Berghahn Books, 2003), pp. 32–42.

Favret, Mary A., *Romantic Correspondence: Women, Politics and the Fiction of Letters* (Cambridge: Cambridge University Press, 1993).

Ferris, Ina, *The Romantic National Tale and the Question of Ireland* (Cambridge: Cambridge University Press, 2002).

Freitag, Sabine, Introduction, in Sabine Freitag (ed.), *Exiles from European Revolutions: Refugees in Mid-Victorian England* (New York and Oxford: Berghahn Books, 2003), pp. 1–16.

Gaylin, Ann Elizabeth, 'The Madwoman Outside the Attic: Eavesdropping and Narrative Agency in *The Woman in White*', *Texas Studies in Literature and Language* 43.3 (2001), pp. 303–33, <https://muse.jhu.edu> (last accessed 27 June 2014).

Gilbert, Sandra M., 'From *Patria* to *Matria*: Elizabeth Barrett Browning's Risorgimento', *PMLA* 99.2 (1984), pp. 194–211, <https://www.jstor.org/stable/462161> (last accessed 27 June 2014).

Goodlad, Lauren M. E., *The Victorian Geopolitical Aesthetic: Realism, Sovereignty and Transnational Experience* (Oxford: Oxford University Press, 2015).

Goodlad, Lauren M. E. and Julia M. Wright, 'Introduction and Keywords', in *Victorian Internationalisms*, Special Issue of *Romanticism and Victorianism on the Net* 48 (2007), n. pag.

Greenaway, Vicky, 'The Italian, the Risorgimento, and Romanticism in *Little Dorrit* and *The Woman in White*', *Browning Society Notes* 33 (2008), pp. 40–57.

Groth, Helen, 'A Different Look – Visual Technologies and the Making of History in Elizabeth Barrett Browning's *Casa Guidi Windows*', *Textual Practice* 14.1 (2000), pp. 31–52, <http://dx.doi.org/10.1080/095023600363337> (last accessed 30 April 2017).

Harris, Leigh Coral, 'From *Mythos* to *Logos*: Political Aesthetics and Liminal Poetics in Elizabeth Barrett Browning's *Casa Guidi Windows*', *Victorian Literature and Culture* 28.1 (2000), pp. 109–31, <https://www.jstor.org> (last accessed 27 June 2014).

Heller, Tamar, *Dead Secrets: Wilkie Collins and the Female Gothic* (New Haven and London: Yale University Press, 1992).

Huggins, Michael, 'A Cosmopolitan Nationalism: Young Ireland and the Risorgimento', in Nick Carter (ed.), *Britain, Ireland and the Italian Risorgimento* (Basingstoke: Palgrave Macmillan, 2015), pp. 33–54, <http://ebookcentral.proquest.com> (last accessed 10 May 2018).

Hughes, Winifred, *The Maniac in the Cellar: Sensation Novels of the 1860s* (Princeton: Princeton University Press, 1980).

Hunt, Lynn, *The Family Romance of the French Revolution* (Berkeley and Los Angeles: University of California Press, 1992).

Huzzard, John A., 'George Meredith and the Risorgimento', *Italica* 36.4 (1959), pp. 241–50, <http://www.proquest.com> (last accessed 14 March 2017).

Hyder, Clyde K., 'Wilkie Collins and *The Woman in White*', *PMLA* 54.1 (1939), pp. 297–303, <https://www.jstor.org> (last accessed 28 September 2015).

Isabella, Maurizio, 'Italian Exiles and British Politics before and after 1848', in Sabine Freitag (ed.), *Exiles from European Revolutions: Refugees in Mid-Victorian England* (New York and Oxford: Berghahn Books, 2003), pp. 59–87.

Isabella, Maurizio, *Risorgimento in Exile: Italian Émigrés and the Liberal International in the Post-Napoleonic Era* (Oxford: Oxford University Press, 2009).

Jackson, Virginia and Yopie Prins, 'Lyrical Studies', *Victorian Literature and Culture* 27.2 (1999), pp. 521–30, <http://www.jstor.org/stable/25058475> (last accessed 23 June 2017).

Johnson, Kristen, 'When "Letter" Becomes "Litter": The (De)construction of the Message from Ann Radcliffe to Wilkie Collins', *Anglophonia* 15 (2004), pp. 153–62.

Jones, Chris, *Radical Sensibility: Literature and Ideas in the 1790s* (London: Routledge, 1993).

Keane, Angela, *Women Writers and the English Nation in the 1790s: Romantic Belongings* (Cambridge: Cambridge University Press, 2000).

Keirstead, Christopher M., *Victorian Poetry, Europe, and the Challenge of Cosmopolitanism* (Columbus: Ohio State University Press, 2011).

Kelly, Gary, *Women, Writing, and Revolution 1790–1827* (Oxford: Clarendon, 1993).

Kendrick, Walter M., 'The Sensationalism of *The Woman in White*', *Nineteenth-Century Fiction* 32.1 (1977), pp. 18–35, <http://www.jstor.org> (last accessed 21 September 2015).

LaCapra, Dominick, *Writing History, Writing Trauma* (Baltimore: Johns Hopkins University Press, 2001).

Langbaum, Robert, *The Poetry of Experience: The Dramatic Monologue in Modern Literary Tradition* (New York: Random House, 1957).

Leighton, Angela, *Elizabeth Barrett Browning* (Brighton: Harvester Press, 1986).

Lew, Joseph W., 'God's Sister: History and Ideology in *Valperga*', in Audrey A. Fisch, Anne K. Mellor and Esther H. Schor (eds), *The Other Mary Shelley: Beyond* Frankenstein (New York and Oxford: Oxford University Press, 1993), pp. 159–81.

Lootens, Tricia, *The Political Poetess: Victorian Femininity, Race, and the Legacy of Separate Spheres* (Princeton and Oxford: Princeton University Press, 2017).

Luzzi, Joseph, 'Italy without Italians: Literary Origins of a Romantic Myth', *MLN* 117 (2002), pp. 48–83, <https://muse.jhu.edu> (last accessed 12 November 2015).

Lynch, Deidre, 'Historical Novelist', in Esther Schor (ed.), *Cambridge Companion to Mary Shelley* (Cambridge: Cambridge University Press, 2003), pp. 135–50.

Lyttelton, Adrian, 'The National Question in Italy', in Mikuláš Teich and Roy Porter (eds), *The National Question in Europe in Historical Context* (Cambridge: Cambridge University Press, 1993), pp. 63–105.

Mack Smith, Denis, 'Britain and the Italian Risorgimento', in Martin McLaughlin (ed.), *Britain and Italy from Romanticism to Modernism: A Festschrift for Peter Brand* (Oxford: Legenda, 2000), pp. 13–31.

Martens, Britta, '"Oh, a Day in the City Square, There is no Such Pleasure in Life!": Robert Browning's Portrayal of Contemporary Italians', *Browning Society Notes* 32 (2007), pp. 4–16, <http://www.proquest.com> (last accessed 29 July 2017).

Marwil, Jonathan, *Visiting Modern War in Risorgimento Italy* (New York: Palgrave Macmillan, 2010).

Masetti, Maurizio, 'The 1844 Post Office Scandal and its Impact on English Public Opinion', in Barbara Schaff (ed.), *Exiles, Emigrés, and Intermediaries: Anglo-Italian Cultural Transactions* (Amsterdam and New York: Rodopi, 2010), pp. 203–14.

Masetti, Maurizio, 'Lost in Translation: "The Italian in England"', *Browning Society Notes* 32 (2007), pp. 17–26, <http://www.proquest.com> (last accessed 29 July 2017).

Matus, Jill L., *Shock, Memory and the Unconscious in Victorian Fiction* (Cambridge: Cambridge University Press, 2009).

Maxwell, Catherine, *The Female Sublime From Milton to Swinburne: Bearing Blindness* (Manchester and New York: Manchester University Press, 2001).

McAllister, Annemarie, *John Bull's Italian Snakes and Ladders: English Attitudes to Italy in the Mid-Nineteenth Century* (Newcastle upon Tyne: Cambridge Scholars, 2007).

Mellor, Anne K., *Mary Shelley: Her Life, Her Fiction, Her Monsters* (New York: Routledge, 1989).

Mellor, Anne K., *Mothers of the Nation: Women's Political Writing in England, 1780–1830* (Bloomington: Indiana University Press, 2000).

Menke, Richard, *Telegraphic Realism: Victorian Fiction and Other Information Systems* (Stanford: Stanford University Press, 2008).

Mermin, Dorothy, *Elizabeth Barrett Browning: The Origins of a New Poetry* (Chicago and London: University of Chicago Press, 1989).

Mighall, Robert, *A Geography of Victorian Gothic Fiction: Mapping History's Nightmares* (Oxford: Oxford University Press, 1999).

Miller, D. A., '*Cage aux Folles*: Sensation and Gender in Wilkie Collins's *The Woman in White*', *Representations* 14 (1986), pp. 107–36, <http://www.jstor.org> (last accessed 27 June 2014).

Montwieler, Katherine, 'Domestic Politics: Gender, Protest, and Elizabeth Barrett Browning's *Poems before Congress*', *Tulsa Studies in Women's Literature* 24.2 (2005), pp. 291–317, <https://www.jstor.org> (last accessed 6 January 2016).

Moskal, Jeanne, 'Gender and Italian Nationalism in Mary Shelley's *Rambles in Germany and Italy*', *Romanticism* 5.2 (1999), pp. 188–201, <https://www.ebsco.com> (last accessed 12 November 2015).

Nail, Thomas, *The Figure of the Migrant* (Stanford: Stanford University Press, 2015).

O'Connor, Anne, 'An Italian Inferno in Ireland: Alessandro Gavazzi and Religious Debate in the Nineteenth Century', in Nick Carter (ed.), *Britain, Ireland and the Italian Risorgimento* (Basingstoke: Palgrave Macmillan, 2015), pp. 127–50, <http://ebookcentral.proquest.com> (last accessed 10 May 2018).

O'Connor, Maura, *The Romance of Italy and the English Political Imagination* (New York: St Martin's, 1998).

Oldstone-Moore, Christopher, 'The Beard Movement in Victorian Britain', *Victorian Studies* 48.1 (2005), pp. 7–34, <https://www.ebscohost.com/academic/mla-international-bibliography> (last accessed 30 November 2011).

Perkins, Pamela and Mary Donaghy, 'A Man's Resolution: Narrative Strategies in Wilkie Collins' *The Woman in White*', *Studies in the Novel* 22.4 (1990), pp. 392–402, <http://www.proquest.com> (last accessed 20 September 2015).

Pfister, Manfred, 'Performing National Identity', in Manfred Pfister and Ralf Hertel (eds), *Performing National Identity: Anglo-Italian Cultural Transactions* (Amsterdam and New York: Rodopi, 2008), pp. 9–28.

Pireddu, Nicoletta, 'Foreignizing the Imagi-Nation: Giovanni Ruffini's Contrapuntal Risorgimento', *Quaderni D'italianistica* 34.1 (2013), pp. 93–114, <http://www.proquest.com> (last accessed 14 March 2017).

Porter, Bernard, *The Refugee Question in Mid-Victorian Politics* (Cambridge: Cambridge University Press, 1979).

Pratt, Mary Louise, *Imperial Eyes: Travel Writing and Transculturation* (London and New York: Routledge, 1992).

Price, Roger, *The French Second Empire: An Anatomy of Political Power* (Cambridge: Cambridge University Press, 2001).

Pykett, Lyn, *The Nineteenth-Century Sensation Novel*, 2nd edn (Horndon, Devon: Northcote, 2011).

Rajan, Tilottama, 'Between Romance and History: Possibility and Contingency in Godwin, Leibniz, and Mary Shelley's *Valperga*', in Betty T. Bennett and Stuart Curran (eds), *Mary Shelley in Her Times* (Baltimore and London: Johns Hopkins University Press, 2000), pp. 88–102.

Rajan, Tilottama, Introduction, in *Valperga*, by Mary Shelley (Peterborough, ON: Broadview Press, 2009), pp. 7–42.

Rajan, Tilottama, 'The Poetry of Philology: Burckhardt's *Civilization of the Renaissance in Italy* and Mary Shelley's *Valperga*', in Frederick Burwick and Paul Douglass (eds), *Dante and Italy in British Romanticism* (New York: Palgrave Macmillan, 2011), pp. 105–16, e-book, DOI: 10.1057/9780230119970 (last accessed 14 April 2016).

Recchia, Stefano and Nadia Urbinati, 'Giuseppe Mazzini's International Political Thought', in Stefano Recchia and Nadia Urbinati (eds), *A Cosmopolitanism of Nations: Giuseppe Mazzini's Writings on Democracy, Nation Building, and International Relations* (Princeton: Princeton University Press, 2009), pp. 1–30.

Reynolds, Matthew, *The Realms of Verse 1830–1870: English Poetry in a Time of Nation- Building* (Oxford: Oxford University Press, 2001).

Riall, Lucy, *Garibaldi: Invention of a Hero* (New Haven and London: Yale University Press, 2007).

Riall, Lucy, *Risorgimento: The History of Italy from Napoleon to Nation State* (Basingstoke: Palgrave Macmillan, 2009).

Robinson, Howard, *The British Post Office: A History* (Westport, CT: Greenwood, 1970).

Ross, Marlon B., 'Romancing the Nation-State: The Poetics of Romantic Nationalism', in Jonathan Arac and Harriet Ritvo (eds), *Macropolitics of Nineteenth-Century Literature: Nationalism, Exoticism, Imperialism* (Philadelphia: University of Pennsylvania Press, 1991), pp. 56–85.

Rossington, Michael, 'Future Uncertain: The Republican Tradition and Its Destiny in *Valperga*', in Betty T. Bennett and Stuart Curran (eds), *Mary Shelley in Her Times* (Baltimore and London: Johns Hopkins University Press, 2000), pp. 103–18.

Rossington, Michael, Introduction, in *Valperga: or, the Life and Adventures of Castruccio, Prince of Lucca*, by Mary Shelley (Oxford: Oxford University Press, 2000), pp. ix–xxiv.

Rotunno, Laura, *Postal Plots in British Fiction, 1840–1898: Readdressing Correspondence in Victorian Culture* (London: Palgrave Macmillan, 2013).

Rowlinson, Matthew, 'Lyric', in Richard Cronin, Alison Chapman and Antony H. Harrison (eds), *A Companion to Victorian Poetry* (Malden, MA: Blackwell, 2002), pp. 59–79.

Rudman, Harry W., *Italian Nationalism and English Letters: Figures of the Risorgimento and Victorian Men of Letters* (New York: Columbia University Press, 1940).

Saglia, Diego, 'Hemans's Record of Dante: "The Maremma" and the Intertextual Poetics of Plenitude', in Frederick Burwick and Paul Douglass (eds), *Dante and Italy in British Romanticism* (New York: Palgrave Macmillan, 2011), pp. 117–31, e-book, DOI: 10.1057/9780230119970 (last accessed 14 April 2016).

Said, Edward W., 'Reflections on Exile', in *Reflections on Exile and Other Essays* (Cambridge, MA: Harvard University Press, 2000), pp. 173–86.

Saville, Julia F. *Victorian Soul-Talk: Poetry, Democracy, and the Body Politic* (Cham, Switzerland: Palgrave Macmillan, 2017).

Schaff, Barbara, 'Italianised Byron – Byronised Italy', in Manfred Pfister and Ralf Hertel (eds), *Performing National Identity: Anglo-Italian Cultural Transactions* (Amsterdam and New York: Rodopi, 2008), pp. 103–21.

Schoina, Maria, 'The "Poetry of Politics" in Shelley's and Byron's Italian Works', *Gramma* 9 (2001), n. pag, <https://genesis.ee.auth.gr/dimakis/Gramma/9/04.html> (last accessed 14 April 2016).

Schoina, Maria, *Romantic 'Anglo-Italians': Configurations of Identity in Byron, the Shelleys, and the Pisan Circle* (Farnham: Ashgate, 2009).

Schor, Esther, 'Acts of Union: Theodosia Garrow Trollope and Frances Power Cobbe on the Kingdom of Italy', in Alison Chapman and Jane Stabler (eds), *Unfolding the South: Nineteenth-Century British Women*

Writers and Artists in Italy (Manchester: Manchester University Press, 2003), pp. 90–109.

Schor, Esther, 'The Poetics of Politics: Barrett Browning's *Casa Guidi Windows*', *Tulsa Studies in Women's Literature* 17.2 (1998), pp. 305–24, <https://www.jstor.org> (last accessed 17 September 2014).

Simpson, Erik, *Literary Minstrelsy, 1770–1830: Minstrels and Improvisers in British, Irish, and American Literature* (Basingstoke: Palgrave Macmillan, 2008).

Sponza, Lucio, *Italian Immigrants in Nineteenth-Century Britain: Realities and Images* (Leicester: Leicester University Press, 1988).

Stabler, Jane, *The Artistry of Exile: Romantic and Victorian Writers in Italy* (Oxford: Oxford University Press, 2013).

Steinmetz, Virginia V., 'Images of "Mother-Want" in Elizabeth Barrett Browning's *Aurora Leigh*', *Victorian Poetry* 21.4 (1983), pp. 351–67, <http://www.jstor.org/stable/40002102> (last accessed 27 June 2014).

Stevenson, Lionel, *The Ordeal of George Meredith* (London: Peter Owen, 1954).

Stewart-Steinberg, Suzanne, *The Pinocchio Effect: On Making Italians (1860–1920)* (Chicago and London: University of Chicago Press, 2007).

Stone, Marjorie, *Elizabeth Barrett Browning* (Basingstoke: Macmillan, 1995).

Stone, Marjorie, 'Joseph Mazzini, English Writers, and the Post Office Espionage Scandal: Politics, Privacy, and Twenty-First Century Parallels', in Dino Franco Felluga (ed.), *BRANCH: Britain, Representation and Nineteenth-Century History*, <http://www.branchcollective.org> (last accessed 4 August 2017).

Sutcliffe, Marcella Pellegrino, *Victorian Radicals and Italian Democrats* (Woodbridge: Boydell, 2014).

Thomas, Kate, *Postal Pleasures: Sex, Scandal, and Victorian Letters* (Oxford: Oxford University Press, 2012).

Thompson, Andrew, *George Eliot and Italy: Literary, Cultural, and Political Influences from Dante to the Risorgimento* (Basingstoke: Macmillan, 1998).

Treves, Giuliana Artom, *The Golden Ring: The Anglo-Florentines 1847–1862*, trans. Sylvia Sprigge (London, New York and Toronto: Longmans, Green and Co., 1956).

Trumpener, Katie, *Bardic Nationalism: The Romantic Novel and the British Empire* (Princeton: Princeton University Press, 1997).

Urry, John, *Mobilities* (Cambridge: Polity Press, 2007).

Wagner, Tamara S., 'Violating Private Papers: Sensational Epistolary and Violence in Victorian Detective Fiction', *Wenshan Review of Literature and Culture* 3.1 (2009), pp. 25–53, <http://www.wreview.org/index.php/archive/32-vol-3-no-1.html> (last accessed 19 October 2015).

Watson, Nicola J., *Revolution and the Form of the British Novel* (Oxford: Clarendon, 1994).

Williams, Ioan, 'Emilia in England and Italy', in Ian Fletcher (ed.), *Meredith Now: Some Critical Essays* (London: Routledge & Kegan Paul, 1971), pp. 144–64.

Wright, Julia M., Introduction, in *The Missionary: An Indian Tale*, by Sydney Owenson [Lady Morgan] (Peterborough, ON: Broadview Press, 2002), pp. 9–57.

Wright, Julia M., 'Nationalist Discourses in the British Isles, 1780–1850', in Elizabeth Sauer and Julia M. Wright (eds), *Reading the Nation in English Literature: A Critical Reader* (London and New York: Routledge, 2010), pp. 164–74.

Index